Vietnam War
Almanac

Vietnam War
Almanac

Kevin Hillstrom
and Laurie Collier
Hillstrom

Diane Sawinski, Editor

AN IMPRINT OF THE GALE GROUP

DETROIT · SAN FRANCISCO · LONDON
BOSTON · WOODBRIDGE, CT

Vietnam War: Almanac

Kevin Hillstrom and Laurie Collier Hillstrom

Staff

Diane Sawinski, *U•X•L Senior Editor*
Gerda-Ann Raffaelle, *U•X•L Editor*
Carol DeKane Nagel, *U•X•L Managing Editor*
Thomas L. Romig, *U•X•L Publisher*

Rita Wimberley, *Senior Buyer*
Dorothy Maki, *Manufacturing Manager*
Evi Seoud, *Assistant Manager, Composition Purchasing and Electronic Prepress*
Mary Beth Trimper, *Manager, Composition and Electronic Prepress*

Sarah Tomasek, *Permissions Specialist*

Michelle DiMercurio, *Senior Art Director*
Kenn Zorn, *Product Design Manager*

Dean Dauphinais, *Senior Editor, Imaging and Multimedia Content*
Pamela A. Reed, *Imaging Coordinator*
Robert Duncan, *Imaging Specialist*
Randy Bassett, *Imaging Supervisor*
Barbara J. Yarrow, *Manager, Imaging and Multimedia Content*

Linda Mahoney, LM Design, *Typesetting*

Laura Exner, XNR Productions, Inc., *Cartographer*

Cover photographs reproduced by permission of AP/Wide World Photos and Archive Photos, Inc.

Library of Congress Cataloging-in-Publication Data

Hillstrom, Kevin, 1963–.
  Vietnam War : Almanac / Kevin Hillstrom and Laurie Collier Hillstrom ; Diane Sawinski, editor.
    p.cm.
  Includes bibliographical references and index.
    ISBN 0-7876-4883-3
      1. Vietnamese Conflict, 1961–1975—Chronology—Juvenile literature. 2. Vietnamese Conflict, 1961–1975—Juvenile Literature. 3. Vietnamese Conflict, 1961–1975—United States—Juvenile literature. [1. Vietnamese Conflict, 1961–1975.] I. Hillstrom, Laurie Collier, 1965– II. Sawinski, Diane M. III, Title.

DS557.7 .H556 2001
959.704'3'0202—dc21
00-056379

Printed in the United States of America

10 9 8 7 6 5 4 3 2 1

Contents

Ho Chi Minh.
Reproduced by permission of Archive Photos.

Bao Dai.
*Reproduced by permission
of Archive Photos.*

President Lyndon B. Johnson.
Reproduced by permission of Corbis-Bettman.

Martin Luther King, Jr.
Reproduced by permission of the Library of Congress.

Vietnam War veteran returning home.
Reproduced by permission of AP/World Wide Photos.

Vietnamese flee fighting.
Reproduced by permission of AP/World Wide Photos.

Visitors at the Vietnam Veterans Memorial Wall.
Unknown source.

Reader's Guide

Vietnam War: Almanac presents a comprehensive overview of the Vietnam War. The volume's sixteen chapters cover all aspects of the conflict, from the reasons behind American involvement, to the antiwar protests that rocked the nation, to the fall of Saigon to Communist forces. The chapters are arranged chronologically, beginning with Vietnam's struggles under French colonial rule, moving through early American involvement into the war itself, and concluding with a look at both the United States and Vietnam since the North Vietnamese victory in 1975. Interspersed are four chapters that cover the growth of the American antiwar movement, the experiences of U.S. soldiers in Vietnam, Vietnam veterans in American society, and the effect of the war on Vietnam's land and people.

Each chapter of the *Almanac* includes "Words to Know" and "People to Know" sections that define important terms and individuals discussed in the chapter for easy reference. In addition, each chapter features informative sidebars containing brief biographies, excerpts from memoirs and important documents, and interesting facts about the issues and events discussed in the main body of the text. Nearly seventy black-and-white photos and maps illustrate the work.

Vietnam War: Almanac also includes a "Vietnam War Timeline" of important events, "Words to Know" and "People to Know" sections that combine those terms from individual chapters, and a list of "Research and Activity Ideas" with suggestions for research efforts, oral and dramatic presentations, and group projects. *Vietnam War: Almanac* concludes with a bibliography of sources for further study and a comprehensive index.

Vietnam War Reference Library

Vietnam War: Almanac is only one component of a three-part Vietnam War Reference Library. The other two titles in this multivolume set include:

- *Vietnam War: Biographies* is a two-volume set featuring profiles of sixty important figures from the Vietnam War era. The essays cover such key people as politicians Ho Chi Minh, Lyndon B. Johnson, Robert S. McNamara, Ngo Dinh Diem, and Richard M. Nixon; military leaders William Westmoreland and Vo Nguyen Giap; antiwar activists Joan Baez, David Dellinger, and Abbie Hoffman; journalists Frances FitzGerald, David Halberstam, and Neil Sheehan; and prominent veterans Ron Kovic, Tim O'Brien, John McCain, and Oliver Stone. The volumes are filled with photographs, sidebars, individual "Where to Learn More" sections, and an index.

- *Vietnam War: Primary Sources* presents thirteen full or excerpted speeches and written works from the Vietnam War era. The volume includes excerpts from civil rights leader Martin Luther King, Jr.'s 1967 antiwar speech at Riverside Church in New York City; President Richard Nixon's 1969 "Silent Majority" speech; Le Ly Hayslip's memoir *When Heaven and Earth Changed Places,* about growing up in a war-torn Vietnamese village and becoming involved with the Viet Cong; and Admiral James Stockdale's memoir about his years in a Vietnamese prisoner-of-war camp, *In Love and War.* Each entry includes an introduction, things to remember while reading the excerpt, information on what happened after the work was published or the event took place, and other interesting facts. Photographs, source information, and an index supplement the work.

- A cumulative index of all three titles in the Vietnam War Reference Library is also available.

Acknowledgments

The authors extend thanks to U•X•L Senior Editor Diane Sawinski and U•X•L Publisher Tom Romig at the Gale Group for their assistance throughout the production of this series; and to copyeditors Kelle Sisung and Nancy Dziedzic for their careful attention to detail.

Comments and Suggestions

We welcome your comments on *Vietnam War: Almanac* and suggestions for other topics in history to consider. Please write: Editors, *Vietnam War: Almanac,* U•X•L, 27500 Drake Rd., Farmington Hills, Michigan 48331-3535; call toll-free 800–877–4253; fax to 248–414–5043; or send e-mail via http://www.galegroup.com.

Vietnam War Timeline

1859 The French capture Saigon.

1862 Under the Treaty of Saigon, Vietnam gives control of three eastern provinces to France.

1863 France makes Cambodia a French colony.

1883 Under the Treaty of Hue, France expands its control over all of Vietnam.

1887 France turns its holdings in Southeast Asia into one colony, called Indochina.

1893 France makes Laos a French colony.

1930 Vietnamese nationalist Ho Chi Minh creates the Indochinese Communist Party to oppose French colonial rule.

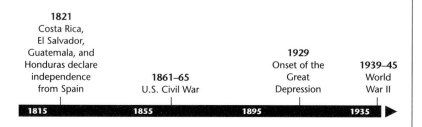

1821
Costa Rica,
El Salvador,
Guatemala, and
Honduras declare
independence
from Spain

1861–65
U.S. Civil War

1929
Onset of the
Great
Depression

1939–45
World
War II

1815   1855   1895   1935 ▶

1940 Japan occupies Indochina during World War II.

1941 The Communist-led Vietnamese nationalist organization known as the Viet Minh is established.

March 1945 Emperor Bao Dai proclaims Vietnam an independent nation under Japan's protection.

April 1945 U.S. President Franklin Roosevelt dies; Harry S. Truman takes office.

August 1945 Japan surrenders to end World War II.

August 1945 Bao Dai is removed from power in the August Revolution.

September 1945 Ho Chi Minh establishes the Democratic Republic of Vietnam and declares himself president. France and most other Western powers do not recognize the new nation.

September 1945 U.S. Army Major A. Peter Dewey becomes the first American soldier to die in Vietnam. Mistaken for a French officer, Dewey was ambushed and killed by a group of Viet Minh soldiers.

March 1946 France declares Vietnam an independent state within the French Union.

November 1946 The First Indochina War begins with a Viet Minh attack on French forces in Hanoi.

1949 France creates the independent State of Vietnam under Bao Dai.

January 1950 Communist countries China, Yugoslavia, and the Soviet Union formally recognize the Democratic Republic of Vietnam under Ho Chi Minh.

February 1950 Democratic countries Great Britain and the United States formally recognize the State of Vietnam under Bao Dai.

1940
B. F. Goodrich exhibits the first commercial synthetic rubber tire

1946
The Cold War between the United States and the Soviet Union begins

1948
Indian independence leader Mohandas Gandhi is assassinated

1949
People's Republic of China proclaimed by Mao Tse-tung

1940   1943   1946   1949

May 1950 The United States begins providing military and economic aid to French forces in Vietnam.

1952 Dwight Eisenhower becomes president of the United States.

March 1954 The Viet Minh set up a siege of the French outpost at Dien Bien Phu.

May 1954 Viet Minh forces defeat the French in the Battle of Dien Bien Phu.

June 1954 Bao Dai selects Ngo Dinh Diem as prime minister of the State of Vietnam.

July 1954 The Geneva Accords divide Vietnam into two sections: North Vietnam, led by Communists under Ho Chi Minh; and South Vietnam, led by a U.S.-supported government under Ngo Dinh Diem.

July 1954 Laos and Cambodia are granted full independence from France.

October 1954 French troops are withdrawn from Vietnam.

July 1955 Ngo Dinh Diem refuses to proceed with national elections required by the Geneva Accords.

October 1955 Diem takes control of the South Vietnamese government from Bao Dai and establishes the Republic of Vietnam.

November 1955 The U.S. Military Advisory Group—Vietnam (MAGV) is formed.

1957 Communist rebels begin fighting for control of South Vietnam.

1959 In neighboring Laos construction begins on the Ho Chi Minh Trail, a major supply and communications route for Communist forces.

French headquarters at Dien Bien Phu captured by Viet Minh.
Reproduced by permission of AP/World Wide Photos.

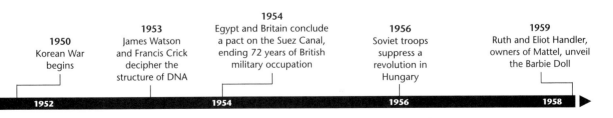

1950 Korean War begins

1953 James Watson and Francis Crick decipher the structure of DNA

1954 Egypt and Britain conclude a pact on the Suez Canal, ending 72 years of British military occupation

1956 Soviet troops suppress a revolution in Hungary

1959 Ruth and Eliot Handler, owners of Mattel, unveil the Barbie Doll

1952   1954   1956   1958

John F. Kennedy."
Reproduced by permission of the John F. Kennedy Library.

Suicide of a Buddhist monk.
Reproduced by permission of AP/World Wide Photos.

Novermber 1960 John F. Kennedy becomes president of the United States.

December 1960 The National Liberation Front is established in North Vietnam to overthrow Diem and reunite the two parts of Vietnam.

1961 Kennedy offers military assistance to Diem and sends the first U.S. advisors to South Vietnam.

1962 U.S. Military Assistance Command—Vietnam (MACV) is established.

1962 The South Vietnam government and the United States' Central Intelligence Agency (CIA) launch the Strategic Hamlets resettlement program to reduce support for Viet Cong guerrillas in rural farming communities.

January 1963 The Battle of Ap Bac brings American public attention to Vietnam.

April 1963 Buddhists begin demonstrating against the Diem government.

June 1963 The suicide of a Buddhist monk draws international attention to the situation in Vietnam.

*November 1963 Diem and other members of his government are assassinated; the Military Revolutionary Council takes control of South Vietnam.

November 1963 Kennedy is assassinated; Lyndon Johnson takes office.

August 1964 North Vietnamese patrol boats reportedly attack American warships in the Gulf of Tonkin.

August 1964 The U.S. Congress passes the Tonkin Gulf Resolution, which allows Johnson to use any means necessary to prevent North Vietnamese aggression.

1960
Theodore Maiman builds the first working laser

1961
CIA-backed invasion of Cuba at the Bay of Pigs

1962
Television satellite Telstar put into orbit by U.S.A.

1963
Freedom March held in Washington, D.C.

1960 1961 1962 1963

November 1964 Johnson is reelected president of the United States.

February 1965 Viet Cong guerillas (small groups of fighters who launch surprise attacks) ambush a U.S. base at Pleiku; the U.S. military retaliates with air attacks.

March 1965 The American bombing campaign known as Operation Rolling Thunder begins over North Vietnam.

March 1965 The first U.S. combat troops are sent to Vietnam.

March 1965 Faculty of the University of Michigan organize a teach-in to protest the war.

August 1965 Henry Cabot Lodge is appointed as American ambassador to South Vietnam.

November 1965 Antiwar demonstrations become widespread in the United States.

September 1967 Nguyen Van Thieu becomes president of South Vietnam.

October 1967 The March on the Pentagon draws 50,000 antiwar protesters to Washington, D.C.

January 1968 The Siege of Khe Sanh (in South Vietnam) begins.

January 1968 North Vietnamese forces launch the Tet Offensive.

January 1968 The Battle for Hue (in South Vietnam) begins.

February 1968 Clark Clifford replaces Robert McNamara as U.S. Secretary of Defense.

March 1968 U.S. troops kill hundreds of Vietnamese civilians in the My Lai Massacre.

March 1968 Johnson announces he will not seek reelection.

April 1968 Civil rights leader, Martin Luther King, Jr., is assassinated.

Shelling of Saigon by North Vietnamese.
Reproduced by permission of Corbis-Bettman.

1964
G.I. Joe toy figure is introduced by toymaker Hasbro

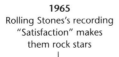

1965
Rolling Stones's recording "Satisfaction" makes them rock stars

1966
Cultural Revolution begins in China

1967
Dr. Christiaan Barnard performs the first human heart transplant

1964   1965   1966   1967

Richard M. Nixon.
Reproduced by permission of the Library of Congress.

Kent State shootings.
Reproduced by permission of Corbis-Bettman.

May 1968 The United States and North Vietnam open peace negotiations in Paris.

June 1968 U.S. Senator and Democratic presidential candidate Robert F. Kennedy is assassinated.

August 1968 Antiwar protesters disrupt the Democratic National Convention in Chicago.

October 1968 Johnson announces an end to the bombing of North Vietnam.

November 1968 Richard M. Nixon is elected president of the United States.

February 1969 Secret bombing of Cambodia begins.

April 1969 U.S. troop levels in Vietnam peak at 543,400.

June 1969 Nixon puts his Vietnamization policy into effect, reducing U.S. troop levels by 25,000.

September 1969 North Vietnamese military leader and president Ho Chi Minh dies.

April 1970 Lon Nol seizes power from Norodom Sihanouk in Cambodia.

April 1970 Nixon authorizes American troops to invade Cambodia.

May 1970 The National Guard kills four student protesters during an antiwar demonstration at Kent State University in Ohio.

June 1970 U.S. troops withdraw from Cambodia.

October 1970 Antiwar groups hold the first Moratorium Day protests.

November 1970 Nixon makes his "Silent Majority" speech.

1968
Ralph Lauren introduces his Polo line of clothing

July 1969
U.S. astronaut Neil Armstrong becomes the first man to walk on the moon

August 1969
Woodstock Music Fair attracts three hundred thousand people

1970
Marxist politician Salvador Allende is elected president of Chile

1971
Greenpeace founded in Vancouver, Canada

1968   1969   1970   1971

November 1970 The My Lai Massacre is revealed to the American people. Lt. William Calley is put on trial for his role in the massacre.

December 1970 The U.S. Congress repeals the Tonkin Gulf Resolution.

1971 The *New York Times* begins publishing the Pentagon Papers.

March 1972 North Vietnamese troops begin the Easter Offensive.

June 1972 Republican agents associated with Nixon break into the Democratic presidential campaign headquarters at the Watergate Hotel in Washington, D.C.

August 1972 The last U.S. combat troops withdraw from Vietnam.

November 1972 Nixon is reelected president of the United States.

December 1972 U.S. warplanes begin the Christmas bombing campaign.

January 1973 The United States and North Vietnam sign the Paris Peace Accords.

February 1973 North Vietnam releases American prisoners of war (POWs).

June 1973 The U.S. Congress passes the Case-Church Amendment, prohibiting further American military involvement in Southeast Asia.

November 1973 The U.S. Congress passes the War Powers Act over Nixon's veto, reducing the president's authority to commit U.S. military forces.

1972
President Nixon makes historic visit to China

1973
Artist Pablo Picasso dies

1974
Anthropologists discover "Lucy," a hominid skeleton more than three million years old

1975
Bill Gates organizes Microsoft Corp.

1972   1973   1974   1975

South Vietnamese fleeing Saigon.
Reproduced by permission of Corbis-Bettman.

August 1974 Threatened with impeachment over the Watergate scandal, Nixon resigns from office; Gerald R. Ford becomes president of the United States.

September 1974 Ford pardons Nixon.

March 1975 North Vietnamese forces capture Hue, Da Nang, and other South Vietnamese cities.

March 1975 President Nguyen Van Thieu orders South Vietnamese forces to withdraw from the central provinces, creating the "Convoy of Tears."

April 1975 The U.S. Embassy in the South Vietnamese capital of Saigon is evacuated by military helicopters.

April 1975 North Vietnamese forces capture Saigon to win the Vietnam War.

April 1975 Communist Khmer Rouge rebels capture the capital of Phnom Penh and take control of Cambodia.

May 1975 Khmer Rouge forces capture the U.S. merchant ship *Mayaguez.*

August 1975 The Communist-led Pathet Lao take control of Laos.

July 1976 Vietnam is reunited as one country under Communist rule, called the Socialist Republic of Vietnam.

November 1976 Jimmy Carter is elected president of the United States.

1977 Carter pardons most Vietnam War draft evaders.

1978 Thousands of refugees known as "boat people" flee from Vietnam, creating an international crisis.

1978 Vietnam invades Cambodia and takes control of the government away from the violent Khmer Rouge.

1976
Viking I and *Viking II* space probes land on Mars

1977
Steven Jobs and Steve Wozniak found the Apple Computer Co.

1978
U.S. Senate ratifies Panama Canal agreement returning waterway to control of Panama

1979
Political action group "Moral Majority" is founded by Jerry Falwell

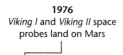

1976   1977   1978   1979

1979 China reacts to the Vietnamese invasion of Cambodia by invading northern Vietnam.

1980 Ronald Reagan is elected president of the United States.

1982 The Vietnam Veterans Memorial is dedicated in Washington, D.C.

1984 American Vietnam veterans reach an out-of-court settlement with chemical companies over health problems related to their wartime exposure to the poisonous herbicide Agent Orange.

1986 Nguyen Van Linh becomes head of the Communist Party in Vietnam and introduces the *Doi Moi* economic reforms.

1988 George Bush becomes president of the United States.

1989 Vietnam withdraws its troops from Cambodia.

1992 Bill Clinton is elected president of the United States.

1993 The United Nations sponsors free elections in Cambodia.

1994 Clinton ends the economic embargo against trade with Vietnam.

1995 The United States restores full diplomatic relations with Vietnam.

July 2000 The United States and Vietnam sign a sweeping trade agreement. Congressional approval was expected.

1981	1990	1997
Acquired Imune Deficiency Virus (AIDS) is identified	Mikhail Gorbachev, president of the Soviet Union is awarded the Nobel Peace Prize	U.S. diplomat Madeline Albright becomes the first woman secretary of state

| 1980 | 1987 | 1994 | 2001 |

People to Know

Bao Dai (1913–): Vietnamese political leader who served as emperor and head of state under French colonial rule, 1926–45 and 1949–55.

George Bush (1924–): President of the United States, 1989–93; also served as vice president under Ronald Reagan, 1981–1989.

Jimmy Carter (1924–): President of the United States, 1977–81. In 1977, he pardoned people who had resisted the draft during the Vietnam War.

Clark Clifford (1906–): U.S. Secretary of Defense under President Lyndon Johnson, 1968–69.

Bill Clinton (1946–): President of the United States, 1993–2000. In 1995, he resumed full diplomatic relations with Vietnam.

Dwight D. Eisenhower (1890–1969): A top American general during World War II who served as president of the United States, 1953–61. Although he was committed to stopping the spread of communism in Asia, he was reluctant to take direct military action in Vietnam.

Barry Goldwater (1909–1998): U.S. senator from Arizona and Republican presidential candidate in 1964. He supported increasing U.S. military involvement in Vietnam during his campaign and was defeated by Lyndon Johnson.

Ho Chi Minh (1890–1969): Vietnamese Communist leader who led Viet Minh forces in opposing French rule. Became the first president of North Vietnam in 1954. He also led the North during the Vietnam War until his death.

Hubert H. Humphrey (1911–1978): Vice president of the United States during the Johnson administration, 1964–68. Became the Democratic presidential nominee in 1968 after Johnson decided not to run for reelection, but lost to Richard Nixon.

Lyndon B. Johnson (1908–1973): After serving as vice president under John F. Kennedy, he became president of the United States after Kennedy was assassinated in 1963. Johnson sent U.S. combat troops to Vietnam. Opposition to his policies convinced him not to seek reelection in 1968.

John F. Kennedy (1917–1963): Served as president of the United States from 1960 until he was assassinated in 1963.

Robert F. Kennedy (1925–1968): Attorney general under his brother President John Kennedy's administration and under President Johnson's administration until 1965. After being elected U.S. senator from New York, he became a leading critic of Johnson's policies during the Vietnam War. Became a Democratic candidate for president in 1968 but was assassinated during his campaign.

Martin Luther King, Jr. (1929–1968): African American leader of the civil rights movement who opposed the Vietnam War. Worked to link the civil rights and antiwar movements before he was assassinated in 1968.

Henry Kissinger (1923–): U.S. national security advisor (1969–75) and secretary of state (1973–77) during Nixon administration. Represented the United States in peace negotiations with North Vietnam.

Le Duc Tho (1911–1990): North Vietnamese Communist leader who represented North Vietnam in peace negotiations with the United States.

Henry Cabot Lodge (1902–1985): U.S. ambassador to South Vietnam during the Kennedy and Johnson administrations, 1963–66.

Lon Nol (1913–1985): Cambodian military and political leader who overthrew the government of Prince Norodom Sihanouk in 1970. Despite U.S. military assistance, he was removed from power by Communist Khmer Rouge forces in 1975.

Madame Nhu (1924–): Served as the unofficial first lady of South Vietnam during the presidency of Ngo Dinh Diem. She was actually the wife of Diem's brother Ngo Dinh Nhu, and her maiden name was Tran Le Xuan.

George McGovern (1922–): U.S. Senator from South Dakota who opposed the Vietnam War. Became the Democratic presidential nominee in 1972 but lost the election to Richard Nixon.

Robert McNamara (1916–): Served as U.S. Secretary of Defense during the Kennedy and Johnson administrations, 1961–68. After helping to shape U.S. policy toward Vietnam, he privately began to doubt that America could win the war.

Napoleon III (1808–1873): Emperor of France during its colonial rule over Vietnam.

Ngo Dinh Diem (1901–1963): Vietnamese political leader who became president of South Vietnam in 1954. He gradually lost the support of the United States and was killed following the overthrow of his government in 1963.

Ngo Dinh Nhu (1910–1963): Known as Brother Nhu, he was the brother and main political advisor of South Vietnamese President Ngo Dinh Diem.

Nguyen Van Thieu (1923–): President of South Vietnam, 1967–73.

Richard Nixon (1913–1994): Elected as president of the United States in 1969, at the height of the Vietnam

War. Resigned from office during the Watergate scandal in 1974.

Pol Pot (1928–1998): Head of the Communist-led Khmer Rouge forces that took control of Cambodia in 1976. As prime minister of Cambodia from 1976 to 1979, he oversaw a violent transformation of society that resulted in the deaths of up to two million citizens.

Ronald Reagan (1911–): President of the United States, 1981–89.

Franklin D. Roosevelt (1882–1945): Served three terms in office as president of the United States, from 1933 until his death in 1945. Led the United States through the Great Depression and World War II.

Norodom Sihanouk (1923–): Member of the royal family that ruled Cambodia, 1941–70. After his government was overthrown by Lon Nol, he supported the Communist Khmer Rouge forces who were trying to take control of Cambodia.

Harry S. Truman (1884–1972): Served as president of the United States, 1945–53. Did not oppose France reclaiming control over Vietnam after World War II.

Vo Nguyen Giap (1911–): North Vietnamese general and Communist Party leader during the First Indochina War and the Vietnam War.

William Westmoreland (1914–): Commander of American military forces in Vietnam, 1964–68.

Words to Know

A

ARVN: The South Vietnamese army, officially known as the Army of the Republic of South Vietnam. The ARVN fought on the same side as U.S. troops during the Vietnam War.

B

Buddhism: A religion based on the teaching of Gautama Buddha, in which followers seek moral purity and spiritual enlightenment.

C

Cambodia: Southeast Asian nation located on the western border of South Vietnam. During the Vietnam War, Cambodia experienced its own civil war between its pro-U.S. government forces and Communist rebels known as the Khmer Rouge.

Cold War: A period of intense rivalry between the United States and the Soviet Union as both nations competed to spread their political philosophies and influence around the world after the end of World War II. The climate of distrust and hostility between the two nations and their allies dominated international politics until the 1980s.

Colonialism: A practice in which one country assumes political control over another country. Most colonial powers established colonies in foreign lands in order to take possession of valuable natural resources and increase their own power. They often showed little concern for the rights and well-being of the native people.

Communism: A political system in which the government controls all resources and means of producing wealth. By eliminating private property, this system is designed to create an equal society with no social classes. However, Communist governments in practice often limit personal freedom and individual rights.

Coup d'état: A sudden, decisive attempt to overthrow an existing government.

D

Dien Bien Phu: A French fort in northwestern Vietnam that was the site of a major battle in the Indochina War in 1954.

Domino Theory: A political theory that held that the fall of one country's government to communism usually triggered similar collapses in neighboring countries, as if the nations were dominoes falling in sequence.

E

Escalation: A policy of increasing the size, scope, and intensity of military activity.

G

Great Society: A set of social programs proposed by President Lyndon Johnson designed to end segregation and reduce poverty in the United States.

H

Hanoi: The capital city of Communist North Vietnam. Also an unofficial shorthand way of referring to the North Vietnamese government.

I

Indochina: The name sometimes given to the peninsula between India and China in Southeast Asia. The term narrowly refers to Cambodia, Laos, and Vietnam, which were united under the name French Indochina during the colonial period, 1893–1954.

Indochina War: Later known as the First Indochina War (the Vietnam War became the Second Indochina War), this conflict took place between France and Communist-led Viet Minh forces in Vietnam, 1946–54.

K

Khmer Rouge: Communist-led rebel forces that fought for control of Cambodia during the Vietnam War years. The Khmer Rouge overthrew the U.S.-backed government of Lon Nol in 1975.

L

Laos: A Southeast Asian nation located on the western border of North Vietnam. During the Vietnam War, Laos experienced its own civil war between U.S.-backed forces and Communist rebels known as the Pathet Lao.

M

MIAs: Soldiers classified as "missing in action," meaning that their status is unknown to military leaders or that their bodies have not been recovered.

Military Revolutionary Council: A group of South Vietnamese military officers that overthrew President Ngo Dinh Diem and took control of South Vietnam's government in 1963.

N

Nationalism: A feeling of intense loyalty and devotion to a country or homeland. Some people argued that nationalism, rather than communism, was the main factor that caused the Viet Minh to fight the French for control of Vietnam.

North Vietnam: The Geneva Accords of 1954, which ended the First Indochina War, divided the nation of Vietnam into two sections. The northern section, which was led by a Communist government under Ho Chi Minh, was officially known as the Democratic Republic of Vietnam but was usually called North Vietnam.

NVA: The North Vietnamese Army, which assisted the Viet Cong guerilla fighters in trying to conquer South Vietnam. These forces opposed the United States in the Vietnam War.

O

Offensive: A sudden, aggressive attack by one side during a war.

P

Pentagon Papers: A set of secret U.S. Department of Defense documents that explained American military policy toward Vietnam from 1945 to 1968. They created a controversy when they were leaked to the national media in 1971.

Post-Traumatic Stress Syndrome (PTSS): A set of psychological problems that are caused by exposure to a dangerous or disturbing situation, such as combat. People who suffer from PTSS may experience symptoms of depression, flashbacks, nightmares, and angry outbursts.

S

Saigon: The capital city of U.S.-supported South Vietnam. Also an unofficial shorthand way of referring to the South Vietnamese government.

Silent Majority: A term used by President Richard Nixon to describe the large number of American people he believed quietly supported his Vietnam War policies. In contrast, Nixon referred to the antiwar movement in the United States as a vocal minority.

Socialist Republic of Vietnam (SRV): The country created in 1976, after North Vietnam won the Vietnam War and reunited with South Vietnam.

South Vietnam: Created under the Geneva Accords of 1954, the southern section of Vietnam was known as the Republic of South Vietnam. It was led by a U.S.-supported government.

T

Tonkin Gulf Resolution: Passed by Congress after U.S. Navy ships supposedly came under attack in the Gulf of Tonkin, this resolution gave President Lyndon Johnson the authority to wage war against North Vietnam.

V

Veteran: A former member of the armed forces.

Veterans Administration: A U.S. government agency responsible for providing medical care, insurance, pensions, and other benefits to American veterans of Vietnam and other wars.

Viet Cong: Vietnamese Communist guerilla fighters who worked with the North Vietnamese Army to conquer South Vietnam.

Viet Minh: Communist-led nationalist group that worked to gain Vietnam's independence from French colonial rule.

Vietnamization: A policy proposed by President Richard Nixon that involved returning responsibility for the war to the South Vietnamese. It was intended to allow the United States to reduce its military involvement without allowing the country to fall to communism.

W

Watergate: A political scandal that forced U.S. President Richard Nixon to resign from office in 1974. In June 1972, Republican agents associated with Nixon's reelection campaign broke into the Democratic campaign headquarters in the Watergate Hotel in Washington, D.C., to gather secret information. Nixon and several members of his administration attempted to cover up the burglary.

Research and Activity Ideas

The following research and activity ideas are intended to offer suggestions for complementing social studies and history curricula, to trigger additional ideas for enhancing learning, and to suggest cross-disciplinary projects for library and classroom use.

Immediately after World War II, U.S. President Harry S. Truman had to decide whether to support Vietnam's bid for independence or France's efforts to resume its colonial power over Indochina. Divide the class into three groups. One group will present the position of Ho Chi Minh and the Vietnamese nationalists. The second group will present the position of the French government. The third group, representing President Truman and his advisors, will listen to the arguments and make a decision.

Ngo Dinh Diem, whose government ruled South Vietnam from 1954 to 1963, was widely viewed as brutal and corrupt. He refused to follow any of the democratic principles that Americans value. So how did the United States end up supporting Diem? Write a report tracing the early history of U.S. involvement in Vietnam. Be sure to discuss the Domino Theory and American fears that arose during the Cold War. Did the United States have other options besides supporting Diem? What would have happened in South Vietnam if the United States had not become involved?

Pretend that you are a 19-year-old American man in 1967. You have just received your draft notice and expect to be sent to Vietnam. What do you do? Your options might include enlisting in the military, joining the National Guard, trying to obtain a legal deferment, filing for conscientious objector status, or fleeing to Canada. Divide the class into groups based on which option they chose. Have each group discuss how their answer would change if they were: 1) an African American follower of Martin Luther King, Jr.; 2) a working-class man whose father had fought in World War II; 3) a wealthy man who planned to attend law school.

Imagine yourself as an American combat soldier in Vietnam. Create a diary of your imaginary experiences as you patrol the Vietnamese countryside, search a village for evidence of Viet Cong activity, or prepare to return to the United States.

When North Vietnam launched the Tet Offensive in 1968, it marked a turning point in the Vietnam War. But historians continue to disagree about whether Tet should be considered a victory or a defeat for the United States. Divide the class into two teams and debate the impact of the Tet Offensive. Be sure to consider the reaction of the American public as well as what happened on the battlefields of Vietnam.

American bombing campaigns took a terrible toll on the land and people in both North and South Vietnam. Draw a map of Vietnam and mark the regions that were most affected by the American bombing, using different colors for the various campaigns. Include the major cities and transportation routes on your map. Where would refugees from the heavily bombed areas likely go in search of safety?

Divide the class into several groups of three or four students. Have each group present a skit about the experience of an American veteran returning home from Vietnam. One group might show the veteran's reaction to an antiwar demonstration, one might show his first meeting with his family, and another might show him struggling with physical or psychological wounds.

People continue to argue about why the United States lost the Vietnam War. The following factors are commonly cited as reasons for the American defeat: timid political leadership; the antiwar movement and lack of public support; media coverage of the war; flawed military strategies; and North Vietnam's dedication to its cause. Assign members of the class to rank these factors in order of importance and then support their rankings orally.

It took twenty years after the end of the Vietnam War for the United States and Vietnam to resume full diplomatic relations. Discuss the pros and cons of reestablishing diplomatic ties from the perspective of a Vietnamese government official, an American business leader, and an American citizen whose son was classified as "missing in action" during the war.

As a class, create a list of the various ways that the Vietnam War has affected the United States since 1975. Be sure to consider both domestic issues and foreign policies. How did the Vietnam Veterans Memorial and the Persian Gulf War change the way Americans felt after Vietnam?

Vietnam War
Almanac

Vietnam and French Colonialism

The Asian nation of Vietnam has had a troubled past. In fact, conquest and rebellion are the central themes of Vietnam's recorded history. In ancient times, the Vietnamese people came under the control of China, the empire to their north. Centuries of Chinese rule did a great deal to shape Vietnam's culture, language, and religion. But even though China had a profound influence on the development of Vietnamese society, it never managed to erase Vietnam's unique sense of identity or its desire for independence from foreign rule.

In the tenth century A.D., Vietnam finally succeeded in casting off Chinese rule. For most of the next 800 years a succession of Vietnamese emperors ruled the country. In the 1800s, however, Vietnam once again came under the control of a foreign power. France, a European nation eager to build a global empire, conquered Vietnam during the 1860s.

Over the next several decades, France became known for its uncaring attitude toward the country's indigenous (native) people. "[France's] rule was often incompetent, usually inconsistent, and regularly harsh," writes Robert D. Schulzinger in *A Time for War*. This treatment, combined with

Words to Know

Buddhism A religion based on the teachings of Siddhartha Gautama (known as the Buddha; c. 563–c. 483 B.C.), in which followers seek moral purity and spiritual enlightenment.

Colonialism A practice in which one country assumes political control over another country. Most colonial powers establish colonies in foreign lands in order to take possession of valuable natural resources and increase their own power. Historically, they showed little concern for the rights and well-being of the native people.

Communism A political system in which the government controls all resources and means of producing wealth. By eliminating private property, this system is designed to create an equal society with no social classes. However, Communist governments in practice often limit personal freedom and rights.

Confucianism A belief system based on the teachings of Confucius (551–479 B.C.) that emphasizes morality, social relationships, and respect for ancestors. The major Confucian virtues include integrity, loyalty, generosity, and politeness.

Indochina The name sometimes given to the peninsula between India and China in Southeast Asia. The term narrowly refers to Cambodia, Laos, and Vietnam, which were united under the name French Indochina during the colonial period, 1893–1954.

Nationalism A feeling of intense loyalty and devotion to a country or homeland. Some people argue that nationalism, rather than communism, was the main factor that caused the Viet Minh to fight the French for control of Vietnam.

Viet Minh Communist-led nationalist movement to gain Vietnam's independence from French colonial rule.

traditional Vietnamese resistance to foreign rule, eventually created a strong movement to force France out of Vietnam.

Location and geography of Vietnam

The country of Vietnam is located along the eastern coast of mainland Southeast Asia, on the eastern side of the Indochina Peninsula. Its neighbor to the north is China, while the nations on its western borders are Laos and Cambodia. Vietnam's eastern and southern boundaries extend to the

South China Sea. The country is shaped roughly like the letter "S" and covers almost 130,000 square miles, making it about the size of California.

Several geographic regions can be found within Vietnam. The country's northern section is known for its annual monsoon seasons, characterized by great quantities of rainfall. The region is dominated by the Red River delta, a watershed that serves as a tremendously fertile farming area. But the north also supports a wide range of rainforest vegetation and wildlife, especially in the mountainous interior. The central section of Vietnam features the highest elevations of the country. It consists mostly of mountains and dense rainforest, and has traditionally been the least populated area of the country. The most famous region of Vietnam's southland is the fertile Mekong River delta. This low-lying area, which has a tropical climate, has historically supported a wide range of farming practices.

Vietnam's northern Red River delta and its southern Mekong delta are connected by the Chaîne Annamatique, a mountain range that runs from north to south along Vietnam's western boundary with Laos and Cambodia. This rugged chain of mountains guards Vietnam's western border all the way from China down through the nation's midsection before fading into the foothills north of the city of Saigon (modern-day Ho Chi Minh City). Over the centuries, these mountains isolated Vietnam from nations to the west, like India. But the Chaîne Annamatique did not protect the country from peoples of the north, like the Chinese. In fact, the mountains seemed to channel Chinese armies, religions, political systems, and other aspects of Chinese culture down into Vietnam over the years.

Vietnam and surrounding countries.
Map by XNR Productions, Inc. Reproduced by permission of Gale Group.

Rebellion against Chinese rule

Legends say that the region that eventually became northern Vietnam was governed in ancient times by a series of hereditary leaders known as the Hung Kings (hereditary means that rule was passed down within a family). These ancient rulers were believed to be indigenous, or native, to the area. Vietnam's recorded history, however, did not begin until 208 B.C., when an outlaw Chinese general named Trieu Da (also known as Chao T'o) took over an area of northern Vietnam known as Au Lac. About 100 years later, in 111 B.C., the region was conquered by China and absorbed into the powerful Han Dynasty (a dynasty is a family that maintains rule over a period of many generations; members of the Han Dynasty ruled from 206 B.C. to A.D. 220). It remained a pro-vince (a territory governed by another country) of China for most of the next thousand years, even though the Vietnamese made periodic attempts to break free from Chinese control.

The Vietnamese people battled China with great determination for centuries. But China's superior military power enabled it to stamp out the uprisings and maintain control of Vietnam and much of the rest of Indochina. During this thousand-year period of Chinese rule, Vietnamese civilization was strongly influenced by China's social customs and values. For example, China introduced Confucianism to Vietnam during its reign. Confucianism is a system of thought and belief based on the teachings of the Chinese philosopher Confucius, who lived during the sixth century B.C. This philosophy, which emphasizes ancestor worship and family relations, became an important aspect of Vietnamese culture, although Buddhism remained the region's dominant religion. "Historians dwell on China's military aggression, [but] it was its cultural aggression that had the most profound effect on the evolution of Vietnamese social and political institutions," writes Harry Summers Jr. in *Historical Atlas of the Vietnam War.* "Chinese culture shaped Vietnamese language, writing, religion, and views on the role and structure of government."

Vietnam's steady resistance to Chinese rule also played a part in the development of its national identity. "China failed to assimilate [absorb] the Vietnamese, who retained their ethnic singularity despite their receptivity [positive attitude] to Chinese innovations," remarks Stanley Karnow in *Vietnam: A History.* "Over the centuries, they would repeatedly challenge Chinese domination. And that hostility entered their historic consciousness."

Confucius (551–479 B.C.).
Reproduced by permission of Archive Photos.

An independent kingdom

China's control over Vietnam came to an end in the tenth century A.D., when its Tang Dynasty (618–907) collapsed. The Vietnamese leader Ngo Quyen (c. 897–944) took advantage of the political problems in China to create a new Vietnamese kingdom that he called Nam Viet. Over the next five centuries, the nation of Nam Viet thrived. Guided by monarchs (rulers) of the Ly Dynasty (1009–1225) and the Tran Dynasty (1225–1400), the Vietnamese kingdom expanded its land holdings throughout Indochina by invading other nations. They also fended off repeated threats from Mongol armies during the thirteenth century. The Mongols were a nomadic people from central Asia who conquered much of Asia and eastern Europe during the thirteenth and fourteenth centuries.

Early in the fifteenth century, however, Vietnamese self-rule came to a crashing halt. Members of China's powerful Ming Dynasty (1368–1644) seized control of Vietnam and instituted an extremely harsh rule. For example, they forced the Vietnamese people to worship Chinese gods and to speak Chinese, and they seized vast quantities of gold, spices, rare woods, and other natural resources for shipment to Chinese ports. "The rule of the Ming was probably worse than anything Vietnam had ever experienced," comments historian Joseph Buttinger in *The Smaller Dragon: A Political History of Vietnam.* "The country was bled white [robbed of its most valuable resources]. Battalions of forced laborers were sent into mines, forests, and to the bottom of the sea to extract Vietnam's natural wealth for China." But China's leadership was unable to keep its grip on the Vietnamese. In 1428, a rebellion led by a wealthy landowner named Le Loi (ruled 1428–1443) finally forced China to recognize Vietnam's independence.

After securing Vietnamese independence, Le Loi established the new capital in Hanoi and launched a dynasty—known as the Le Dynasty—that endured for the next 400 years. During this period, effective leaders like Le Thanh Tong (ruled 1460–1497) strengthened Vietnam's social and economic foundations. They also expanded the nation's borders by taking control of the Mekong River delta and the Ca Mau Peninsula (the southernmost regions of modern Vietnam). Only the central highlands, inhabited by non-Vietnamese tribal peoples, remained largely unsettled.

Vietnam and European colonialism

The Vietnamese people first made contact with Europe in the sixteenth century, when Portuguese merchants and Christian missionaries from several countries landed on their shores. During this period, European fleets were sailing all around the world in search of wealth and people to convert to Christianity. The various European nations (primarily Portugal, Spain, England, France, and the Netherlands) were engaged in fierce competition with one another for economic and political superiority. They saw Vietnam and many other regions of the world, such as Africa and Central America, as places of potentially great economic and strategic value.

In many instances, however, the European nations that led this period of exploration did not establish equal trading partnerships with the peoples they visited. Instead, European powers introduced a practice known as colonialism, in which one country assumes political control over another. Usually, these European nations took over a country in order to take ownership of its existing riches or take possession of its valuable natural resources, such as gold, cotton, or cash crops, including sugar, tea, and rubber. They believed that they could increase the size and power of their empires through such strategies. Colonialism was also encouraged by Europe's Roman Catholic and Protestant Christian leaders, who believed that it was their holy duty to spread their religious beliefs to other nations and eliminate non-Christian religions.

Europe did not pay much attention to Vietnam during the seventeenth and eighteenth centuries. Instead, the main European powers concentrated their efforts on controlling other regions of the world that were thought to be of greater economic or strategic value. Nonetheless, Vietnam endured long periods of internal political unrest and economic turbulence during this time. Squabbling between northern and southern clans, or families, even split the country in two for a time, until Nguyen Hue (ruled 1788–1793) reunited the nation during the so-called Tay Son Rebellion of 1771. By 1778, Nguyen Hue had declared himself emperor of Vietnam and established his own Nguyen Dynasty.

Suspicious of French influence

Nguyen Hue died in 1792, leaving a void at the top of Vietnam's power structure. Several factions (a group organized in opposition) tried to seize control of the troubled nation, but by 1802 Nguyen Anh (1762–1820; ruled 1802–1820) had emerged as the new emperor. Nguyen Anh was the sole surviving heir of a family that had ruled the south during much of the previous century. Upon assuming power, he quickly moved the capital to Hue in central Vietnam in order to symbolize the reunification of the nation's southern and northern sections.

Nguyen Anh had been assisted in his rise to power by Pigneau de Béhaine, a French missionary and adventurer who hoped to increase his country's influence in Southeast Asia. While Nguyen Anh appreciated de Béhaine's efforts on his behalf, he and his son and successor, Minh Mang (1792–1841), did not trust the French missionaries or traders operating in their kingdom. They knew that Vietnam had been controlled by foreign powers in the past, and they wanted to make sure that such a situation did not develop again. As a result, they placed restrictions on French activities in Vietnam and tried to push French missionaries out of the country.

The Nguyen government also grew hostile toward religious organizations. As a result, they harassed Vietnamese who had converted to Christianity. Vietnamese who followed Buddhism or Confucianism, the main belief systems of the region, also were mistreated.

By the 1850s, French businessmen and churches were asking the French government to intervene in Vietnam. At the same time, French emperor Napoleon III (1808–1873) became concerned about British colonization efforts elsewhere in Southeast Asia. He decided that France needed to establish a base of power in the area in order to keep pace with England. He subsequently ordered a French fleet to sail to Vietnam, punish the government for its actions, and force the Vietnamese leadership to accept a French presence in the country.

The naval expedition arrived off Vietnam's shores in 1858. The French military quickly made its presence felt. By 1862, the French had conquered the Mekong delta area and forced Vietnamese Emperor Tu Duc (1829–1883; ruled 1847–1883) to sign the Treaty of Saigon. Under the terms of this agreement, Tu Doc gave up control of a large section of southern Vietnam to France. The French government renamed this area Cochin China and immediately established programs designed to benefit French businesses and churches in the region. This event marked the beginning of the French colonialism era in Vietnam.

French colonialism arrives in Vietnam

During the last half of the nineteenth century, France took strong measures to establish colonial control over Vietnam and the rest of the Indochina Peninsula. For example, both Cambodia and Laos became French protectorates during this period (in 1863 and 1893 respectively; a protectorate is a country that is under official protection and control of another country). France recognized, however, that Vietnam was the biggest prize in Indochina. After all, it had large expanses of fertile farmland, and its location on the South China Sea made it an attractive destination for traders operating throughout Southeast Asia and Indonesia.

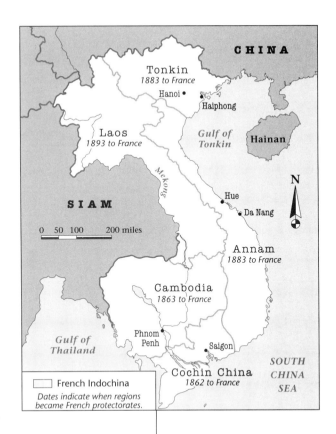

French colonialism in Southeast Asia.
Map by XNR Productions, Inc. Reproduced by permission of Gale Group.

In the years following the 1862 Treaty of Saigon, France used its superior economic and military power to increase its influence. From their base in southern Vietnam, the French steadily pushed northward into the rest of the country. By the mid-1880s it was clear to Vietnam's rulers that they could not resist France's military advances. In 1884, they reluctantly accepted French rule over the remainder of the country. France divided the newly acquired territory into two protectorates—Tonkin in the north and Annam along the central coast.

During the last years of the nineteenth century, France transformed Vietnam and its western neighbors, Cambodia and Laos, into a single possession—called the Indochinese Union—so that it could more easily maintain control over the region's affairs. French authorities permitted Vietnam to keep its traditional emperor. But the emperor held no real power under French rule, and most Vietnamese mourned the loss of their independence.

Life in French-controlled Vietnam

When France imposed colonial rule in Southeast Asia, it removed the name "Vietnam" from official use because the

Vietnamese people associated the word with self-rule. It then began the process of transforming Vietnam into the sort of country that French business, military, and religious leaders wanted. As part of this transformation, French authorities launched a series of ambitious construction projects throughout the country, including extensive road and railway networks and sophisticated irrigation systems. In addition, France funded projects that dramatically increased the region's industrial and agricultural output.

Colonial officials also created a primitive school system for Vietnamese children and introduced medical treatments that helped people combat malaria (an infectious, sometimes fatal, disease spread by mosquitoes) and other diseases. France received assistance from a variety of Vietnamese businessmen, officials, and wealthy landowners in all of these efforts. Before long, this sub-class of the Vietnamese population became an important asset to France in its management of the country.

As time passed, defenders of French colonialism pointed to its educational programs and development schemes as evidence that France had not entered Vietnam just to enrich itself. They argued that France helped to "civilize" the Vietnamese people by establishing new industrial and agricultural practices and introducing them to Christianity. But historians generally agree that French officials usually acted in their own interests rather than those of the Vietnamese people.

The benefits of colonialism were not apparent to most Vietnamese. For example, French-sponsored agricultural projects and irrigation projects opened up a lot of land for farming, but most Vietnamese families could not afford to buy the land. Instead, French landowners and a small number of wealthy Vietnamese bought up all this valuable property. The average Vietnamese farmer, meanwhile, was taxed at such a high rate that he often fell into deep debt. Many peasant families were forced to abandon their farms—many of which had been tended by their ancestors for many generations—to take jobs at the huge French-owned rubber and tea plantations that popped up along the eastern coastline. As time passed, French systems of taxation, land distribution, and economic policy all combined to create "pervasive [widespread] misery among peasants throughout Vietnam," according to Gabriel Kolko, author of *Anatomy of a War.*

The Father of Vietnamese Nationalism

One of Vietnam's early leaders in the nationalist movement was Phan Boi Chau (1867–1941). The son of a Vietnamese scholar, Phan Boi Chau was born in Nghe An, a central province that was known for its resistance to French colonial rule. As he grew older, he became very bitter about the impact of colonialism on his people, and he eventually emerged as an early advocate of violent rebellion. He also argued that once Vietnam achieved independence, it should establish a democratic system of government similar to those in place in the United States and other Western nations.

In the early 1900s, Phan Boi Chau worked tirelessly for the cause of Vietnamese independence. He wrote several books explaining his views on Vietnamese history. He also established a political organization, called the Association for the Modernization of Vietnam (Viet Nam Duy Tan Hoi), that worked to unite Vietnamese students, businessmen, and professionals for the cause of independence. In addition, he helped create a group called the East Asia United League, which brought together nationalist political leaders from China, Japan, Korea, India, and other places that had been threatened by European colonialism. These activities have led some historians to call Phan Boi Chau the father of Vietnamese nationalism.

Not surprisingly, French colonial officials viewed Phan Boi Chau as a dangerous threat. French agents drove him into exile and chased him all around Southeast Asia, forcing him to live an unsettled existence. In 1914, Chinese authorities imprisoned him for three years at the request of France. Upon his release, however, Phan Boi Chau continued with his anticolonialist activities. In 1925, French agents captured him in China and brought him back to Vietnam. He lived under house arrest (forced confinement in one's own home) in Hue for the next sixteen years, until his death in 1941.

The quality of life for Vietnamese who lived in cities also declined under French colonialism. As French industrialization and economic policies transformed the country, large numbers of Vietnamese had little choice but to accept work in factories or coal mines, where they endured long hours in terrible conditions for low wages. As time passed, it became harder and harder for parents in the cities to provide their families with good food and shelter. In addition, bitter Vietnamese felt that France's so-called "improvements" to their society often were exaggerated. For example, many Vietnamese observed that the school system introduced by the French did not benefit many children. Most children received some basic elementary school education, but very few received the opportunity to gain a higher education.

Finally, most Vietnamese simply resented being under the control of a foreign power. Convinced that French colonialism exploited the Vietnamese people and the nation's natural resources, increasing numbers of Vietnamese turned to nationalistic dreams of independence. Nationalism is a movement in which a nation or ethnic group believes that their future should be based on their common history and culture rather than that of some outside group or nation. This feeling of nationalism, which had been a part of Vietnamese society since the Chinese first conquered their land thousands of years before, flared up again during the era of French colonialism.

Organized opposition to colonialism

The first organized groups dedicated to ending French colonial rule in Vietnam appeared in the 1920s. Several of these nationalistic organizations were led by well-educated Vietnamese students and intellectuals who had lived in Europe, where they experienced greater freedoms than they had ever known in their homeland. Their travels in Europe also exposed these patriotic Vietnamese to a range of political and economic philosophies, from American-style democracy to communism. (Democracy is a form of government in which the power lies in the hands of the people, who govern either directly, or indirectly through elected representatives. Communism is a political system in which the resources and property of a people are owned by the government rather than by individuals. Under this system, the government controls all the farms and factories and is responsible for providing jobs and distributing the wealth for the common good of its people.) Many of these students and intellectuals returned to their homeland determined to gain Vietnamese independence from colonial rule. One of these students was Ho Chi Minh (1890–1969), a young advocate of communism who eventually became the most influential figure in modern Vietnamese history.

Bao Dai, emperor and head of state under French colonial rule.
Reproduced by permission of Archive Photos.

By the late 1920s, many anti-French secret societies had sprouted throughout Vietnam. Some of these groups wanted to change the existing political structure in Vietnam through peaceful protest, but others favored more violent revolution. The most important of these groups was the Indochinese Communist Party (ICP), founded by Ho Chi Minh in 1930 (an early version of this group, called Thanh Nien, was founded by Ho Chi Minh in 1925).

Political unrest surged in Vietnam in the early 1930s. In 1930, the French smashed both armed rebellions and peaceful protests with brutal force. But France's policy of military repression failed to destroy Vietnam's nationalist movement. Instead, the French efforts to wipe out the "troublemakers" merely forced them underground, where they continued to plot against their colonial masters.

In 1932, meanwhile, Vietnam's emperor, Bao Dai (1913–), returned to the country after several years of schooling in France. He tried to gain greater control over internal affairs in the country, but France continued to hold the reins of power. The French colonialists continued with their policies of economic development and improvements, devoting their attention to massive industrial projects like the Trans-Indochina Railroad, which was completed in 1937. As before, they rarely took the well-being of the Vietnamese people into consideration when planning these projects.

Japanese occupation during World War II

The situation in Vietnam changed dramatically during World War II (1939–45). In June 1940, Germany defeated France and assumed control over the nation's internal affairs. The Germans seized control over northern France, and installed a pro-German government in the country's southern territory. Later that year, Germany's military ally, Japan, forced the French government to give them free use of Indochina's airfields and other resources. In exchange, Japan agreed to recognize France's continued sovereignty (rule) over Vietnam and the rest of Indochina.

By July 1941, however, it was clear that Japan held primary authority over Vietnam and the rest of Indochina. At that time, Japanese military leaders forced France to sign an agreement providing for the "common defense of French Indochina." Japan then stationed large numbers of troops in the region and assumed control of all major railroads, harbors, and airfields. These steps placed Japan in firm control of the country.

Japan's actions encouraged Vietnam's anticolonial movement, which had been forced into hiding by France's military crackdown. They saw that France's hold over the country had weakened, and they felt the turmoil might provide an opportunity to expand their influence. The rebels subsequently carried out a range of guerrilla activities (surprise attacks launched by small groups of fighters) from bases in the mountains of north Vietnam. The most important of these groups united Vietnamese Communists and nationalists for a single cause. Led by Ho Chi Minh, it was known as the Vietnam Independence League (Viet Nam Doc Lap Dong Minh, or Viet Minh for short).

During the remainder of the war, Vietnam's nationalist guerrillas fought against both the French and the Japanese. At times they even received assistance from U.S. intelligence officials, who encouraged Viet Minh troops to resist Japan's occupying force. The primary U.S. agency involved in this effort was the Office of Strategic Services (OSS), which later became the Central Intelligence Agency (CIA). Ho Chi Minh welcomed their assistance and worked hard to convince OSS agents that the United States should support Vietnam's efforts to end French colonial rule. As the United States fought against Japan in World War II, Ho Chi Minh's relationship with the OSS became so valuable that he was given an official appointment as an OSS agent.

Between 1944 and 1945, the situation in Vietnam turned terribly grim. Poor harvests and wartime disruptions in transportation triggered a tremendous famine that washed over the entire country (see box titled "Terrible Famine in Vietnam"). Historians estimate that between 350,000 and one million Vietnamese died of starvation and malnutrition during this period. Many Vietnamese blamed the tragedy on Japanese and French policies. As a result, the event dramatically increased the popularity of the country's nationalist movement.

At the same time, Ho Chi Minh's Communist Viet Minh organization became firmly established as the largest, most effective, and best organized of the nationalist groups operating in Vietnam. Historians agree that Ho Chi Minh's success in building this organization was due in large part to his decision to emphasize Vietnamese nationalism and patriotism instead of the group's communist philosophy. Ho Chi Minh believed deeply in the ideas and principles of commu-

Terrible Famine in Vietnam

During the early 1940s, Vietnam's agricultural economy was devastated by poor crop harvests, French tax policies, and transportation problems associated with World War II (1939–45). By 1944, these conditions created famine conditions throughout the country. This famine, which lasted through the first part of 1945, caused the deaths of hundreds of thousands of Vietnamese men, women, and children. In the following excerpt from *Before the Revolution: The Vietnamese Peasants Under the French* (1973), a Vietnamese writer named Ngo Vinh Long recalls those awful months:

> The Vietnamese people are accustomed to leading a hard working, frugal, and patient life. They believe that if they eat less, save some money, and work hard, then no matter how difficult life is for them, they can still "patch things up" and somehow manage to have at least one meal of greens and one meal of rice gruel each day. The changes in the economy of Vietnam between 1940 and 1945, however, greatly disrupted the people's livelihood, worst of all in the countryside . . . .

> During the seasonal harvest of 1944 the wage for a harvester or a rice grinder was two meals of rice and salted cucumbers, an extra bowl of rice, and one piaster [a small unit of money] per day. A very strong laborer could earn only enough to feed himself, to say nothing of the taxes he had to pay or provision for his parents, wife, and children.

> From May through September 1944 there were three typhoons in the coastal areas of Bac Viet [northern Vietnam]. In normal times this kind of catastrophe would

nism. But he knew that the best way to gain new followers was to appeal to his people's sense of patriotism and their desire to be free of colonial rule.

In early 1945, Japan became concerned that American and French Resistance forces were on the verge of staging a big attack on Japanese positions in Indochina (the French Resistance included forces within France that opposed German occupation and French forces that had been stationed in France's colonial possessions when the war broke out). On March 9, 1945, Japan reacted to this threat by seizing outright control of Vietnam from the country's French administrators. "The French wolf was finally devoured by the Japanese . . . hyena," remarked Ho Chi Minh when he heard about the takeover.

be enough to put the population in an impossible situation. But now the disaster fell upon them during wartime and during a time of economic disorder. Worst of all, the French colonizers were plotting to destroy the very vitality of the population, to increase starvation in every possible way so as to be able to neutralize the traditional unyielding spirit of the Vietnamese people, and thus to rule them easily. For this reason, from September and October of 1944 onward, everybody realized that the tragedy of all times could not be avoided.

In normal times harvest season in the countryside was bustling with the activities of rice pounding and grinding. But during the seasonal harvest of the year 1944 things were completely different. The farmers went out into the fields, cried to the heavens, and moaned. People looked at each other with all hope drained from their eyes and uttered words that made it seem that they were saying farewells to one another . . . .

The starvation began in early October. Earlier than any other year the weather was cuttingly cold. The north wind howled, and it pierced through the rags worn by the hungry and the poor. It penetrated their flesh and their bones and their weak insides . . . . It rained continuously, day and night, and the dampness seeped into the very marrow [core] of the hungry . . . . The days and months dragged by slowly. Rain, wind, hunger, and cold seemed to slow down the wheels of time. It was so cold that people would lie in haystacks, covering themselves up with banana leaves. They were so hungry that they had to eat marsh pennywort [a plant found in the wild], potato leaves, bran, banana roots, and the bark of trees. The villagers—fathers and sons, brothers and sisters, husbands and wives, all of them alike—could no longer save one another. Regardless of the time of day or night, the hungry people, over and over again, would hug each other and would moan tragically.

Ho Chi Minh takes over

Japan's decision to seize formal control over Vietnam had little practical impact on the war. By this point, the United States, Great Britain, the Soviet Union, and other military partners—collectively known as the Allied Forces—were on the verge of defeating both Germany and Japan. As the Allied Forces continued to register big victories in Europe and Southeast Asia, it became clear that Japan would not be able to maintain its grip on Indochina for very long.

Ho Chi Minh and other Viet Minh leaders decided to take advantage of Japan's crumbling authority. In May 1945, they organized the Vietnam Liberation Army, a military force that became the foundation of North Vietnam's army during the Vietnam War. The Viet Minh hoped to use this army to

The first president of North Vietnam, Ho Chi Minh, led the North during the Vietnam War until his death in 1969.

Reproduced by permission of Archive Photos.

take control of the country before French forces could re-establish colonial rule.

In August 1945, Japan fled Indochina for good (it formally surrendered to Allied Forces on September 2, 1945). Ho Chi Minh and the Viet Minh immediately seized control of several major Vietnamese cities, including Hanoi and Hue. Ho Chi Minh's Communist nationalists then took steps to install a new government and consolidate their power. On August 25, 1945, Bao Dai stepped down as emperor, announcing that he would instead serve as an advisor to Ho Chi Minh's government. Bao Dai's decision convinced many Vietnamese people to view Ho Chi Minh as their country's rightful leader.

France looks to reclaim Vietnam

On September 2, 1945, Ho Chi Minh established the Democratic Republic of Vietnam. He declared that the new nation would be ruled by its own citizens and that it would be independent from France and other foreign powers. He even used words from America's famous Declaration of Independence in his speech, comparing the Vietnamese struggle for freedom with the United States' successful bid for independence two centuries earlier.

France, however, wanted to regain control of Vietnam. Most of Europe—including France—had been devastated by World War II. Many of Europe's cities had been badly damaged during the conflict, and the economies of France and other nations were in terrible condition. Most French leaders believed that the resources of Vietnam and their other colonial territories could help France rebuild its cities and industries. They argued that repossession of Vietnam was essential if they hoped to recover from their war wounds.

This situation left U.S. political leaders in a difficult position. They understood the French position, but many people in the United States believed that people in Vietnam and other countries under colonial rule deserved to govern themselves. U.S. President Franklin D. Roosevelt (1882–1945), who served as president from 1933 until his death on April 12, 1945, even commented once that "after 100 years of French rule in Indochina, the inhabitants were worse off than they had been before." Other American officials thought that returning Vietnam to the French would spark years of violence and instability in the region. They believed that the Vietnamese people would not accept a return to French rule.

After weighing arguments on both sides, U.S. President Harry Truman (1884–1972; president 1945–1963), who succeeded Roosevelt after his death, decided to support France's efforts to regain Vietnam. He knew that the plan to reintroduce colonial rule was a risky one. But as Robert D. Schulzinger notes in *A Time for War,* the "political, economic, and even spiritual lives [of Europe's nations] had been broken by the war, and the highest-level American officials believed that the restoration of their health represented the first priority of the United States in the postwar world." Consequently, the United States did not object when France initiated military operations in its old colonial territory.

French forces return to Vietnam

In late 1945, French forces managed to push the Viet Minh out of most major urban centers in Vietnam's southern provinces. Ho Chi Minh and his Communist nationalist army retreated to bases in the rural north, where they enjoyed greater popular support. They also lobbied the United States and other nations for formal recognition of Vietnamese independence. In fact, Ho Chi Minh wrote letters to Truman on eight different occasions, each time asking him to recognize Vietnamese self-rule. But the United States and other nations refused to extend this recognition.

In 1946, French and Viet Minh negotiators reached a compromise. Under this agreement, France agreed to acknowledge the Democratic Republic of Vietnam as a "free state" with its own government, army, and treasury. In return, Vietnam agreed to remain a part of the French empire and permit a French military presence. But the agreement fell apart a few months later in a flurry of broken promises and disagreements over Vietnam's status. In December 1946, the Viet Minh launched a series of deadly attacks on French installations throughout Hanoi. The long-standing hostilities between French and Viet Minh forces had finally erupted into all-out war.

Sources

Buttinger, Joseph. *The Smaller Dragon: A Political History of Vietnam*. New York: Praeger, 1958.

Duiker, William J. *The Communist Road to Power in Vietnam*. 2nd ed. Boulder, CO: Westview Press, 1996.

Dunn, Peter M. *The First Vietnam War*. New York: St. Martin's Press, 1985.

Karnow, Stanley. *Vietnam: A History*. Rev. ed. New York: Penguin Books, 1997.

Kolko, Gabriel. *Anatomy of a War: Vietnam, the United States, and the Modern Historical Experience*. New York: New Press, 1994.

Marr, David G. *Vietnamese Anticolonialism 1885–1925*. Berkeley: University of California Press, 1971.

Ngo Vinh Long. *Before the Revolution: The Vietnamese Peasants Under the French*. Cambridge, Massachusetts: MIT Press, 1973.

Schulzinger, Robert D. *A Time for War: The United States and Vietnam, 1941–1975*. New York: Oxford University Press, 1997.

Summers, Harry Jr. *Historical Atlas of the Vietnam War.* Boston: Houghton Mifflin, 1995.

Wiegersma, Nancy. *Vietnam: Peasant Land, Peasant Revolution.* New York: St. Martin's Press, 1988.

The Indochina War (1946–54)

2

In 1946, the struggle between Vietnam's French colonial rulers and its Communist-supported nationalist movement finally erupted into all-out war. This war—known as the Indochina War or the First Indochina War (the Vietnam War is sometimes referred to as the Second Indochina War)—lasted for eight long years. It finally ended in 1954, after France suffered a humiliating defeat in an area of northern Vietnam known as Dien Bien Phu.

Stalemate in the early years

From 1946 to 1949 French occupation forces and the Viet Minh waged bitter war, with neither side able to gain a meaningful advantage. The nation of France entered the Indochina War willingly. Both its government and its military believed that controlling Vietnam was crucial to France's postwar economic recovery, and they expressed confidence that their superior weaponry and resources would lift them to victory.

But the Viet Minh forces proved to be a dedicated and skilled enemy. Operating in small units that specialized

Words to Know

Cold War A period of intense rivalry between the United States and the Soviet Union, as both nations competed to spread their political philosophies and influence around the world after the end of World War II (1939–45). The climate of distrust and hostility between the two nations and their allies dominated international politics until the 1980s.

Communism A political system in which the government controls all resources and means of producing wealth. By eliminating private property, this system is designed to create an equal society with no social classes. However, Communist governments in practice often limit personal freedom and rights.

Domino Theory A political theory that holds that the fall of one country's government to communism usually triggers similar collapses in neighboring countries, as if the nations were dominoes falling in sequence.

Dien Bien Phu A French fort in northwestern Vietnam that, in 1954, was the site of a major battle in the Indochina War.

Indochina War Later known as the First Indochina War (the Vietnam War became the Second Indochina War), this conflict took place between France and Communist-led Viet Minh forces in Vietnam, 1946–54.

Nationalism A feeling of intense loyalty and devotion to a country or homeland. Some people argue that nationalism, rather than communism, was the main factor that caused the Viet Minh to fight the French for control of Vietnam.

Viet Minh Communist-led nationalist group that worked to gain Vietnam's independence from French colonial rule.

in guerrilla warfare (surprise attacks and sabotage), these troops assumed control of significant areas of the countryside in northern and central Vietnam. They also mounted occasional strikes in the south, despite the heavy French military presence.

In addition, France underestimated Ho Chi Minh's (1890–1969) popularity in many Vietnamese communities. His message of national independence and his promises of land reform appealed to many Vietnamese, despite their war weariness and reservations about Viet Minh methods (some peasants, for example, were forcibly drafted into the army). In 1949, France tried to reduce popular support for Ho Chi Minh by introducing a new Vietnamese government headed by Bao Dai (1913–), who had previously ruled as emperor from 1926 to 1945. But most people recognized that this new regime (government) was still under the control of the French, and the strategy failed.

As the months passed with no apparent progress in its efforts to smash the Vietnamese rebellion, France became divided over whether to continue its efforts. After all, the Viet Minh continued to operate throughout the north, and the guerrilla movement seemed to be growing in the south as well. Moreover, the French troops found it very difficult to distinguish between peaceful Vietnamese and those that actually carried out Viet Minh missions. "The Viet Minh were like fish in water," recalled one Viet Minh official. "That was our slogan. Our fighters moved and worked among the people like fish in water."

The Cold War

As the Indochina War dragged on, it became part of a larger struggle that was taking shape at the same time between the United States and the Union of Soviet Socialist Republics (USSR), also known as the Soviet Union. This struggle, which developed in the months immediately after World War II (1939–45) and quickly grew into the dominant factor in international politics for the next four decades, was known as the "Cold War."

People to Know

Bao Dai (1913–) Vietnamese political leader who served as emperor and head of state under French colonial rule, 1926–1945 and 1949–1955.

Dwight D. Eisenhower (1890–1969) A top U.S. general during World War II (1939–45) who served as the 34th president of the United States, 1953–1961. Although he was committed to stopping the spread of communism in Asia, he was reluctant to take direct military action in Vietnam.

Ho Chi Minh (1890–1969) Vietnamese Communist leader who led Viet Minh forces in opposing French rule and became the first president of North Vietnam in 1954. He also led the North during the Vietnam War until his death.

Richard M. Nixon (1913–1994) U.S. vice president under Eisenhower. Elected as the 37th president of the United States in 1969, at the height of the Vietnam War. Resigned from office during the Watergate scandal in 1974.

Harry S. Truman (1884–1972) Served as the 33rd president of the United States, 1945–1953. Did not oppose France reclaiming control over Vietnam after World War II (1939–45).

Vo Nguyen Giap (1911–) North Vietnamese general and Communist Party leader during the First Indochina War and the Vietnam War.

First American Casualty in Vietnam

In September 1945, Army Major A. Peter Dewey became the first American soldier to die in Vietnam. Dewey had been assigned to Vietnam as part of a U.S. effort to search for American troops who had been captured by the Japanese or disappeared in Southeast Asia during World War II (1939–45). At the same time, British forces poured into the country in order to disarm the few remaining Japanese troops in the region. These British troops also helped French forces re-establish control of Saigon and other important areas in mid-1945.

As he traveled around Vietnam, Dewey became alarmed at the chaotic conditions in some areas of the country and the hatred that many Vietnamese expressed for the French. "Cochinchina is burning, the French and British are finished here, and we [the United States] ought to clear out of Southeast Asia," he stated in one report. British Major General Douglas D. Gracey, commander of the British mission to disarm the Japanese, grew angry with the American's criticism of France's operations in the country. He finally ordered Dewey out of Vietnam because of concerns that the major was actually sympathetic to the Viet Minh.

On the morning of September 26, 1945, Dewey set out for the Saigon airport to return to the United States. En route to the airport, however, he was ambushed by a small number of Viet Minh who mistakenly identified him as a French officer. They killed him with a burst of machine gun fire, making him the first of nearly 60,000 Americans to lose their lives in Vietnam.

The Cold War was essentially an intense rivalry between two dramatically different political and economic philosophies. The United States and its allied nations (nations that join together for a common cause) believed in principles of democracy and capitalism. In contrast, the Soviet Union and some other countries, including China, supported communism. These differences created extreme distrust and hostility on both sides. Before long, the United States and the USSR were engaged in a fierce competition to establish their political philosophies and influence in all corners of the world. As this political battle unfolded, both sides also raced to develop their military forces and weaponry. When this "arms race" developed, the two sides became even more suspicious and fearful of one another.

By 1947, U.S. President Harry Truman (1884–1972; president 1945–1963) had become convinced that the Soviet Union and its Communist philosophy posed a tremendous threat to the safety and well-being of the United States and its allies. The Soviets had helped bring Communist governments to power in a number of Eastern European countries, and they seemed intent on expanding their influence in other areas of the globe as well. In response to the growing Soviet sponsorship of Communist activities around the world, Truman devised a policy that came to be known as the "containment doctrine." It authorized the United States to provide financial and/or military aid to any nation threatened by Communist forces.

Truman's policy was widely supported by the American public. It also was praised by most U.S. military and political leaders. These leaders had been profoundly disturbed by the flood of new Communist governments in Eastern Europe. They saw Truman's containment doctrine as the United States' best defense against the "Domino Theory," a political theory that had rapidly gained acceptance in U.S. military and government circles. According to this theory, the loss of one country to communism usually triggered similar collapses in neighboring countries, as if the nations were dominoes falling against one another in succession. By the early 1950s, this theory had become an essential factor in most U.S. foreign policy decisions.

Former U.S. President Harry Truman.
Reproduced by permission of the Library of Congress.

United States provides active support to France

In 1949 and 1950, several significant political changes took place around the world. In 1949, Communists under the leadership of Mao Zedong (1893–1976) took control of China

President Eisenhower and the Domino Theory

U.S. President Dwight Eisenhower (1890–1969; president 1953–1961) was a firm believer in the so-called "Domino Theory." This theory stated that when one country in a region fell to communism, other nations in that region came under much greater risk of falling to communism as well. In April 1954, he held a press conference in which he explained the theory and his views on Indochina to the American public. At one point, a reporter asked Eisenhower to explain the strategic importance of China to the United States and other democratic nations. Eisenhower gave the following response:

You have, of course, both the specific and the general when you talk about such things. First of all, you have the specific value of a locality in its production of materials that the world needs. Then, you have the possibility that many human beings pass under a dictatorship that is inimical [harmful] to the free world.

Finally, you have broader considerations that might follow what you would call the 'falling domino' principle. You have a row of dominoes set up, you knock over the first one, and what will happen to the last one is the certainty that it will go over very quickly. So you could have a beginning of a disintegration that would have the most profound influences.

Now, with respect to the first [consideration], two of the items from this

particular area that the world uses are tin and tungsten. They are very important. There are others, of course, the rubber plantations and so on.

Then with respect to more people passing under this domination, Asia, after all, has already lost some 450 million of its peoples to the Communist dictatorship, and we simply can't afford greater losses.

But when we come to the possible sequence of events, the loss of Indochina, of Burma, of Thailand, of the Peninsula, and Indonesia following, now you begin to talk about areas that not only multiply the disadvantages that you would suffer through loss of materials, sources of materials, but now you are talking about millions and millions and millions of people.

Finally, the geographical position achieved [by controlling Indochina] does many things. It turns the so-called island defensive chain of Japan, Formosa, of the Philippines . . . to the southward; it moves in to threaten Australia and New Zealand [with communism].

[The loss of Indochina to communism] takes away, in its economic respects, that region that Japan must have as a trading area or Japan, in turn, will have only one place in the world to go—that is, toward the Communist areas in order to live.

So, the possible consequences of the loss [of Indochina to communism] are just incalculable [beyond calculation] to the free world.

after a long war. A few months later, both China and the Soviet Union formally recognized Ho Chi Minh and his Communist leadership as the rightful rulers of Vietnam. Then, in June

1950, North Korea's Communist government attacked U.S.-supported South Korea, apparently with the approval of the Soviets. The attack by North Korea triggered the Korean War (1950–53), in which American-led forces defended South Korea against the Communist armies of both North Korea and China.

These events convinced the United States that it needed to focus greater attention on the French-Viet Minh conflict in Vietnam. All of Southeast Asia seemed to be in danger of being swallowed up by communism, and Vietnam suddenly loomed as a key strategic country in the fight to contain it. American policymakers condemned Ho Chi Minh as a Soviet-sponsored agent of communism and assured France that the United States was willing to step forward and help them in their battle to regain possession of Vietnam.

On February 7, 1950, the United States formally recognized the French-controlled government of Bao Dai as the legitimate government of Vietnam. By the spring of 1950, the United States was providing direct political, economic, and military support to French forces in Vietnam. Despite such aid, however, many leaders harbored doubts about getting involved in the region. In fact, many officials did not believe that the United States would be able to help transform Vietnam into a peaceful, anticommunist nation. For example, analyst Raymond B. Fosdick argued that "whether the French like it or not, independence is coming to Indochina. Why, therefore, do we tie ourselves to the tail of their battered kite?" Most U.S. officials, however, believed that the threat posed by communism was so great that the United States had to side with the French.

French support for war fades

U.S. military and economic assistance provided a much-needed boost to the French war effort in Vietnam. Despite the influx of U.S. aid, however, the Viet Minh managed to strengthen their hold over the country's northern provinces. They were able to do this in large part because the rise to power of the Communists in China, Vietnam's neighbor to the north, gave Ho Chi Minh and his forces a valuable ally. In fact, the Chinese Communists provided the Viet Minh

Captured French soldiers marching through fields after surrendering to the Vietnamese.
Reproduced by permission of AP/World Wide Photos.

with considerable military assistance throughout the remainder of the Indochina War.

With the help of Chinese weapons and other equipment, the Viet Minh expanded quickly into a significant military force. As their army grew in size, the Vietnamese Communists showed a greater willingness to confront the French in bigger battles, especially in the thick jungles of northern

Vietnam. The Viet Minh continued to strengthen their hold over the region's rural areas, and in the fall of 1950 they launched successful strikes against French military positions and supply routes throughout the area.

The assaults resulted in the death or capture of approximately 6,000 French troops in October alone, and ultimately forced French troops to abandon large expanses of territory along the Chinese border. "That was the first disaster of the war," confirmed French historian Jean Lacouture. "[It] gave the idea that the war was nearly impossible to win because the Viet Minh, with China behind it, had a great enormous sanctuary. So the war became more and more unpopular from 1950—and very expensive, though of course the United States paid."

By the end of 1950, the Viet Minh forces—commanded by General Vo Nguyen Giap (1911–)—seemed to be on their way to eventual victory. "Giap could feel satisfied with his achievements in 1950," writes Phillip B. Davidson, author of *Vietnam at War: The History 1946–1975*. "He demonstrated the effectiveness of his Main Force units; he seized the initiative; and he demoralized the French command. Beyond that, he had unnerved the French government, which now realized that there was no way to win Indochina without a massive effort, and this was politically impossible."

Vo Nguyen Giap was the leader of the North Vietnamese military forces for more than thirty years. One of his greatest achievements came in the decisive battle of Dien Bien Phu, which ended the Indochina War in 1954. *Reproduced by permission of Archive Photos.*

American aid not enough

From 1950 to 1954, the United States steadily increased the amount of financial assistance it provided to France's military operations in Vietnam. By 1954, the U.S. aid total reached almost $3 billion, an amount that covered about 80 percent of all French military spending in the Indochina War. This was even more aid than France received from the

Marshall Plan, a massive U.S. program of financial assistance designed to help European nations rebuild after the devastation of World War II.

Nonetheless, the war continued to swing in favor of the Viet Minh. By the end of 1952, French casualties (dead, wounded, and missing) had reached 80,000 to 90,000, and the Communists showed no signs of letting up. In fact, the Viet Minh made good use of traditional Vietnamese hostility toward France in their efforts to gain new recruits to their cause. Ho Chi Minh also continued to present the Viet Minh as a primarily nationalistic—rather than Communist—force that was fighting to restore Vietnamese independence. This message appealed to many young men. It also made it very difficult for France to gain the support of Vietnamese communities, most of which just wanted an end to the war.

The battle of Dien Bien Phu

As 1953 unfolded, France continued to lose ground. By late 1953, French territorial control had been reduced to positions around Hanoi, Haiphong, Saigon, and a smattering of other areas.

And in May 1954, France's dream of re-establishing colonial rule over Vietnam finally came to an end, as the French suffered one of the most significant defeats in modern military history.

In late 1953, a large French military force had been assigned to Dien Bien Phu, a military post in northwestern Vietnam. The French troops were sent there in order to prevent the Viet Minh Communists from taking control of the Mekong River valley and the nearby region that bordered the country of Laos. By this time, however, war-weary France was already preparing to negotiate an end to the war. In fact, Viet Minh and French negotiators were scheduled to join other international officials in Geneva, Switzerland, on May 7, 1954, to discuss terms of a peace treaty. But French General Henri Navarre, who ordered the deployment to Dien Bien Phu, reasoned that if the French military still held strong positions in Vietnam when the negotiations began, France would be able to negotiate a treaty that would be more beneficial to its interests. As U.S. official

Walter Medell Smith remarked at Geneva, "You don't win at the conference table what you've lost on the battlefield."

Navarre's plan underestimated the size and strength of Viet Minh forces in the area surrounding Dien Bien Phu. In early 1954, the Viet Minh successfully isolated the garrison (military post) from other French troops, and in March they launched a fierce siege on the stronghold. Over the next two months, Viet Minh units battered the trapped French soldiers with artillery, antiaircraft guns, and automatic weapons fire. France tried to provide the garrison with supplies by parachute, but this strategy did not work very well. Many parachute drops missed their mark, and Viet Minh antiaircraft guns shot down several French transport planes.

As the siege dragged on, conditions inside Dien Bien Phu decayed rapidly. Outnumbered and outgunned, the garrison's defenders—which also included Vietnamese troops from Bao Dai's government—suffered terrible casualties, especially as food,

A Vietnamese soldier waving a flag over the captured headquarters of the French army at Dien Bien Phu.
Reproduced by permission of AP/World Wide Photos.

medicine, ammunition, and other supplies dwindled away. "The surgeons at Dien Bien Phu are reaching the limit of their endurance, and the overflow of wounded are waiting on the ground for their dressings to be changed," reported the French magazine *Le Monde* at the height of the siege. "The water of the river in which bodies float can be filtered only in eyedrop amounts. There is just enough water to give the men when they get delirious from thirst."

Alarmed by the deteriorating situation, some top U.S. generals and advisors, including Vice President Richard Nixon (1913–1994), recommended that the United States begin military air strikes on Communist positions throughout northern Vietnam. President Dwight Eisenhower (1890–1969; president 1953–1961), who succeeded Truman as president in 1953, gave serious consideration to the proposal. After all, he firmly believed that if the Communists gained control of Vietnam, other Southeast Asian nations might also turn to communism. But despite his belief in the Domino Theory, Eisenhower decided that direct military involvement in Vietnam was too risky. His refusal to order air strikes greatly angered the French government, which realized that a major disaster was unfolding at the remote outpost.

On May 7, 1954, the garrison at Dien Bien Phu was finally overrun by Viet Minh forces. An estimated 8,000 Viet Minh were killed in the siege and battle, and another 15,000 troops were injured during the campaign. By comparison, only 2,200 French troops died in the clash (another 6,000 were wounded, and 10,000 were captured). But despite these statistics, the Battle of Dien Bien Phu was universally regarded as a tremendous Viet Minh victory, and as a shocking defeat for France. In fact, the loss of Dien Bien Phu triggered a tremendous shakeup in the French government and created an outcry against the war throughout France that could not be ignored. On July 20, 1954, France agreed to permanently withdraw from Vietnam under terms of an agreement known as the Geneva Accords.

"The battle of Dien Bien Phu . . . ranks with Agincourt, Waterloo, and Gettysburg as one of the great military engagements in history," writes Stanley Karnow in Howard Simpson's *Dien Bien Phu: The Epic Battle America Forgot*. "It spelled the end of France's crumbling empire in Asia, and while nobody foresaw the possibility then, it eventually opened the way for America's commitment to the region over the years that followed. So it was a decisive episode that indirectly set in motion a process that was to have profound and pervasive consequences for the United States."

Sources

Billings-Yun, Melanie. *Decision Against War: Eisenhower and Dien Bien Phu, 1954.* New York: Columbia University Press, 1988.

Buttinger, Joseph. *The Smaller Dragon: A Political History of Vietnam.* New York: Praeger, 1958.

Davidson, Phillip B. *Vietnam at War: The History 1946–1975.* Novato, CA: Presidio Press, 1988.

Duiker, William J. *The Communist Road to Power in Vietnam.* 2nd ed. Boulder, CO: Westview Press, 1996.

Dunn, Peter M. *The First Vietnam War.* New York: St. Martin's Press, 1985.

Fall, Bernard. *Hell in a Very Small Place: The Siege of Dien Bien Phu.* Philadelphia: J. B. Lippincott, 1966.

Karnow, Stanley. *Vietnam: A History.* Rev. ed. New York: Viking, 1991.

Olson, James, and Randy Roberts. *Where the Domino Fell: America and Vietnam, 1945–1990.* New York: St. Martin's Press, 1996.

Simpson, Howard R. *Dien Bien Phu: The Epic Battle America Forgot.* Washington, DC: Brassey's, 1994.

Early American Involvement in Vietnam (1954–62)

3

In 1954, France gave up its colonial claims on Vietnam. But even as France prepared to leave the region, the United States and other democratic nations continued to assert influence on the internal affairs of the country. Specifically, they forced Ho Chi Minh's Vietnamese Communists to accept a treaty that divided Vietnam in half.

Throughout the late 1950s and early 1960s, Ho Chi Minh (1890–1969) established a Communist government in North Vietnam. At the same time, the United States government worked hard to support a non-Communist government in South Vietnam. Ignoring the 1954 Geneva Accords—which called for reunification of the country in 1956 after nation-wide elections—U.S. officials threw their support behind an anti-Communist politician named Ngo Dinh Diem (1901–1963). At first, Diem's government seemed like a strong candidate for U.S. financial and military support. But as time passed, Diem's style of governing and the growth of political opposition to his regime (government) sparked great concern in the United States.

Words to Know

ARVN The South Vietnamese army, officially known as the Army of the Republic of South Vietnam. The ARVN fought on the same side as U.S. troops during the Vietnam War.

Buddhism A religion based on the teachings of Siddhartha Gautama (known as the Buddha; c. 563–c. 483 B.C.), in which followers seek moral purity and spiritual enlightenment. Buddhism was the religion of the majority of citizens of South Vietnam.

Communism A political system in which the government controls all resources and means of producing wealth. By eliminating private property, this system is designed to create an equal society with no social classes.However, Communist governments in practice often limit personal freedom and rights.

Hanoi The capital city of Communist North Vietnam. Also an unofficial shorthand way of referring to the North Vietnamese government.

North Vietnam The Geneva Accords of 1954, which ended the First Indochina War (1946–54), divided the nation of Vietnam into two sections. The northern section, which was led by a Communist government under Ho Chi Minh, was officially known as the Democratic Republic of Vietnam, but was usually called North Vietnam.

Saigon The capital city of U.S.-supported South Vietnam. Also an unofficial shorthand way of referring to the South Vietnamese government.

South Vietnam Created under the Geneva Accords of 1954, the southern section of Vietnam was known as the Republic of South Vietnam. It was led by a U.S.-supported government under Ngo Dinh Diem.

Viet Cong Vietnamese Communist guerilla fighters who worked with the North Vietnamese Army to conquer South Vietnam.

Viet Minh Communist-led nationalist group that worked to gain Vietnam's independence from French colonial rule.

The division of Vietnam

The year 1954 marked a major turning point in the history of Vietnam. France reluctantly prepared to give up control of the country, which it had held since the late nineteenth century. At the same time, Viet Minh forces led by Ho Chi Minh hoped to establish Communist rule over the entire nation. After all, the Viet Minh had seized control of much of

People to Know

Bao Dai (1913–) Vietnamese political leader who served as emperor and head of state under French colonial rule, 1926–1945 and 1949–1955.

Dwight D. Eisenhower (1890–1969) A top U.S. general during World War II (1939–45) who served as the 34th president of the United States, 1953–1961. Although he was committed to stopping the spread of communism in Asia, he was reluctant to take direct military action in Vietnam.

Ho Chi Minh (1890–1969) Vietnamese Communist leader who led Viet Minh forces in opposing French rule and became the first president of North Vietnam in 1954. He also led the North during the Vietnam War until his death.

John F. Kennedy (1917–1963) Served as the 35th president of the United States from 1960 until he was assassinated in 1963.

Ngo Dinh Diem (1901–1963) Vietnamese political leader who became president of South Vietnam in 1954. He gradually lost the support of the United States and was killed following the overthrow of his government in 1963.

Ngo Dinh Nhu (1910–1963) Known as Brother Nhu, he was the brother and main political advisor of South Vietnamese President Ngo Dinh Diem.

Madame Nhu (1924–) Served as the unofficial first lady of South Vietnam during the presidency of Ngo Dinh Diem. She was actually the wife of Diem's brother Ngo Dinh Nhu; her maiden name was Tran Le Xuan.

the country by this time. But the United States and other democratic nations objected to this plan because they did not want Vietnam controlled by Communists. As a result, Ho Chi Minh and the Vietnamese Communists were forced to accept a compromise.

This compromise, drawn up at the Geneva Conference of July 1954, temporarily divided Vietnam into northern and southern sections. The Viet Minh received the northern half of the country above the 17th parallel. The southern portion of the country below the 17th parallel went to non-Communists. According to the Geneva Accords, however, this arrangement was only supposed to be temporary. The treaty called for

national elections to be held in both zones in 1956 to create a united Vietnamese government.

As soon as the Geneva settlement was reached, both North and South Vietnam scrambled to strengthen their positions and establish their governments. As the leader of the Viet Minh forces that had forced France to surrender its grip on Vietnam, Ho Chi Minh was the obvious choice to take over leadership of North Vietnam. In the South, meanwhile, the United States wanted to make sure that the government had a strong anti-Communist leader. They pressured Emperor Bao Dai (1913–), who held little actual political power, to appoint a man named Ngo Dinh Diem as prime minister.

Ngo Dinh Diem served as the president of South Vietnam during the early years of the Vietnam War. Diem initially gained the support of the United States because of his strong opposition to communism. *Reproduced by permission of the Library of Congress.*

Ngo Dinh Diem becomes leader of South Vietnam

The United States government liked Ngo Dinh Diem for several reasons. A strong anti-Communist and opponent of French rule, Diem was viewed as someone who had always been dedicated to creating a united and independent Vietnam. In addition, he had become acquainted with many U.S. religious and political leaders during the early 1950s, when fears about his safety in French-ruled Vietnam led him to relocate to Europe and the United States. American officials believed that he might represent a legitimate "third force" in Vietnamese politics—a figure who was neither a Communist nor connected to the nation's unpopular French colonial governments.

On July 7, 1954, Bao Dai appointed Diem as prime minister. Upon assuming power, Diem worked with the United States' Central Intelligence Agency (CIA) to increase political support for his government. They agreed that one of the best ways to do this was to convince Vietnamese Catholics living in the North to relocate to the South. Diem was a member of the Roman Catholic religious faith. Buddhists, however, accounted for ninety to ninety-five percent of the South's total population. This concerned Diem, who believed that he could broaden support for his government by convincing other Catholics to come to South Vietnam.

Diem knew, however, that he only had a limited amount of time to convince northern Catholics to relocate. According to the terms of the Geneva Accords, both North and South Vietnam agreed to hold off on formally establishing the boundary dividing the two nations until October 1954. The two sides agreed to this provision so that French troops still in the North could withdraw peacefully and so that Vietnamese people could move from one region to the other if they wished.

Approximately 80,000 people from South Vietnam went north during this time. Most of these people were Viet Minh fighters who wanted to live in Ho Chi Minh's Communist society. But a far greater number of Vietnamese traveled from north to south. The majority of these people were Catholics who left North Vietnam for a variety of reasons. Some expressed fears about religious persecution at the hands of the Communist government. Others were lured by Diem's promises of valuable land grants or frightened by CIA warnings that North Vietnam might someday be the target of an American nuclear attack.

The promises and scare tactics employed by the Diem government and the CIA worked extremely well. Over several weeks, an estimated 850,000 people migrated south, most of them Catholics and small land owners. The South Vietnamese and American governments later claimed that this mass exodus from the North showed that the Vietnamese people did not want to live under Communist rule.

Diem's family dominates government

As both prime minister and president of South Vietnam, Diem held enormous influence over the nation's government. After settling in the capital city of Saigon, he quickly appointed close family members to many of the most important positions in his new government. In many cases, however, these appointments were not good for the country. For example, Diem made his brother Ngo Dinh Nhu (1910–1963) his most important political advisor and chief of the country's secret police.

Nhu—known as "Brother Nhu" to the international media—was an intelligent, educated man. But he quickly gained a reputation as a corrupt and ruthless official who resorted to terror and murder to protect his many criminal activities. Brother Nhu's wife, Madame Nhu (maiden name Tran Le Xuan), acted as first lady and official hostess for South Vietnam's unmarried president. Ambitious and energetic, Madame Nhu soon became known both for her beauty and her greedy and vengeful personality. Together, Nhu and his wife exercised considerable control over Diem and his government.

Other members of Diem's family held important positions as well. His brother Ngo Dinh Can controlled the region around Hue, Vietnam's second largest city. Diem's older brother, Ngo Dinh Thuc, was an important bishop in South Vietnam's Catholic Church. And many of Diem's cousins and in-laws were given important national and provincial government posts. These arrangements further strengthened Diem's hold over the South Vietnam government. But many of these appointments ultimately proved disastrous for the nation. A number of Diem's relatives were terribly corrupt, and many of his closest relatives did not have the skills or personalities to manage their important responsibilities. "[Diem and his family were] the most neurotic family I've ever known, *even in history*," recalled *Time* reporter Charles Mohr. "They simply were a bunch of dingbats."

Diem establishes Republic of Vietnam

The 1954 Geneva Accords called for national elections to be held in Vietnam's two zones in 1956. The winner of these elections would then take control of the entire nation, which would be reunified. But Diem and his U.S. supporters ignored this provision of the agreement. They feared that if these elections were held, North Vietnam's Communist government would win. In fact, the United States never actually signed the Geneva Accords—although it pledged to honor the agreement—because of these fears. As U.S. President Dwight Eisenhower (1890–1969; president 1953–1961) later admitted, "if the elections had been held in 1956, Ho Chi Minh would have won 80 percent of the vote."

Instead, Diem devoted his energies to consolidating his power in the South. During the spring of 1955, Diem mounted effective attacks on a number of ethnic minorities and criminal sects, which had built their own private armies over the years. His main targets were the Cao Dai and Hoa Hao religious sects and the Binh Xuyen force, which controlled many of Saigon's underworld criminal activities. He also made sure that Roman Catholics occupied most of South Vietnam's important political and military positions. This favoritism triggered considerable anger among the country's non-Catholic Buddhist majority, but Diem believed that he would be more secure if he was surrounded by Catholics.

As the months passed, Diem ignored North Vietnamese efforts to make arrangements for the 1956 elections. Instead, he and his American allies moved ahead with their own plan. In October 1955, Diem defeated Bao Dai in a presidential election to determine future leadership of South Vietnam. Diem received better than ninety-eight percent of the vote in the contest, for which Bao Dai did not actively campaign. In fact, Bao Dai remained in his home in France throughout this time. Nonetheless, some historians suggest that the vote may have been rigged in Diem's favor.

A few days after the election, on October 26, 1955, Diem established South Vietnam as a separate country formally known as the Republic of Vietnam. Over the next several months he formed a permanent National Assembly to serve as the country's main legislative body. He also took steps to strengthen the South Vietnamese army, known as the ARVN (Army of the Republic of South Vietnam). Diem was helped in this effort by an American military unit called Military Assistance Advisory Group-Vietnam (MAAG-Vietnam). This group was formed in November 1955 to provide military training, aid, and support to the South Vietnamese army. By early 1956, Ngo Dinh Diem's political and military maneuverings had placed him firmly in control of South Vietnam.

Violence in North Vietnam

Diem's strong performance frustrated North Vietnam's Communist leaders, who had thought that his government would collapse. And his refusal to hold elections to reunite the country infuriated Ho Chi Minh and other Communist officials. North Vietnam's prime minister Pham Van Dong, for example, called it "a blatant violation of the Geneva Agreements." But at first, the North Vietnamese government, based in Hanoi, decided not to launch any violent campaigns to disrupt Diem's rule. As former CIA Director William Colby recalls in *The Bad War: An Oral History of the Vietnam War,* "The Communists had a full job organizing North Vietnam for the first two or three years. They went through land reform that managed to create an enormous famine. They killed a lot of landlords and things of this nature."

Indeed, the situation in North Vietnam became very grim in the mid-1950s. After the Geneva Accords of 1954, Ho Chi Minh and other Communist leaders concentrated on building a socialist society in the North (socialism is a political doctrine that calls for state ownership and control of industry, agriculture, and distribution of wealth). North Vietnamese leaders subsequently worked to replace the region's village and family-oriented economies with government-controlled industries and agricultural practices.

As part of this plan, the Communists started a land reform campaign in the mid-1950s. These programs were meant to distribute privately owned land to poor and landless people. But the land reform campaign soon turned vicious. Thousands of people who had previously owned land or were thought to be unfriendly to communism were put in prison or executed. Estimates of the numbers of Vietnamese killed during this period range from 30,000 to as many as 100,000.

In October 1956, the government finally ended the bloody program. It then launched a "rectification of errors" program to punish people who had gotten carried away during the land reform campaign. This program resulted in the imprisonment of another 12,000 people branded as "exploiters" and the dismissal of many party officials.

During the late 1950s, the situation in North Vietnam stabilized. The country, now formally known as the Democratic Republic of Vietnam (DRV), completed its transition to a communist way of life. The nation's economic development during this time was guided by government strategies known as the Three-Year-Plan (1958–60) and the Five-Year-Plan (1961–65). These plans were meant to increase the North's industrial base by nationalizing former French-owned industries and developing mining and hydroelectric projects throughout the country. The Communists were helped in these efforts by both the Chinese and Soviet governments.

Growing American doubts about Diem

When Ngo Dinh Diem assumed power in the mid-1950s, the United States viewed him as the best candidate to keep South Vietnam out of Communist hands. With that in mind, America provided him with a great deal of political, economic, and military assistance. Led by U.S. Secretary of State John Foster Dulles (1888–1959), the United States even created a regional alliance called the Southeast Asia Treaty Organization (SEATO). This organization extended U.S. protection to South Vietnam and the neighboring countries of Cambodia and Laos in case of Communist "subversion" (attempts to overthrow their governments).

As time passed, however, U.S. officials became divided about the wisdom of supporting the Diem government. They liked his fierce anti-Communist views and his swift steps to stabilize the government in South Vietnam. But Diem's government also came to be viewed as a secretive and corrupt one that resisted American calls to give the South Vietnamese people increased personal rights and economic opportunities.

The attitudes displayed by members of Diem's government caused concern among some American military leaders and diplomats. In 1955, for example, General Joseph L. Collins recommended reducing U.S. support because of Diem's refusal to make democratic reforms. "I am . . . convinced Diem does not have the knack of handling men nor the executive capacity truly to unify the country and establish an effective government," he said.

Two years later, Eldridge Durbrow, who served as U.S. ambassador to South Vietnam from 1957 to 1961, voiced similar doubts. "Diem has avoided making decisions required to build the economic and social foundations necessary to secure Viet Nam's future independence and strength," wrote Durbrow. "He has made it clear that he would give first priority to the build-up of his armed forces regardless of the country's requirements for economic and social development." Durbrow

Dwight D. Eisenhower (1890–1969)

Dwight D. Eisenhower served the United States as both a military general and president, making him one of the most important public figures of the mid-twentieth century. Born in Texas and raised in Kansas, he chose a career in the U.S. military. In World War II (1939–45) he became supreme commander over all Allied forces in Europe, ultimately guiding them to victory over Germany. After World War II, he became the first commander of the North Atlantic Treaty Organization (NATO), a military alliance of European and North American nations (including the United States) against the Union of Soviet Social Republics (USSR) and other Communist powers.

In 1952, Eisenhower won the Republican nomination for the U.S. presidency, and in November of that year he defeated Democratic candidate Adlai Stevenson (1900–1965) to succeed outgoing president Harry Truman (1884–1972; president 1945–1953). In early 1953, Eisenhower was sworn in as America's 34th president.

Eisenhower served two four-year terms as president before leaving office in 1961. He was a popular president who led the United States during a period of general economic prosperity. During his presidency, America created the national highway system, built the St. Lawrence Seaway, and experienced great economic growth. Eisenhower also used federal troops to enforce Supreme Court rulings calling for integration of schools and other public institutions in the United States.

Eisenhower is perhaps best remembered, however, for his Cold War attitudes and policies. Eisenhower distrusted the Soviet Union and hated communism, and he actively worked against Communist governments and organizations throughout his presidency. For example, he approved significant financial assistance to French military forces engaged in Vietnam throughout the second half of the Indochina War (1946–54).

But Eisenhower resisted calls from some U.S. congressmen for massive increases in military spending, and he

also claimed that Diem's reliance on Catholics and wealthy land owners for support was alienating the rest of the South Vietnamese population.

But Diem and his family continued to resist American calls to implement democratic reforms. They wanted the financial aid from the United States, but they did not want to be told

Dwight D. Eisenhower, speaking with a group of paratroopers. *Reproduced by permission of the National Archive Photos and Records Administration.*

turned down U.S. military recommendations that he launch first-strike nuclear attacks against the Soviets. The Eisenhower administration also clashed with Senator Joseph McCarthy (1908–1957) over his controversial investigations of alleged Communist activity within the U.S. government (McCarthy's ruthless efforts to uncover Communists are now regarded as an unfortunate chapter in American history).

Eisenhower's stands on these issues were based on his belief that if communism was simply contained—rather than destroyed—it would eventually collapse because of its own faults. "This will take a long time," he said, "but our most realistic policy is holding the line until the Soviets manage to educate their people. By doing so, they will sow the seeds of their own destruction."

After leaving office, Eisenhower publicly supported the Vietnam policies of presidents John F. Kennedy (1917–1963; president 1960–1963) and Lyndon B. Johnson (1908–1973; president 1963–1969). Privately, however, he complained that neither leader used sufficient military force in Vietnam. As the war progressed, Eisenhower also became fiercely hostile to the views and activities of many members of America's antiwar movement. He supported U.S. involvement in the Vietnam War up until his death in 1969.

how to run their country. As time passed, the Diem government continued to make policies that troubled U.S. officials. For example, much of the country's wealth and power remained in the hands of a small Catholic minority, most of whom lived in Saigon and a couple of other cities. In addition, Diem took ruthless steps to stamp out Communist political opposition.

As Diem's last military chief, General Tran Van Don, later wrote in *Our Endless War: Inside Vietnam,* Diem and his family "resorted to arbitrary arrests, confinement in concentration camps for undetermined periods of time without judicial guarantees or restraints, and assassinations of people suspected of Communist leanings. Their use of Gestapo-like police raids and torture were known and decried everywhere." Soon, the government began using these tactics against non-Communists as well. "The repression . . . spread to people who simply opposed their regime, such as heads or spokesmen of other political parties, and against individuals who were resisting extortion [use of force or intimidation to obtain wealth or cooperation] by some of the government officials," said the general.

Despite concerns about some aspects of Diem's rule, however, most American officials believed that he was their only hope for keeping South Vietnam out of Communist hands. As a result, the Eisenhower administration declared its continued support for his government. In May 1957, for example, Diem was invited to address a joint session of the U.S. Congress. At the same session, President Eisenhower proclaimed that "the cost of defending freedom, of defending America, must be paid in many forms and many places. Vietnam cannot at this time produce and support the military formations essential to its survival. Military as well as economic help is currently needed in Vietnam."

Problems in the countryside

During the late 1950s, the situation in South Vietnam became more explosive. In late 1957, southern Communists assassinated several hundred village officials and schoolteachers around the country in retaliation for Diem's crackdown. In January 1958, these guerrillas (small groups of fighters who launch surprise attacks), who were the last remnants of the Viet Minh forces that had helped end French rule, attacked a number of Diem supporters living in the Saigon area. These raids angered and worried Diem, who introduced the term "Viet Cong" to describe the attackers. This term, an abbreviation for Vietnamese Communists, quickly became the most widely used term for the Vietnamese Communist fighters operating in the South.

Most historians believe that North Vietnam still hoped to unite the country through an election rather through warfare during this period. Communist leaders worried that if they tried to take South Vietnam by force, the United States would use its military might on behalf of Diem. With this in mind, in March 1958, the North suggested holding new talks with the South to iron out their differences and plan for an eventual reunification. But Diem flatly rejected any such discussions until North Vietnam adopted "democratic liberties similar to those existing in the South." This language was a little embarrassing to America, since Diem had resisted all U.S. advice to make South Vietnam more democratic. But the United States supported Diem's stand because it still feared that a unified Vietnam would choose a Communist government.

In 1959, the Viet Cong increased their activities in rural areas of South Vietnam, where dissatisfaction with Diem was strongest. These regions were populated by Buddhists and ethnic minorities who felt as though Diem's government was mistreating them and ignoring their needs in favor of its wealthy, Catholic supporters. This anti-Diem atmosphere made it possible for the Viet Cong to gain control of significant sections of the countryside. At the same time, the Viet Cong continued to lobby the North Vietnamese government for military assistance. The North's political leadership finally agreed that the only way they would be able to reunite the divided country would be to take up arms once again. From this point forward, North Vietnam began preparing for war.

Communists mobilize against Diem

In May 1959, North Vietnam began building a trail that would allow it to secretly transport supplies, troops, and communications into South Vietnam and back into the North. General Vo Bam supervised the construction of this trail, which officials called the Truong Son Route. The pathway eventually became better known as the Ho Chi Minh Trail.

The Ho Chi Minh Trail was built in Laos, the country immediately to the west of Vietnam. It extended down the spine of the Chaîne Annamitique mountains in eastern Laos to supply stations in the jungles of South Vietnam. By the time it was completed in the mid-1960s, it was 12,500 miles long and

"Secret War" in Laos

During the 1950s and early 1960s in Indochina, armed struggle between Communist and non-Communist forces was not limited to Vietnam. This fight could also be seen in Laos, a country along the northwestern border of Vietnam.

Laos is a country with a history similar to that of Vietnam in several important respects. Both countries enjoyed a long period of self-rule that ended in the nineteenth century, when European colonialism swept through Southeast Asia. By the late nineteenth century, both Laos and Vietnam were controlled by France. And like Vietnam, Laos also was occupied by Japanese forces during World War II (1939–45).

In 1947, France gave Laos limited independence, and six years later it granted the Laotian people full independence. But once Laos received its independence, it became paralyzed by violent disputes between various political factions. The main groups in this battle for control of the nation were the Pathet Lao (Lao Nation), a Communist movement that received support from Ho Chi Minh's Communist Vietnamese forces, and the Royal Lao, a non-Communist government supported by France.

In 1954, the Geneva Conference was held in an effort to end the Indochina War (1946–54) in Vietnam. During this meeting, Laos' opposing forces and other countries interested in the conflict reached an agreement to end the war and withdraw all foreign troops from the country. But the Pathet Lao soon broke the

included underground barracks, hospitals, and other facilities. This intricate network of paths, invisible from the air because of the thick jungle foliage, became a vital supply route and communication lifeline for the Communists.

At the same time that the North Vietnamese military began hacking the Ho Chi Minh Trail out of the jungle, it also sent agents into the South to lead many of the Viet Cong guerrilla groups. Many of these men were recruited from southern Viet Minh troops who had moved north after the Geneva Accords. In December 1960, meanwhile, opponents of the Diem government united to form an organization called the National Liberation Front (NLF). This group was dedicated to the overthrow of Diem. It included members of a wide range truce and resumed its rebellion with the help of North Vietnam.

The struggle for control of Laos continued until 1962, by which time both the United States and the Soviet Union were inching closer to involvement. In 1962, another round of peace talks was held in Geneva in an effort to end the fighting. In the final agreement, the Communists guaranteed the neutrality of western Laos. In exchange, the United States guaranteed that it would not invade eastern Laos. America's promise to remain neutral and stay out of eastern Laos was very important to Ho Chi Minh and the Vietnamese Communists because the region contained a large section of the Ho Chi Minh Trail, North Vietnam's primary supply and communication line into South Vietnam.

Many of the Laotian people hoped that the 1962 Geneva Conference would bring an end to the years of fighting. But their hopes were soon dashed, as the Pathet Lao and their North Vietnamese allies resumed their push to replace the existing government with a Communist one. The fight for control of the kingdom continued throughout the mid-1960s, with both the Soviets and the Americans providing military aid and supplies to their respective allies. The United States, however, provided its military and financial aid to the Laotian government in secret because of its 1962 Geneva Conference pledge to remain neutral. The United States' various efforts to aid anti-Communist forces in Laos without being detected eventually became known as America's "Secret War in Laos."

of groups who were unhappy with South Vietnam's government, but its activities were ultimately directed by North Vietnam's Communist leadership.

Kennedy pledges support

By 1960, a growing number of American observers were expressing grave doubts about Diem's government, even though the United States continued to provide economic and military aid. In fact, it doubled the number of military advisors provided to the South Vietnamese military in 1960. But many military officers and government leaders wondered about the long-term stability of the Diem regime.

American involvement in Vietnam increased during President John F. Kennedy's administration.
Reproduced by permission of the John F. Kennedy Library.

Those concerns led some U.S. officials to suggest that the United States should consider withdrawing its support for Diem and lending its help to some new leader. Other policymakers defended Diem as a good leader who was making the best of a difficult situation. But Diem sensed that U.S. support for his regime was weakening, and this realization made him even more insecure and stubborn. "The [Diem] family had survived . . . for two reasons," writes William Prochnau in *Once Upon a Distant War.* "American support and an almost total lack of credible alternative leadership in a country created by outside powers after the French defeat. Diem could be such a troublesome client, however, that the American support was not always so unstinting [reliable]—and Saigon's plotters knew it."

In November 1960, John F. Kennedy (1917–1963; president 1960–1963) was elected to succeed Eisenhower as America's next president. A few days later, a group of angry South Vietnamese paratroopers launched a coup (takeover) attempt against Diem that nearly succeeded. Diem slipped out of danger and maintained control of the government. Nonetheless, the incident demonstrated that the situation in his country was tense and unpredictable.

When Kennedy took over the presidency in January 1961, he emphasized the need for continued U.S. support of South Vietnam. Like many other people in the United States, he feared that the loss of Vietnam to the Communists would trigger a wave of Communist aggression across the globe. "No other challenge is more deserving of our every effort and energy [than Vietnam]," he said. Kennedy added that if South Vietnam was lost to the Communists, "our [nation's] security may be lost piece by piece, country by country."

In April 1961, Diem was re-elected president by an overwhelming majority. Defenders of the president claimed that these results showed he had the support of the South Vietnamese people. One month later, Kennedy declared at a press conference that he was willing to consider the use of American military forces "to help South Vietnam resist Communist pressures." In late 1961, the Kennedy administration swallowed its doubts about deepening U.S. involvement in the country and established a new military command—called the Military Assistance Command, Vietnam (MACV)—to direct the activities of U.S. troops stationed in South Vietnam.

Mounting criticism of Diem government

Throughout 1961, the debate over the situation in South Vietnam intensified in American political and military circles. Nearly everyone agreed that the United States needed to make sure that South Vietnam did not fall to the Communists. But people disagreed wildly about whether Diem's regime and U.S. military and economic aid was succeeding in that regard.

Some officials, such as U.S. Ambassador Frederick Nolting, offered unwavering support of Diem and his government. In his memoirs, Nolting calls President Diem "an honest and dedicated man" who was "very much concerned with the welfare of his people." Others, such as U.S. General Paul Harkins, who served as commander of MACV from 1962 to 1964, insisted that the Diem government was stable and that the Viet Cong would soon be destroyed. But other U.S. officers and members of the Kennedy administration were not so optimistic. They charged that Harkins and other Saigon-based officials were not providing an accurate picture of events in South Vietnam. This concern was partly due to increasingly critical press coverage in the *New York Times* and other newspapers.

During this period, the U.S. government provided optimistic accounts of events in Vietnam in order to maintain public support for their efforts there. Many reporters filed stories that reflected the U.S. government's description of events. But some members of the American and international press corps based in South Vietnam suggested that the country was in serious trouble. These accounts, filed by veteran correspondents such as Homer Bigart and David Halberstam (both of the *New York Times*), indicated that Diem's government was corrupt and unpopular. They noted that significant sections of

The Quiet American

One of the first people to warn Americans about the potential problems of getting involved in Vietnam was the British novelist Graham Greene (1904–1991). Greene was stationed in Vietnam as a war correspondent in the early 1950s, during the First Indochina War (1946–54). During this conflict, Vietnamese Communist forces known as the Viet Minh tried to take control of the country away from France, which had ruled Vietnam as a French colony for many years.

As the U.S. government grew concerned about the spread of communism following World War II (1939–45), they decided to support France in the First Indochina War. By 1954, however, the Viet Minh had scored several important victories, and France decided to negotiate a settlement. But rather than allow the Communists to take over Vietnam, the United States began sending military advisors to establish a separate, democratic government in the South.

In 1955, Greene published a novel based on his experiences in Vietnam during the transition from French control to U.S. involvement. *The Quiet American* tells the story of an idealistic U.S. military advisor, Alden Pyle, who secretly tries to create a new, democratic government in Vietnam. Pyle is willing to use any means to accomplish his mission, including violence. In fact, Pyle helps a terrorist group plant bombs in busy areas of Saigon. When the bombs kill innocent people, they blame the violence on the Viet Minh. In this way, Pyle hopes to increase support for a U.S.-friendly government.

Greene used the character of Pyle to show his feelings about U.S. policies toward Vietnam. After spending time in the country, the author came to love and respect the Vietnamese people and culture.

the country were controlled by the Viet Cong, at least during the nighttime. They also reported that the South Vietnamese army—known as the ARVN—was completely dependent on U.S. military equipment and intelligence. Finally, many press reports indicated that ARVN commanders were afraid to risk a defeat against Viet Cong forces because of Diem's reputation for punishing officers who reported casualties. These factors made it impossible for U.S. military advisors to organize any effective counterattack on the growing Viet Cong presence in South Vietnam's rural villages and towns.

Novelist Graham Greene.
Reproduced by permission of AP/World Wide Photos.

He believed that the U.S. government misunderstood the Viet Minh and the nature of their revolution against French rule. He felt that the Viet Minh were driven to make war because of nationalism (an intense loyalty and devotion to their

country and way of life) rather than a desire for communism. For this reason, Greene believed that the United States was wrong to interfere in Vietnamese attempts to overthrow the French and establish their own, independent government.

The Quiet American created quite a stir when it was published in 1955. Many reviewers criticized it as "anti-American" and "pro-Communist." In fact, leaders of the Soviet Union praised the novel and even published excerpts in the Communist newspaper *Pravda.* But as time passed, more and more of the things Greene predicted in his novel came true. As the United States increased its military involvement in Vietnam during the 1960s, the country also started feeling some of the negative effects that Greene had warned about. Later reviewers praised the novel for its accurate predictions of the tragic consequences of American military involvement in Vietnam.

Even though they were mostly accurate, such reports angered U.S. military leaders based in Saigon and Kennedy administration officials in Washington, D.C. The officials wanted the press to repeat their reassuring public statements that the Diem government was prospering and the Viet Cong threat was fading away. But the reporters refused to go along. Instead, they continued to submit stories that showed their own impressions of the situation in South Vietnam. At this point, few reporters questioned America's decision to become involved in Vietnam. But their observations led them to believe that the early strategies taken by Diem and U.S. policymakers to protect South Vietnam were ineffective. In any case, these critical reports soon created a hostile relationship between the American press and the U.S. military that endured throughout most of the Vietnam War.

Not surprisingly, the negative American press coverage angered Diem and his family as well. He repeatedly contacted American officials and demanded an end to the critical press reports. Of course, U.S. government officials responded that they did not have the power to silence them. As Prochnau writes, "Diem could never understand why the Americans could not control their reporters the same way he controlled his."

United States increases military and financial aid

Throughout 1961, U.S. President Kennedy received conflicting advice on how to handle the military and political situation in South Vietnam. Some people encouraged him to abandon Diem and withdraw from South Vietnam. Others insisted that the nation could be saved from the Communists by an increase in American military and economic aid.

In October 1961, Kennedy sent General Maxwell Taylor and advisor Walt Rostow to Saigon on a fact-finding mission. When they returned, they advised Kennedy to increase the U.S. military presence in South Vietnam in order to reassure Diem and scare the Viet Cong. They also told Kennedy that the country remained a vital prize in the battle against communism, but that the risk of being drawn into a long war there was small.

After discussing the Taylor-Rostow Report with his advisors, Kennedy decided to boost financial aid to Diem. He also provided the South Vietnamese with a wide range of new military equipment, and sent the first American helicopter units, called Eagle Flights, to South Vietnam. The 300 American pilots of these aircraft received orders to lead Vietnamese troops into battle but not engage in combat themselves, unless in self-defense.

In addition, the president ordered more U.S. military advisors into South Vietnam, including a detachment of Special Forces soldiers known as Green Berets. These Green Beret units—so-called because of their distinctive headgear—were designed to organize and train guerrilla bands behind enemy lines. The number of U.S. troops in Vietnam thus increased from 600 to about 15,000 within one year. Many of these new troops became actively involved in combat direction, even though they were technically just "advisors" to the ARVN.

This infusion of new U.S. personnel, equipment, and financial aid provided a needed lift to the Diem regime. But even so, the South Vietnamese leader's grip on power continued to slip. On February 27, 1962, a few dissatisfied South Vietnamese air force officers bombed Diem's presidential palace. American and international reporters seized upon the bombing as evidence that popular support for Diem had collapsed.

Strategic Hamlets Program

In early 1962, the South Vietnam government and the CIA launched a controversial program designed to reduce support for Viet Cong guerrillas in rural farming communities, where they had become a major presence. This effort was a new version of a short-lived 1959 program called Agroville, in which rural villagers were uprooted and forced to build new villages designed to isolate them from the Viet Cong. The Agroville program, however, had been quickly abandoned because of peasant resistance.

The 1962 initiative, called the Strategic Hamlets Program, was similar to the Agroville plan in most respects. It moved rural communities from traditional villages into government-sponsored concrete villages, where the people were trained to defend themselves. By the end of 1962, more than 3,000 strategic hamlets had been built under the supervision of Ngo Dinh Nhu (Brother Nhu).

Supporters of the Strategic Hamlets plan argued that these fortified villages, some of which included ARVN troops, would serve as a network of forts against Viet Cong forces operating in the countryside. But the villagers bitterly resented these forced relocations. Many of the peasants worked land that had belonged to their families for many generations. They did not want to leave their traditional homes to go live in unfamiliar concrete villages surrounded by barbed wire.

Critics of the Strategic Hamlets Program insisted that the whole scheme was a disaster. They claimed that the concrete hamlets resembled concentration camps, and that most of the villagers who were forced to move into them were deeply unhappy. Opponents of the plan even argued that it increased peasant hostility toward the South Vietnam government and made them more likely to side with the Communists. Finally, they claimed that the hamlets did not even succeed in their basic goal of separating the villagers from the Viet Cong. They cited numerous instances in which Viet Cong forces entered the hamlets, either to terrorize the occupants or to recruit new soldiers. "The Viet Cong claim we use U.S. barbed wire and iron stakes to confine the people," wrote South Vietnamese General Nguyen Huu Co. "With the loathing and hatred the people already have, when they hear the seemingly reasonable Viet Cong propaganda, they turn to the side of the Viet Cong and place their confidence in them."

At first, high-level representatives of the United States and South Vietnam praised the Strategic Hamlets Program. Gradually, however, American and South Vietnamese officials were forced to admit that the program was a failure. Efforts to maintain the program ended by late 1963, and occasional efforts to revive it later never succeeded.

Increase involvement or withdraw?

As debate raged over the effectiveness of the Strategic Hamlets Program, the Kennedy administration worked very hard to determine the true situation in South Vietnam. But military officers, diplomats, and other officials continued to offer dramatically different interpretations of Diem's government and the progress of the campaign against the Viet Cong. For example, White House aide Arthur J. Schlesinger recalled an early 1963 meeting of the National Security Council. During this meeting, the council and President Kennedy heard reports from two men who had recently returned from South Vietnam, General Victor Krulak and State Department official Joseph A. Mendenhall. "Krulak said that everything in Vietnam was going fine," recalls Schlesinger. According to Krulak's report, "Diem is a much loved figure, the morale is high, and all we need do is just back him to the end and he will win the war.

Then Mendenhall reported and said Diem was extremely unpopular, the regime was in a very precarious state, the Buddhists dislike him, the liberal democrats dislike him and he does not provide any kind of possible basis for a successful American policy. President Kennedy listened very carefully and said finally, 'Were you two gentleman in the same country?'"

Sources

Anderson, David L. *Trapped by Success: The Eisenhower Administration and Vietnam, 1953–1961*. Lawrence: University Press of Kansas, 1991.

Dareff, Hal. *The Story of Vietnam: A Background Book for Young People*. New York: Parents Magazine Press, 1966.

Halberstam, David. *The Making of a Quagmire: America and Vietnam During the Kennedy Era*. Rev. ed. New York: Knopf, 1988.

Herring, George C. *America's Longest War: The United States and Vietnam, 1950–1975*. 3rd ed. New York: McGraw Hill, 1996.

Kahin, George M. *Intervention: How America Became Involved in Vietnam*. Garden City, NY: Doubleday, 1987.

Karnow, Stanley. *Vietnam: A History*. Rev. ed. New York: Penguin Books, 1997.

Maclean, Michael. *The Ten Thousand Day War: Vietnam, 1945–1975*. New York: St. Martin's Press, 1980.

Nolting, Frederick E., Jr. *From Trust to Tragedy: The Political Memoirs of Frederick Nolting, Kennedy's Ambassador to Diem's Vietnam*. New York: Praeger, 1988.

Prochnau, William. *Once Upon a Distant War*. New York: Times Books, 1995.

Rust, William J. *Kennedy in Vietnam*. New York: Scribner's, 1985.

Willenson, Kim. *The Bad War: An Oral History of the Vietnam War*. New York: New American Library, 1987.

The Fall of Diem (1963)

4

During 1963, American dissatisfaction with Ngo Dinh Diem's (1901–1963) government in South Vietnam continued to grow. At the beginning of the year, the United States' policy of providing military and financial aid to Diem remained in place. But as the months passed, U.S. President John Kennedy (1917–1963; president 1960–1963) and his administration reluctantly concluded that the Diem government was too deeply flawed to survive.

One primary reason for American unhappiness with Diem was the growing strength of Viet Cong Communists operating in South Vietnam. But an even bigger cause for alarm was Diem's response to a massive uprising by the country's Buddhist majority population, which finally became fed up with Diem's anti-Buddhist views and policies. Diem's brutal crackdown against the demonstrators kept him in power for another few months. But it also convinced the United States that Diem would never be able to rally his people against the Communist threat. As a result, the United States did not interfere when several South Vietnamese generals engineered the overthrow of Diem's government in November 1963.

Words to Know

ARVN The South Vietnamese army, officially known as the Army of the Republic of South Vietnam. The ARVN fought on the same side as U.S. troops during the Vietnam War.

Buddhism A religion based on the teachings of Siddhartha Gautama (known as the Buddha; c. 563–c. 483 B.C.), in which followers seek moral purity and spiritual enlightenment. Buddhism was the religion of the majority of citizens of South Vietnam.

Communism A political system in which the government controls all resources and means of producing wealth. By eliminating private property, this system is designed to create an equal society with no social classes. However, Communist governments in practice often limit personal freedom and rights.

Coup d'état A sudden, decisive attempt to overthrow an existing government.

North Vietnam The Geneva Accords of 1954, which ended the First Indochina War (1946–54), divided the nation of Vietnam into two sections. The northern section, which was led by a Communist government under Ho Chi Minh, was officially known as the Democratic Republic of Vietnam, but was usually called North Vietnam.

South Vietnam Created under the Geneva Accords of 1954, the southern section of Vietnam was known as the Republic of South Vietnam. It was led by a U.S.-supported government.

Viet Cong Vietnamese Communist guerilla fighters who worked with the North Vietnamese Army to conquer South Vietnam.

Viet Cong gains in the countryside

During the early 1960s the Communist guerrillas known as the Viet Cong continued to make military gains throughout South Vietnam (guerrillas are small groups of fighters who launch surprise attacks). Relying on terrorism and widespread dissatisfaction with Ngo Dinh Diem's government, the Viet Cong successfully recruited large numbers of South Vietnamese from both rural villages and urban areas. They also launched periodic attacks on targets throughout South Vietnam, including government installations, military outposts, villages, and strategic hamlets (fortified villages created by the Diem government). All of these efforts were actively supported by the Communist government of North Vietnam.

Around this same time, the performance of the South Vietnamese army came under increasingly harsh criticism. Many U.S. military advisors stationed in the country complained that Diem and the military leadership of the South Vietnamese army—formally known as the Army of the Republic of Vietnam or ARVN—were reluctant to move aggressively against the Viet Cong. The advisors also noted that South Vietnamese officers were afraid that Diem would punish them if their troops suffered many casualties. Some U.S. observers even came to believe that the ARVN contained significant numbers of secret Viet Cong agents. "The whole country had been penetrated [by the Viet Cong], from the palace down to the platoons," claims historian Bruce Palmer in *The 25-Year War: America's Military Role in Vietnam.* "The Vietnamese could not put out their orders the way we would. They did not trust their own chain of command. They wouldn't tell the troop commanders where they were going until the last minute. And I think that when we [the United States] went in there, we didn't really realize the extent of the subversion.'"

By early 1963, the United States had stationed more than 12,000 American advisors and pilots in South Vietnam to help the country defend itself from the Communists. Despite this assistance, however, the ARVN continued to struggle in its campaign against the Viet Cong. "One had a sense on all sides of the . . . incompetence and unpopularity of the [Diem] government at the time," recalled presidential advisor John Kenneth Galbraith. "Here were just a few thousand Vietcong guerrillas

People to Know

John F. Kennedy (1917–1963) Served as the 35th president of the United States from 1960 until he was assassinated in 1963.

Henry Cabot Lodge (1902–1985) U.S. ambassador to South Vietnam during the Kennedy and Johnson administrations, 1963–66.

Ngo Dinh Diem (1901–1963) Vietnamese political leader who became president of South Vietnam in 1954. He gradually lost the support of the United States and was killed following the overthrow of his government in 1963.

Ngo Dinh Nhu (1910–1963) Known as Brother Nhu, he was the brother and main political advisor of South Vietnamese President Ngo Dinh Diem.

Madame Nhu (1924–) Served as the unofficial first lady of South Vietnam during the presidency of Ngo Dinh Diem. She was actually the wife of Diem's brother Ngo Dinh Nhu; her maiden name was Tran Le Xuan.

U.S. paratroopers jumping over a trench.
Reproduced by permission of AP/World Wide Photos.

scattered over that still quite huge country and a vast array of armed men already incapable of doing anything about them."

Battle of Ap Bac

American concern about the capabilities of South Vietnam's army intensified after an early 1963 clash known as the Battle of Ap Bac. This battle took place on January 2, 1963, at the small town of Ap Bac, about thirty-five miles southwest of Saigon. During the course of this fight, a Viet Cong battalion defeated a much larger South Vietnamese force that was supported by armored vehicles, heavy artillery, and U.S. Army helicopters. The South Vietnamese army performed very poorly in this battle, and the Viet Cong escaped after shooting down several helicopters and inflicting heavy casualties.

American military advisor John Paul Vann witnessed the entire battle at Ap Bac. After the fight was over, he submitted an angry report in which he harshly criticized the South Vietnamese army for its "damn miserable" performance. He charged that the officers were cowards and claimed that the entire ARVN force showed no willingness to fight. A few days later, Vann became further outraged when he learned that the South Vietnamese military lied about what happened in order to claim victory.

It then became clear that U.S. Ambassador Frederick Nolting and other American officials in Vietnam had no intention of telling the public the true story. So Vann secretly informed several American reporters about the disastrous battle. After hearing Vann's account, these reporters began to doubt the word of U.S. and South Vietnamese military officials, who continued to insist that the war against the Viet Cong was going well.

Armed with Vann's inside information, reporters told the American public about the loss at Ap Bac. The news stunned the American people, many of whom had paid little attention to U.S. involvement in Vietnam until this time. "Ap Bac . . . was a decisive battle," writes *New York Times* reporter Neil Sheehan in *A Bright Shining Lie*. "Ap Bac was putting Vietnam on the front pages and on the television evening talk shows with a drama no other event had yet achieved. The dispatches, [full of] details of cowardice and bumbling, were describing the battle as the worst and most humiliating defeat ever inflicted on the Saigon [South Vietnamese] side."

American worries about Diem continue

As America's worries about South Vietnam's military increased, so did U.S. concerns about the stability of President Ngo Dinh Diem's government. Throughout the spring of 1963,

American officials tried to convince Diem to make changes in the way he was ruling South Vietnam. They wanted him to introduce policies that would help the nation's struggling peasant population and stamp out widespread corruption in the military and other branches of government. They also urged Diem, who was Catholic, to show respect for Buddhism, the religion practiced by most South Vietnamese families. The United States hoped that by making these changes, the Diem government could reverse its drop in popularity and strengthen its grip on power.

But Diem ignored most U.S. efforts to get him to change his ways, and the military situation continued to deteriorate. "The military leadership of the ARVN seemed more interested in preserving its own privileges than in fighting the war," states Robert D. Schulzinger in *A Time for War: The United States and Vietnam, 1941–1975.* "For his part, Diem worried more about disloyal army officers threatening his regime [government] than he did about fighting the Vietcong."

By mid–1963, members of the Kennedy administration were fiercely divided over whether the United States should continue to support Diem's presidency. "We had a big battle all that summer between [the Department of] State and the National Security Council," former Central Intelligence Agency (CIA) Director William Colby recalls in *The Bad War: An Oral History of the Vietnam War.* "State's position was that you cannot hope to win with Diem because he cannot generate popular support. That was an honest appreciation. The other side, people at Defense and in CIA who'd been there, believed you weren't going to get much different government from anybody else." General Maxwell D. Taylor agreed that "there was a strong group [of Kennedy advisors] that had picked up the slogan 'You can't win with Diem.' The other group, to which I belonged, argued maybe we can't win with Diem, but if not Diem—who? And the answer was complete silence."

The Buddhist crisis

In early May President Diem traveled to the city of Hue to celebrate the 25th anniversary of his brother Ngo Dinh Thuc's promotion to archbishop in the Catholic Church. As part of the celebration, Catholic-themed flags were strung along the city's streets. A few days later, however, the Diem government banned members of the city's majority Buddhist population from flying their own banners in celebration of one of their religious holidays. This discriminatory treatment outraged the Buddhists in Hue, one of the historical centers of Vietnamese Buddhism. Thousands of Buddhist demonstrators soon took to the streets in a major protest against Diem's government. On May 8, 1963, the protest in Hue ended in terrible violence. Diem's soldiers attacked the crowds with clubs, tear gas, and gunfire, killing a number of people (reports range from eight to forty people killed) and wounding and jailing many others.

The Diem government blamed Viet Cong guerrillas for the violence in Hue and never admitted responsibility for its actions. But the nation's general population was not fooled, and new demonstrations organized by Buddhist leaders quickly spread throughout the country. Within a matter of days, the Buddhists were joined by several other South Vietnamese groups who opposed Diem's government. In *The Making of a Quagmire: America and Vietnam during the Kennedy Era*, *New York Times* reporter David Halberstam describes these protests against the Diem regime as an ominous sign of "deep-rooted discontent [anger] among a religious group [the Buddhists] that constitutes about 70 percent of the country's population. What started as a religious protest has become predominantly political . . . the Buddhists are providing a spearhead for other discontented [groups]."

Buddhist suicide shocks the world

On the morning of June 11, 1963, a 73-year-old Buddhist bonze (monk) named Quang Duc sat down in the middle of a busy Saigon intersection. He folded his hands in prayer and crossed his legs in the lotus position of meditation, while another monk poured gasoline over his shaven head and orange robe. The old monk then lit a match and set himself on fire to protest Diem's repression of the Buddhist religion.

Shocking pictures of the monk's suicide quickly appeared in the United States and all around the world. The photographs persuaded many stunned Americans to focus greater attention on their country's involvement in South Vietnam. The pictures also triggered a wave of intense inter-

Buddhist monk Quang Duc burns himself to death in 1963 in protest of the persecution of Buddhists by the South Vietnamese government.
Reproduced by permission of AP/World Wide Photos.

national criticism against Diem's government and its treatment of Vietnamese Buddhists. U.S. President John Kennedy commented that "no news picture in history has generated as much emotion around the world as that one."

President Diem and his ruling family reacted defiantly to the criticism, however. Diem's brother Ngo Dinh Nhu (1910–1963) insulted the country's followers of Buddhism and proclaimed that "if the Buddhists want to have another barbecue, I will be happy to supply the gasoline." Diem's sister-in-law, Madame Nhu, made similar statements. She indicated that she would cheer if other monks committed suicide, adding that "if they [the Buddhists] burn thirty women we shall go ahead and clap our hands."

These remarks horrified President Kennedy and other U.S. officials. They told Diem that "Madame Nhu is out of control" and urged him to send her out of the country. U.S. diplomats also told Diem that Ngo Dinh Nhu should be removed from the government, citing his corrupt ways and his brutal use of the nation's secret police to silence political opposition. American advisors warned the South Vietnamese president that if he did not exercise greater control over Madame Nhu and Ngo Dinh Nhu, his government would become even more unpopular. But Diem relied heavily on his brother and sister-in-law, and he disregarded the warnings.

Demonstrations across South Vietnam

Over the next several weeks, six other monks and nuns in South Vietnam committed suicide by setting themselves on fire in ritual ceremonies. As the summer months passed, the demonstrations against the Diem regime continued to grow in size and intensity. On July 30, for instance, Buddhists and university students launched massive protests in Saigon and four other cities in South Vietnam. "The Buddhist movement became a rallying point for all of the discontent that had been accumulating against the ruling family among urban Vietnamese since 1954," explains Neil Sheehan in *A Bright Shining Lie.*

During this time, the Diem government used violence in an effort to stop the unrest. Peaceful demonstrators were sometimes attacked by soldiers and police armed with rifles, clubs, and tear gas. Other protestors, including monks and students who were believed to be leaders of the demonstrations, were kidnaped in the middle of the night and never seen again. Nonetheless, the government was unable to stop the demonstrations. According to Sheehan, Diem and the other members of his ruling family "did not understand that each act of repression bred more followers for the Buddhists."

On August 21, 1963, the Diem government declared

Henry Cabot Lodge served as the U.S. ambassador to South Vietnam in the mid-1960s. During his first stay in Saigon, Lodge helped convince the U.S. government to support the coup that removed Ngo Dinh Diem from power. *Reproduced by permission of the Library of Congress.*

martial law (meaning that the military took charge of the nation) and launched a massive crackdown across South Vietnam in an effort to stamp out the Buddhist-led demonstrations once and for all. Ngo Dinh Nhu's U.S.-trained military troops stormed Buddhist temples—known as pagodas—all across the country. They arrested approximately 1,400 monks and nuns in these raids. The attacks were especially bloody in Hue. About 30 monks and student followers were shot or clubbed to death in assaults on Buddhist temples in the ancient city. Madame Nhu personally observed a raid on one of the main Buddhist temples in Saigon. She later called it "the happiest day of my life."

But the government crackdown failed to silence the anti-Diem protestors. Instead, riots broke out at several places across the country, including Saigon University. Diem promptly closed the university, only to see several Saigon high schools erupt in riots. Many of these schoolchildren were the children of important Vietnamese officials and businessmen. Around this same time, Madame Nhu's father, Tran Van Chuong, resigned from his post as ambassador to the United States. He announced that there was "not one chance in a hundred for victory" over the Communists with his daughter, her husband, and brother-in-law in power. Observers saw these developments as further signs that Diem's rule was in grave danger.

Henry Cabot Lodge arrives in Vietnam

In August 1963, the same month that Diem and his ruling family launched their desperate crackdown on the demonstrators, a new U.S. ambassador to South Vietnam arrived in the country. Henry Cabot Lodge (1902–1985) replaced Frederick Nolting, a longtime defender of Diem's government. After

Diem Makes a Final Appeal for Help from America

As the coup that toppled the Diem government was launched, President Ngo Dinh Diem (1901–1963) made a telephone call to U.S. Ambassador Henry Cabot Lodge (1902–1985). The transcript of this last communication makes it clear that Diem feared for his life. It also shows that while the United States was willing to take steps to protect Diem if he promptly resigned, America would not intervene in the coup attempt.

Ngo Dinh Diem: Some units have made a rebellion and I want to know what is the attitude of the U.S.?

Ambassador Lodge: I do not feel well enough informed to be able to tell you. I have heard the shooting, but am not acquainted with all the facts. Also it is 4:30 a.m. in Washington and the U.S. Government cannot possibly have a view.

Diem: But you must have some general ideas. After all, I am a chief of state. I have tried to do my duty. I want to do now what duty and good sense require. I believe in duty above all.

Lodge: You have certainly done your duty. As I told you only this morning, I admire your courage and your great contributions to your country. No one can take away from you the credit for all you have done. Now I am worried about your physical safety. I have a report that those in charge of the current [coup] activity offer you and your brother safe conduct out of the country if you resign. Had you heard this?

Diem: No. (Diem then pauses before continuing.) You have my telephone number.

Lodge: Yes. If I can do anything for your physical safety, please call me.

Diem: I am trying to re-establish order.

reviewing the situation in Saigon, Lodge quickly concluded that Diem's regime was doomed. A week after his arrival, he sent President Kennedy a top-secret message in which he said, "We are launched on a course from which there is no respectable turning back: the overthrow of the Diem government. There is no possibility, in my view, that the war [against the Communists] can be won under a Diem administration."

Lodge's report disturbed Kennedy, who had hoped that the Diem government could be saved. But other reports confirmed Lodge's view of the situation. The entire length of

South Vietnam, from its riot-torn cities to its Viet Cong-threatened rural areas, seemed to be on the verge of collapse. Some intelligence reports even suggested that Diem and his brother Nhu had entered into secret negotiations with North Vietnam in an effort to hold on to their positions. Determined to keep the country out of Communist hands, the Kennedy administration began preparing for the end of the Diem regime.

Diem's last days

In early September 1963, Kennedy publicly expressed his concerns about events in South Vietnam during an interview with newsman Walter Cronkite. "I don't think that unless a greater effort is made by the government to win popular support that the war can be won out there [in South Vietnam]," Kennedy said. "In the final analysis, it is their war. They are the ones who have to win it or lose it. We can help them, we can give them equipment, we can send our men out there as advisors, but they have to win it, the people of Vietnam, against the Communists. We are prepared to continue to assist them, but I don't think that the war can be won unless the people support the effort and, in my opinion, in the last two months, the government has gotten out of touch with the people."

Around this same time, a group of South Vietnamese military officers joined together in a plot to overthrow Diem and take control of the government. The leaders of this group were General Duong Van Minh, General Tran Van Don, and General Le Van Kim. In October, Lodge secretly informed the officers that the United States would not oppose a change of leadership of the South Vietnam government. "It seems at least an even bet that the next government would not bungle and stumble as much as the present one has," Lodge told the Kennedy administration.

After the United States extended its promise not to interfere in the coup (attempt to overthrow the government), the generals set their plan in motion. On November 1, 1963, they used a strong military force to seize control of several strategically important outposts in Saigon and other areas of South Vietnam. Initially, Diem and his brother refused to surrender. When it became clear that they could not stop the coup from succeeding, however, the brothers used a secret exit to escape the presidential palace after dark. But they proved unable to elude their pursuers, and were captured a few hours later at a Catholic church in Saigon. A short time later, Duong Van Minh—also known as "Big Minh"—ordered the execution of both men and assumed leadership of the country. Madame Nhu, meanwhile, escaped capture and possible execution only because she was in the United States at the time of the coup.

President Kennedy was stunned and upset when he learned of Diem's murder. He believed that South Vietnam was better off with new leadership, but he had wanted the South Vietnamese generals to simply remove Diem from office, not assassinate him. "It was a shock to all of us," said General Maxwell Taylor. "But I think perhaps to the President more than any of us—because he didn't realize that we were all playing with fire when we were at least giving tacit [implied or understood] encouragement to the overthrow of this man."

Today, the United States' role in the overthrow of the Diem government continues to be fiercely debated by government officials and historians alike. Some people claim that it was necessary for the Kennedy administration to withhold support for Diem during the coup. They insist that the Communists probably would have seized control of South Vietnam in a matter of months if Diem had remained in power. But other observers strongly disagree. For example, General William C. Westmoreland called the U.S. approval for the overthrow of the Diem government a "grievous mistake." Westmoreland, who commanded U.S. military forces in Vietnam from 1964 to 1968, claimed that "action morally locked us in Vietnam. If it had not been for our involvement in the overthrow of President Diem, we could perhaps have gracefully withdrawn our support when South Vietnam's lack of unity and leadership became apparent."

Sources

Halberstam, David. *The Making of a Quagmire: America and Vietnam during the Kennedy Era*. Rev. ed. New York: Knopf, 1988.

Hammer, Ellen J. *Death in November: America in Vietnam, 1963*. New York: Dutton, 1987.

Karnow, Stanley. "The Fall of the House of Ngo Dinh." *Saturday Evening Post* (December 21, 1963).

McMahon, Robert J., ed. *Major Problems in the History of the Vietnam War.* Lexington, MA: D. C. Heath, 1995.

Nolting, Frederick E., Jr. *From Trust to Tragedy: The Political Memoirs of Frederick Nolting, Kennedy's Ambassador to Diem's Vietnam.* New York: Praeger, 1988.

Palmer, Bruce, Jr. *The 25-Year War: America's Military Role in Vietnam.* Lexington, KY: University Press of Kentucky, 1984.

Schulzinger, Robert D. *A Time for War: The United States and Vietnam, 1941–1975.* New York: Oxford University Press, 1997.

Sheehan, Neil. *A Bright Shining Lie: John Paul Vann and America in Vietnam.* New York: Random House, 1988.

Willenson, Kim. *The Bad War: An Oral History of the Vietnam War.* New York: New American Library, 1987.

Lyndon Johnson and the Tonkin Gulf Resolution (1964)

5

In 1964, political chaos continued to grip South Vietnam. The nation's efforts to achieve political stability floundered, as military and civilian leaders battled for power and influence. At the same time, Communist Viet Cong forces continued to make gains in the country's rural areas and expand their operations in Saigon (the capital of South Vietnam) and other urban centers. These advances convinced many U.S. officials that the Communists who ruled North Vietnam were on the verge of seizing control of the South as well.

In August 1964, a mysterious clash between Communist and U.S. Navy forces took place in the waters of the Tonkin Gulf, off the shores of North Vietnam. American President Lyndon B. Johnson (1908–1973; president 1963–1969)—who became president after John F. Kennedy (1917–1963; president 1960–1963) was assassinated in November 1963—took advantage of this controversial event. Seizing on fears of Communist aggression, Johnson and his administration convinced Congress to approve expanded U.S. military action in Vietnam. The administration hoped that the warning of military intervention would help South Vietnam halt the Communist threat.

Words to Know

Communism A political system in which the government controls all resources and means of producing wealth. By eliminating private property, this system is designed to create an equal society with no social classes. However, Communist governments in practice often limit personal freedom and rights.

Coup d'etat A sudden, decisive attempt to overthrow an existing government.

Great Society A set of social programs proposed by U.S. President Lyndon Johnson designed to end segregation and reduce poverty in the United States.

Military Revolutionary Council A group of South Vietnamese military officers that overthrew Vietnamese President Ngo Dinh Diem and took control of South Vietnam's government in 1963.

North Vietnam The Geneva Accords of 1954, which ended the First Indochina War (1946–54), divided the nation of Vietnam into two sections. The northern section, which was led by a Communist government under Ho Chi Minh, was officially known as the Democratic Republic of Vietnam, but was usually called North Vietnam.

South Vietnam Created under the Geneva Accords of 1954, the southern section of Vietnam was known as the Republic of South Vietnam. It was led by a U.S.-supported government.

Tonkin Gulf Resolution Passed by Congress after U.S. Navy ships supposedly came under attack in the Gulf of Tonkin, this resolution gave U.S. President Lyndon Johnson the authority to wage war against North Vietnam.

Viet Cong Vietnamese Communist guerrilla fighters who worked with the North Vietnamese Army to conquer South Vietnam.

The assassination of Kennedy

On November 22, 1963, U.S. President John F. Kennedy was assassinated by gunman Lee Harvey Oswald (1939–1963) while riding in a motorcade in Dallas, Texas. The murder stunned people all around the world. As Americans mourned the loss of their president, they also wondered how the nation's domestic and foreign policy might change under Lyndon B. Johnson, who had been Kennedy's vice president. According to U.S. law, Johnson immediately became the new president of the United States when Kennedy was killed.

Upon taking office, President Johnson (commonly known by his initials, "LBJ") ordered an investigation into rumors that Oswald had been part of a conspiracy to kill Kennedy. This investigation, headed by Chief Justice Earl Warren (1891–1974), determined that Oswald had acted by himself. But some people continued to believe that others had been involved in the assassination.

As he settled into his new duties, Johnson promised the American people that he would continue Kennedy's policies, which included providing support for South Vietnam in its fight against communism. He even retained most of Kennedy's staff and administration as part of an effort to keep the U.S. government operating smoothly. The assassination had shocked and horrified people all across America, and Johnson wanted to reassure them that the United States and its democratic institutions remained strong.

Johnson and the "Great Society"

As president, Johnson expressed great interest in correcting some social problems that persisted across most of the United States. For example, he believed that prejudice against minorities was a major problem in America. Johnson promised to pass laws to eliminate segregation and other racist practices that separated minorities from whites in the nation's schools, restaurants, businesses, and other institutions. In addition, Johnson believed that far too many people were living in poverty in the United States.

 People to Know

Barry Goldwater (1909–1998) U.S. senator from Arizona and Republican presidential candidate in 1964. He supported increasing U.S. military involvement in Vietnam during his campaign; he was defeated by Lyndon Johnson.

Lyndon B. Johnson (1908–1973) After serving as vice president under John Kennedy, he became the 36th president of the United States after Kennedy was assassinated in 1963. Johnson sent U.S. combat troops to Vietnam. Opposition to his policies convinced him not to seek re-election in 1968.

John F. Kennedy (1917–1963) Served as the 35th president of the United States from 1960 until he was assassinated in 1963.

Robert McNamara (1916–) Served as U.S. secretary of defense during the Kennedy and Johnson administrations, 1961–1968. After helping to shape U.S. policy toward Vietnam, he privately began to doubt that America could win the war.

The Kennedy family at the funeral of John F. Kennedy, November 1963.

Reproduced by permission of Archive Photos.

He promised the American public that he would wage war on poverty by increasing educational and business opportunities for poor families.

Johnson proposed to end segregation and reduce poverty through a set of ambitious government programs. He claimed that once these programs were put in place, a "Great Society" would develop in the United States. But soon after taking office, Johnson recognized that the unsettled situation in South Vietnam might endanger his vision for a more prosperous America. He knew that the government might not have enough funds to finance his social programs if the United States devoted large amounts of money to the conflict in Vietnam.

During his first months as president, however, Johnson refused to reduce the U.S. military and economic aid to South Vietnam. Johnson and most other officials in his administration feared that if the United States abandoned its position in Vietnam, the government in Saigon would quickly come under the control of the North Vietnamese Communists. They believed that a Communist victory in South Vietnam might then trigger a wave of Communist aggression all across Asia.

Continued political problems in Saigon

During the winter of 1963–1964, the Johnson administration's concerns about the stability of South Vietnam's government continued to grow. After President Ngo Dinh Diem's (1901–1963) regime (government) was overthrown in November 1963, the United States had hoped that it might be replaced by a more effective government. As the weeks passed, however, it became clear that South Vietnam's new military rulers lacked political experience. These officers—known as the Military Revolutionary Council—quarreled over how best to lead the country. Many of them used their power to increase their personal wealth or plot against their political enemies.

U.S. advisors tried to convince the military rulers and community leaders to work together to address the country's social and military problems, but the bickering continued. This lack of leadership in Saigon further damaged the morale of South Vietnam's long-suffering people. Confused and bitter, many South Vietnamese became passive observers in the ongoing struggle between the nation's military and the Communist Viet Cong guerrillas (small groups of fighters who launch surprise attacks).

In the first weeks of 1964, some members of the Military Revolutionary Council suggested that South Vietnam negotiate an end to the war with the Communists. The Viet Cong forces operating in the South openly supported this idea. They proposed that South Vietnam hold free elections that would allow people to elect a new government of their choosing. But the United States fiercely opposed this proposal, because they worried that such an election would install a Communist government. U.S. officials also expressed great anger that South Vietnam would even consider negotiating with North Vietnam's Communist leaders. American intelligence experts and advisors viewed the proposed negotiations as further evidence that the new government was unfit to lead South Vietnam.

On January 29, 1964, General Nguyen Khanh seized control of South Vietnam's government. He pushed the council out of power in a bloodless coup (takeover). The United States reacted cautiously to this latest change in political leadership. After all, American officials did not know whether Khanh had the ability to hold power or fight the Viet Cong effectively. But when Khanh indicated that he would rely heavily on U.S. political and military assistance, the Johnson

As John F. Kennedy's vice president, Lyndon B. Johnson assumed the presidency after Kennedy was assassinated in 1963. *Reproduced by permission of AP/World Wide Photos.*

U.S. Secretary of Defense (1961–68) Robert McNamara.
Reproduced by permission of AP/World Wide Photos.

administration sent a new wave of American advisors into the country.

Warnings of collapse

During the spring of 1964, Johnson received a number of reports about the situation in South Vietnam. When Defense Secretary Robert McNamara (1916–) returned from a trip to the troubled country, he told the president that the Viet Cong had established control over large sections of South Vietnam, including areas surrounding the capital city of Saigon. "Large groups of the population are now showing signs of apathy and indifference," McNamara stated. He added that the South Vietnamese army was struggling to stay at full strength because of high desertion rates (soldiers leaving the armed forces illegally before their terms of service had ended) and widespread "draft dodging" (avoiding the military draft). At the same time, he noted that "the Viet Cong are recruiting energetically and effectively." McNamara and most other advisors warned Johnson that unless the situation changed in a hurry, the Viet Cong might take control of South Vietnam within a matter of months.

As Johnson and his advisors debated over how to proceed in South Vietnam, everyone agreed that none of the options was very appealing. The Americans did not want to pull out of the country, because they were certain that the Communists would take it over within weeks of their departure. After all, South Vietnam's government was in terrible shape, and its military seemed dazed and discouraged by the deadly guerrilla campaigns of the Viet Cong. But Johnson and other top U.S. military and political leaders were also reluctant to devote more troops, equipment, and funds to such a messy situation.

Not surprisingly, many members of the Johnson administration adopted a very negative view of South Vietnam as a whole around this time. As Robert Shulzinger writes in *A Time for War*, "the frustrations of U.S. officials boiled over into a contempt for the South Vietnamese, the very people they ostensibly [outwardly] wanted to help with their program of assistance and military activities in the war."

By mid-1964, the Johnson administration concluded that it would probably have to take a more active role in Vietnam. "One by one, President Johnson's advisors lobbied him to send American ground forces and warplanes to Vietnam," writes Elizabeth Becker in *America's Vietnam War*. "They believed that if the United States did not fight the war and win it, the South Vietnamese would fight it and lose, dragging down the United States and most of the free world."

Vietnam and the 1964 presidential election

At the same time, the Johnson administration had begun planning for a wide range of operations related to the war in Vietnam. These activities included instituting a military draft to boost the size of the U.S. military, launching bombing campaigns against North Vietnam, and sending American ground troops to protect South Vietnam from the Viet Cong. The officials hoped to avoid using these "contingency plans," (plans that are devised to prepare for possible emergencies or events in the future) but they wanted to be ready if necessary.

President Johnson, however, did not publicize these contingency plans. He faced a tough presidential election campaign against Senator Barry Goldwater (1909–1998) of Arizona, the Republican Party nominee. Johnson did not want to bring Vietnam to the attention of the American public, which still viewed the struggle there as a minor conflict. After all, Vietnam was on the other side of the world, and U.S. military personnel stationed there were serving as advisors rather than combat troops. Fortunately for Johnson, Goldwater quietly agreed not to argue about America's military presence in Vietnam. Goldwater was fiercely anti-Communist, and he believed that U.S. involvement in Vietnam was necessary.

Freed from defending American policies in Vietnam, Johnson campaigned on his "Great Society" plans. He guided a variety of education, anti-poverty, and anti-discrimination legislation into law during this time, including the Civil Rights

An "Undeclared War"

The Vietnam War is often referred to as an "undeclared war." The U.S. Constitution gives Congress the power to declare war. It also grants the president of the United States special powers during times of war as commander in chief of the American military. But the president does not have the power to decide, by himself, whether or not the nation goes to war.

In August 1964, U.S. warships operating off the coast of Vietnam in the Gulf of Tonkin reportedly came under attack from North Vietnamese torpedo boats. Even though it was unclear what actually happened, U.S. President Lyndon Johnson (1908–1973; president 1963–1969) chose to view this incident as an act of war by North Vietnam against the United States. He asked Congress to pass a resolution that would authorize him to take "all necessary measures" against further attacks.

After Congress passed the Tonkin Gulf Resolution, Johnson used it as permission to send troops to Vietnam. From this point on, he and President Richard Nixon (1913–1994; president 1969–1974) used their war powers as if Congress had issued a formal declaration of war. But the United States never did declare war against North Vietnam. For this reason, critics of U.S. policy toward Vietnam have often referred to the conflict as an "undeclared war."

Bill of 1964 (a wide-reaching law that banned discrimination in voting, jobs, and public institutions). Meanwhile, he privately expressed hope that he could avoid making big decisions on Vietnam until after the election. He did not want to lose South Vietnam to the Communists before the election. At the same time, however, he did not "want to get the country into war" before the vote either. The president knew that either development would probably cost him a lot of votes.

The Gulf of Tonkin incident

On July 28, 1964, the U.S. Navy destroyer *USS Maddox* was ordered to sail to the Gulf of Tonkin, a part of the South China Sea. The ship's mission was to provide support for South Vietnamese commando raids along the North Vietnamese

coast. These raids were designed to gather intelligence on radar sites and other defenses in North Vietnam.

The *Maddox*'s first few days in the Gulf of Tonkin passed quietly. On August 2, however, three North Vietnamese torpedo boats attacked the *Maddox* while it was on patrol. The destroyer returned fire, sinking two boats. The last boat then sailed off, chased by American fighter planes from a nearby U.S. Navy aircraft carrier. On August 3, the *Maddox* was joined by

The Tonkin Gulf Resolution

In early August 1964, a U.S. Navy destroyer called the *Maddox* and a handful of North Vietnamese torpedo boats engaged in a brief fight in the Gulf of Tonkin, off the shores of North Vietnam. Two days later, the U.S. Navy incorrectly reported that its ships had been attacked by Communist forces for a second time. The U.S. Senate and House of Representatives reacted to this news by overwhelmingly approving the Tonkin Gulf Resolution. Over the next several years, U.S. President Lyndon Johnson (1908–1973; president 1963–1969) and his administration used this resolution to dramatically increase U.S. military involvement in Vietnam.

What follows is the full text of the Tonkin Gulf Resolution:

To promote the maintenance [continuation] of international peace and security in southeast Asia.

Whereas naval units of the Communist regime in Vietnam, in violation of the principles of the Charter of the Union Nations and of international law, have deliberately and repeatedly attacked United States naval vessels lawfully present in international waters, and have thereby created a serious threat to international peace; and

Whereas these attacks are part of a deliberate and systematic [organized] campaign of aggression that the Communist regime [government] in North Vietnam has been waging against its neighbors and the nations joined with them in the collective defense of their freedom; and

Whereas the United States is assisting the peoples of southeast Asia to protect their freedom and has no territorial, military, or political ambitions in that area, but desires only that these people should be left in peace to work out their own destinies in their own way: Now, therefore, be it Resolved by the Senate and House of Representatives of the United States of America in Congress assembled, That the Congress approves and supports the determination of the President, as Commander in Chief, to take all necessary measures to repel [resist] any armed attack against the forces of the United States and to prevent further aggression.

Sec. 2. The United States regards as vital to its national interest and to world peace the maintenance of international peace and security in southeast Asia. Consonant [in agreement] with the Constitution of the United States and the Charter of the United Nations and in accordance [agreement] with its obligations under the Southeast Asia Collective Defense Treaty, the United States is, therefore, prepared, as the President determines, to take all necessary steps, including the use of armed force, to assist any member or protocol state of the Southeast Asia Collective Defense Treaty requesting assistance in defense of its freedom.

Sec. 3. This resolution shall expire when the President shall determine that the peace and security of the area is reasonably assured by international conditions created by action of the United Nations or otherwise, except that it may be terminated earlier by concurrent [simultaneous] resolution of the Congress.

another destroyer called the USS *Turner Joy.* One night later, the two ships, relying on radar information, reported that North Vietnamese ships had launched a second attack. The American destroyers returned fire based on their radar readings. They also requested assistance from the aircraft carrier *Ticonderoga,* which promptly sent fighter planes to the area.

Reports of this second attack by North Vietnamese forces triggered a strong response from President Johnson. Stung by criticism that he should have reacted more strongly to North Vietnam's August 2 torpedo boat attack, Johnson took advantage of the reports of a second attack to order an immediate aerial assault on the North Vietnamese coastline. A short time later, fighter bombers from U.S. aircraft carriers stationed in the South China Sea struck North Vietnamese patrol boat bases and an oil storage facility along the coast. The attack was America's first major air strike on North Vietnam.

The Tonkin Gulf Resolution

Johnson also used reports of the second attack to ask Congress for special authority to take additional military action against North Vietnam if it became necessary in the future. Working together, the president and members of Congress composed a resolution that would give Johnson the power to "take all necessary measures to repel an armed attack against the forces of the United States and to prevent further aggression."

Johnson and his allies told the American people that Congress's vote on this resolution—known as the Tonkin Gulf Resolution—was very important. They presented the vote as a test of U.S. unity in the face of an "unprovoked attack" (an attack for no reason) on American forces. Johnson and other lawmakers hoped that the Tonkin Gulf Resolution would scare the North Vietnamese into accepting the division of the country into North and South once and for all.

"[The Johnson administration] made it appear that this was very important to support the President and that if he had the backing of this great country, that we could make North Vietnam understand that the United States couldn't be pushed around in this fashion and that they would in effect sue for peace, and it would end the thing there," confirmed Senator William Fulbright in *The Bad War: An Oral History of the Vietnam War.* "That was the main reason for the urgency, to create the psychological impact."

The Tonkin Gulf Resolution passed easily. It passed in the U.S. House of Representatives by a unanimous 416 to 0 vote. It also passed overwhelmingly in the Senate by an 88 to 2 vote. Only two senators—Democrats Ernest Gruening of Alaska and Wayne Morse of Oregon—voted against the resolution. Gruening called U.S. involvement in Vietnam a "putrid mess" and argued that "all Vietnam is not worth the life of a single American boy." Morse was outspoken in his criticism as well. But they remained alone in their opposition, and Johnson signed the resolution on August 10.

Attack probably never happened

In the meantime, a U.S. Navy investigation into the events of August 4 revealed that reports of a North Vietnamese attack on the *Maddox* and the *Turner Joy* were almost certainly wrong. Investigators discovered that stormy weather, false radar readings made by inexperienced personnel, and misunderstood North Vietnamese radio messages all combined to convince the ships that they were under attack, when actually they were in no danger. But Johnson chose to keep this information quiet. He wanted the increased military authority that would come with passage of the Tonkin Gulf Resolution.

As it turned out, the Tonkin Gulf Resolution failed to convince the Communists in Vietnam to halt their efforts to take over the South. The Viet Cong and their North Vietnamese allies realized that the United States was a mighty military power. Despite the threat of increased American military involvement, however, they continued trying to unite Vietnam under a single Communist government. Viet Cong operations proceeded without pause, supported by North Vietnam.

Passage of the Tonkin Gulf Resolution did end up being a very important event in the Vietnam War, however. In the years following its passage, the Johnson administration used the authority granted by the resolution to increase American military involvement in South Vietnam. These new activ-

ities ranged from launching massive bombing campaigns against North Vietnam to sending U.S. combat troops into the conflict. In effect, the Tonkin Gulf Resolution granted Johnson the legal right to wage war without actually declaring war. Years later, however, Johnson admitted that the initial reason for the resolution—the alleged North Vietnamese attack of August 4—probably never even took place. "For all I know, our navy was shooting at whales out there," he said.

Lyndon Johnson (left), sitting with Robert McNamara, reacts to new problems in Vietnam. *Reproduced by permission of Corbis-Bettman.*

Johnson beats Goldwater

As the 1964 presidential election approached, Johnson did not reveal his plans for Vietnam. He told voters that he was determined to use the American military to help South Vietnam defend itself from Communist aggression. But he also reassured them that the war would have to be won by South Vietnamese troops rather than U.S. soldiers. "We are not about

Barry Goldwater, a strong opponent of communism, was defeated by Johnson for the U.S presidency in 1964. *Reproduced by permission of Archive Photos.*

to send American boys away from home to do what Asian boys ought to be doing for themselves," Johnson declared in October 1964.

In the meantime, Republican candidate Barry Goldwater made strong anti-Communist statements during the presidential campaign. In fact, he once remarked that the United States should have dropped an atomic bomb on North Vietnam ten years earlier. Such comments allowed Johnson to position himself as the so-called "peace" candidate. As the election grew near, the American public saw him as someone who would be less likely than Goldwater to involve the United States in war, whether in Vietnam or elsewhere.

Boosted by public approval for his "Great Society" programs and voter distrust of Goldwater's conservative political views, Johnson marched to an easy victory in the 1964 presidential election. He won 61.2 percent of the popular vote and helped the Democratic Party gain big majorities in both the Senate and the House of Representatives.

Johnson prepares to increase American presence in Vietnam

After his election victory, Johnson turned his attention once again to South Vietnam. By this time, American officials viewed General Khanh as a corrupt dictator who had no idea how to beat the Viet Cong. In addition, widespread demonstrations against Khanh's government showed that he had no popular support. Torn by economic, military, and social problems, South Vietnam seemed paralyzed by what U.S. Ambassador Maxwell Taylor called "war weariness and hopelessness." Not surprisingly, these reports convinced the Johnson administration that the Saigon government was on the verge of political collapse.

In December 1964, a group of South Vietnamese military officers known as the "Young Turks" seized control of the government in yet another coup. But American officials did not believe that this new leadership was any better than the old government. During this period, a few people advised Johnson to withdraw American military support for South Vietnam and accept the fact that the nation was doomed to fall to the Communists. Senator Mike Mansfield, for instance, warned Johnson in December that "we remain on a course in Vietnam which takes us further and further out onto the sagging limb."

Some officials also told the president that the expense of increasing U.S. involvement in Vietnam might prevent him from pursuing his domestic programs. This possibility pained Johnson greatly. "If I left the woman I really loved—the Great Society—in order to get involved with that . . . war on the other side of the world, then I would lose everything at home," Johnson later stated. "All my programs. All my hopes to feed the hungry and shelter the homeless. All my dreams to provide education and medical care to the browns and the blacks and the lame and the poor. But if I left that war and let the Communists take over South Vietnam, . . . there would follow in this country an endless national debate—a mean and destructive debate—that would shatter my Presidency, kill my administration, and damage our democracy."

After weighing his options, Johnson reluctantly prepared to increase U.S. military involvement in Vietnam. He decided that America's political interests and international reputation would not allow him to pull out of the war-torn country.

But even as the Johnson administration prepared to expand the U.S. military role in Vietnam, Communist victories mounted. By late 1964, many provinces in the South were under the practical control of the Viet Cong. Even the heavily populated cities, with their large South Vietnamese military presence, were not immune from Viet Cong activity. On Christmas Eve 1964, a Viet Cong bomb destroyed a U.S. officer barracks in downtown Saigon, killing two soldiers and wounding dozens of other soldiers and civilians. Such incidents made it clear that America's looming battle against the Viet Cong and their North Vietnamese leadership was going to be a grim and bloody one.

Sources

Becker, Elizabeth. *America's Vietnam War: A Narrative History.* New York: Clarion, 1992.

Gardner, Lloyd C. *Pay Any Price: Lyndon Johnson and the Wars for Vietnam.* Chicago: Ivan Dee, 1995.

Goulden, Joseph C. *Truth Is the First Casualty: The Gulf of Tonkin Affair—Illusion and Reality.* Chicago: Rand-McNally, 1969.

Halberstam, David. *The Best and the Brightest.* New York: Random House, 1972.

Herring, George. *LBJ and Vietnam: A Different Kind of War.* Austin: University of Texas Press, 1994.

Johnson, Lyndon B. *The Vantage Point: Perspectives of the Presidency, 1963–1969.* New York: Holt, Rinehart & Winston, 1971.

McNamara, Robert S., with Brian VanDeMark. *In Retrospect: The Tragedy and Lessons of Vietnam.* New York: Times Books, 1995.

Schulzinger, Robert D. *A Time for War: The United States and Vietnam, 1941–1975.* New York: Oxford University Press, 1997.

VanDeMark, Brian. *Into the Quagmire: Lyndon Johnson and the Escalation of the Vietnam War.* New York: Oxford University Press, 1991.

Willenson, Kim. *The Bad War: An Oral History of the Vietnam War.* New York: New American Library, 1987.

Vietnam Becomes an American War (1965–67)

6

Beginning in 1965, the United States dramatically increased its involvement in the war in Vietnam. U.S. officials and military leaders supported this "escalation" in American activity because they worried that South Vietnam's crumbling government would otherwise fall to the North Vietnamese Communists. "South Vietnam's accelerating crisis alarmed American policymakers, driving them to deepen U.S. involvement considerably in an effort to arrest Saigon's political failure," writes Brian VanDeMark in *Into the Quagmire*. "Abandoning the concept of [establishing] stability in the South *before* escalation [of the war] against the North, policymakers now embraced the concept of stability *through* escalation, in the desperate hope that military action against Hanoi would prompt [create] a stubbornly elusive political order in Saigon."

Over the next few years, so-called "Americanization" of the Vietnam War developed rapidly. The United States launched a long and deadly air bombing campaign against North Vietnam during this time. It also sent hundreds of thousands of American soldiers into South Vietnam to fight Viet Cong guerrillas (small groups of fighters who launch surprise

Words to Know

ARVN The South Vietnamese army, officially known as the Army of the Republic of South Vietnam. The ARVN fought on the same side as U.S. troops during the Vietnam War.

Communism A political system in which the government controls all resources and means of producing wealth. By eliminating private property, this system is designed to create an equal society with no social classes. However, Communist governments in practice often limit personal freedom and individual rights.

Great Society A set of social programs proposed by U.S. President Lyndon Johnson designed to end segregation and reduce poverty in the United States.

Hanoi The capital city of Communist North Vietnam. Also an unofficial shorthand way of referring to the North Vietnamese government.

North Vietnam The Geneva Accords of 1954, which ended the First Indochina War (1946–54), divided the nation of Vietnam into two sections. The northern section, which was led by a Communist government under Ho Chi Minh, was officially known as the Democratic Republic of Vietnam, but was usually called North Vietnam.

NVA The North Vietnamese Army, which assisted the Viet Cong guerrilla fighters in trying to conquer South Vietnam. These forces opposed the United States in the Vietnam War.

Saigon The capital city of U.S.-supported South Vietnam. Also an unofficial shorthand way of referring to the South Vietnamese government.

South Vietnam Created under the Geneva Accords of 1954, the southern section of Vietnam was known as the Republic of South Vietnam. It was led by a U.S.-supported government.

Viet Cong Vietnamese Communist guerrilla fighters who worked with the North Vietnamese Army to conquer South Vietnam.

attacks) and North Vietnamese troops. Finally, U.S. officials continued with their efforts to rebuild South Vietnam's weak and unpopular government.

Despite all of these activities, however, the Communists remained strong. Dedicated to their cause, they used guerrilla tactics to neutralize America's huge advantages in mobility and firepower. By the end of 1967, the war had become a military stalemate (a standstill, with no side emerging victorious) in Vietnam and a source of explosive unrest back in the United States.

Operation Rolling Thunder

In early 1965, the United States took a bold step forward in its defense of South Vietnam by launching a sustained campaign of bombing attacks against North Vietnam. This campaign was triggered by a February Viet Cong attack on American barracks in the South Vietnamese city of Pleiku. U.S. and South Vietnamese planes responded by bombing several targets in the North. America's military leadership then halted the bombing. But as it turned out, the bombing stopped for only a few weeks.

One month later, on March 2, 1965, Operation Rolling Thunder began. This U.S. air bombing campaign against targets in North Vietnam remained in place, with occasional interruptions, for the next three and a half years. Experts estimate that from 1965 to 1968 alone, American Navy and Air Force fighter planes dropped 643,000 tons of bombs on North Vietnam. This amount was greater than all the bombs dropped in the Pacific "theatre" (a geographic area where war is conducted) during World War II (1939–45). North Vietnam responded by building a deadly air defense system that shot hundreds of U.S. planes out of the sky. The pilots of these downed planes accounted for many of America's prisoners of war (POWs) in Vietnam (see box titled "American Prisoners of War (POWs)" in Chapter 10, "Coming Home: Vietnam Veterans in American Society").

People to Know

Ho Chi Minh (1890–1969) Vietnamese Communist leader who led Viet Minh forces in opposing French rule and became the first president of North Vietnam in 1954. He also led the North during the Vietnam War until his death.

Lyndon B. Johnson (1908–1973) After serving as vice president under John Kennedy, he became the 36th president of the United States after Kennedy was assassinated in 1963. Johnson sent U.S. combat troops to Vietnam. Opposition to his policies convinced him not to seek re-election in 1968.

Robert McNamara (1916–) Served as U.S. secretary of defense during the Kennedy and Johnson administrations, 1961–1968. After helping to shape U.S. policy toward Vietnam, he privately began to doubt that America could win the war.

William Westmoreland (1914–) Commander of American military forces in Vietnam, 1964–1968.

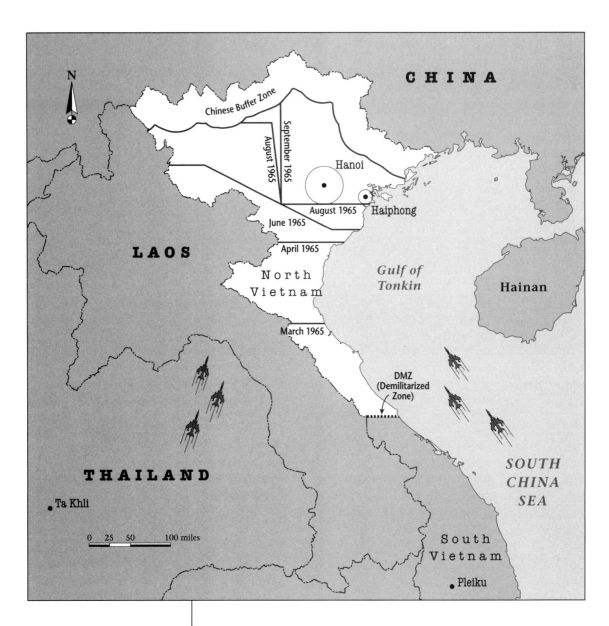

CHINA

Chinese Buffer Zone

September 1965

August 1965

Hanoi

August 1965

Haiphong

June 1965

April 1965

LAOS

North
Vietnam

Gulf of
Tonkin

Hainan

March 1965

DMZ
(Demilitarized
Zone)

THAILAND

SOUTH
CHINA
SEA

Ta Khli

0 25 50   100 miles

South
Vietnam

Pleiku

**Operation Rolling
Thunder. U.S. bombing
missions were usually
launched from Thailand and
the South China Sea.**
*Map by XNR Productions, Inc.
Reproduced by permission
of Gale Group.*

The United States launched Operation Rolling Thunder for several reasons. It hoped that the deadly bombing runs would destroy the North's ability to supply soldiers and equipment to Communists in the South. American officials also hoped that the bombings, which continued day after day, would ruin the morale of the people of North Vietnam and convince them to negotiate an end to the war. Still, President Lyndon Johnson (1908–1973; president 1963–1969) and

One North Vietnamese Villager Remembers Rolling Thunder

In early 1965, the United States launched an ongoing air bombing campaign against strategic targets throughout North Vietnam. This campaign—code-named Operation Rolling Thunder—lasted for more than five years, with only brief interruptions. The bombing caused terrible damage to North Vietnam's military facilities, factories, towns, and countryside. It also inflicted heavy casualties on the North's civilian population, even though American political and military leaders insisted that they did not want to harm innocent people.

Years after the end of the Vietnam War, a villager named Ho Thanh Dam told Stanley Karnow, author of *Vietnam: A History,* how it felt when American planes bombed his small town in July 1967:

The bombing started at about eight o'clock in the morning and lasted for hours. At the first sound of explosions, we rushed into the tunnels, but not everyone made it. During a pause in the attack, some of us climbed out to see what we could do, and the scene was terrifying. Bodies had been torn to pieces—limbs hanging from trees or scattered around the ground. Then the bombing began again, this time with napalm, and the village went up in flames. The napalm hit me, and I must have gone crazy. I felt as if I were burning all over, like charcoal, and I lost consciousness. Comrades took me to the hospital, and my wounds didn't begin to heal until six months later. More than two hundred people died in the raid, including my mother, my sister-in-law, and three nephews. They were buried alive when their tunnel collapsed.

Defense Secretary Robert McNamara (1916–) spared some targets, such as power plants, oil storage facilities, and military airfields, from bombing. Johnson and McNamara hoped that the threat of destroying these valuable facilities might also help convince the North to end hostilities.

As time passed, however, the bombings failed to meet American goals. Soldiers and supplies continued to pour into South Vietnam from the North, and the Communist government took a number of steps to protect itself and its people from the bombings. Northern leaders supervised the construction of a large system of bomb-proof shelters and tunnels. They also dispersed people and industries from the cities to locations all across the country so that enemy planes could not concentrate their fire on a few areas. Finally, they rebuilt highways, railroad bridges, and other targets during the night as fast as the United States could blow them up. The North was aided in all of these efforts by the Communist governments of China and the Soviet Union.

As the Rolling Thunder bombings continued, the Northern Communists actually became more determined to continue the fight. This situation never changed, even after the United States increased the force of its attacks. "The Americans thought that the more bombs they dropped, the quicker we would fall to our knees and surrender," recalled one North Vietnamese citizen. "But the bombs heightened rather than dampened our enthusiasm." In fact, the Rolling Thunder campaign intensified anti-American feelings and made it easier for North Vietnam President Ho Chi Minh (1890–1969) to characterize the war as a battle between the Vietnamese people and a foreign invader. "To oppose the United States and save the country is the most sacred task of every Vietnamese patriot," he claimed.

U.S. combat troops arrive in Vietnam

The first American combat troops arrived in South Vietnam in the spring of 1965. Of course, thousands of U.S. advisors, clerks, pilots, and other military personnel had served in Vietnam prior to 1965. But they had been responsible only for assisting the South Vietnamese military and government. They had not been ordered to Vietnam to fight the Viet Cong (VC) or North Vietnamese military. When U.S. marines arrived in Vietnam on March 8 to guard important facilities, a new stage of the war began.

Over the next few months, General William Westmoreland (1914–)—who was commander of U.S. forces in Vietnam—urged President Johnson to send additional combat troops to Vietnam and allow them to fight in battles against the Communists. Many advisors and military experts like the Joint Chiefs of Staff (composed of the heads of the four branches of the American armed forces and an overall chairman) supported this request. They argued that the time had come to either abandon South Vietnam to the Communists— an option that they saw as humiliating—or use America's awesome military power directly.

President Johnson granted both of Westmoreland's requests, even though he harbored great concerns about expanding America's military role in Vietnam. First, the president approved the commitment of thousands of new troops to Vietnam. Then, on April 6, Johnson authorized U.S. ground troops to engage in direct combat operations in Vietnam. Three months later, he announced an expansion of the military "draft"—a system in which citizens are legally required to provide military service—so that the United States could increase its troop strength in Vietnam. By the end of 1965, more than 180,000 American troops had been transferred to the troubled Southeast Asian nation.

Westmoreland's plan

As American forces poured into South Vietnam, General Westmoreland expressed great confidence that the United States would whip the Viet Cong and their NVA (North Vietnamese Army) allies. He planned to use some of his American troops to defend important U.S. bases and fortify strategic areas of the South like the Central Highlands, located in the heart of the country. He then planned to launch a series of "search-and-destroy" missions, using America's tremendous advantages in weapons, helicopters, airplanes, and other resources to locate and wipe out the enemy. Finally, he intended to introduce a new "pacification" scheme in the South's Viet Cong-infested rural areas.

Westmoreland and other American officials hoped that this new military, economic, and social program would "pacify," or calm, South Vietnamese peasants and persuade them to support the Saigon government. Westmoreland believed that his plan, combined with the bombing campaign against North Vietnam, would eventually prove too much for the Communists to withstand. "We'll just go on bleeding them until Hanoi wakes up to the fact that they have bled their country to the point of national disaster for generations," he said.

Westmoreland's confidence was shared by most of the rest of the American military as well, from generals to ordinary soldiers. "When we marched into the rice paddies on that damp March afternoon [in 1965], we carried, along with our packs and rifles, the implicit [unspoken but understood] convictions that the Vietcong would be quickly beaten," American Marine Philip Caputo recalls in his memoir *A Rumor of War*. Their confidence was understandable. After all, America had never lost a war, and the U.S. military held huge advantages over the Viet Cong and North Vietnamese forces in firepower, mobility, and technology. With all of these advantages, they could not imagine losing in Vietnam.

Continued troubles in Saigon

As America's military leadership prepared to take outright command of the war against the Communists in South Vietnam, U.S. advisors continued trying to breathe new life into the nation's government. With each passing month, however, the generals and politicians who ruled Saigon relied more heavily on American military and economic aid. This situation created significant tensions between the two groups. "[South Vietnam's leaders] repeatedly tried to assert their sovereignty [independence] by defying the Americans in disputes that often resembled quarrels between an adolescent and a parent," reports Stanley Karnow in *Vietnam: A History*. "They would sulk or rebel or maneuver mysteriously, their petulance [immature behavior] betraying an uncomfortable sense of dependence and frustration with the growing American intrusion into their affairs. The more they resisted American guidance, however, the more the U.S. commanders bypassed them in the planning and pursuit of the war." After a while, the Americans practically ignored the Saigon government when making their war plans.

The American military leadership also worked to improve the performance of South Vietnam's armed forces. But many of the South's officers were corrupt or showed little motivation to fight. In addition, most South Vietnamese troops received poor equipment, low pay, and little respect from their superiors. By 1966, many South Vietnamese soldiers relied on extra supplies of American rice for their meals. Not surprisingly, some members of the South Vietnamese army became reluctant to risk their lives for a government that did not seem to care about them. Finally, some of these soldiers had been waging war against the Viet Cong for years, and they were weary of all the bloodshed and violence.

Over time, these factors made many American military leaders and soldiers view the South Vietnamese as poor and undependable fighters. The U.S. forces became unwilling to rely on them. As a result, most South Vietnamese units were reduced to security duties and occasional support of American-led search-and-destroy operations. During this time they played a minor role in American military strategy, even though the war was taking place in their country.

Early American successes

In 1965 and 1966, America's armed forces claimed several significant military triumphs in Vietnam. For instance, U.S. and South Vietnamese naval forces established control over much of Vietnam's coastline. This prevented North Vietnam from sending supplies by sea to Viet Cong and NVA troops operating in the South. In addition, U.S. Navy gunboat patrols loosened the Communist grip on the rivers, canals, and delta areas of South Vietnam, especially in the Mekong Delta region.

U.S. troops also won a number of notable clashes with the enemy during this period. For example, in November 1965, U.S. forces met the North Vietnamese Army at the Battle of Ia Drang, a longtime Communist sanctuary. This was the first major engagement between U.S. troops and NVA troops in the Vietnam War. NVA troops had begun moving into the South in late 1964, when Ho Chi Minh and other North Vietnamese leaders decided that the Viet Cong needed additional help.

Operating from their base in the Ia Drang Valley, these NVA forces hoped to sweep eastward through South Vietnam and attack populated areas along the coastline. But the American forces destroyed this plan in its early stages. Over four days of savage battle, the U.S. troops stood firm, using superior artillery and air strikes to inflict terrible casualties on the Communists. The North Vietnamese finally retreated from the field, fleeing for secret bases in nearby Cambodia or remote jungle hideouts. This victory boosted the morale of the American forces. The presence of NVA troops at the battle also supported U.S. claims that North Vietnam—not the South Vietnamese people—was the main force behind efforts to topple the government in Saigon.

A frustrating enemy

Despite these triumphs, however, the American forces struggled in other aspects of the war. For example, they failed to shut down the Ho Chi Minh Trail, the primary route used by Communists to transport soldiers and supplies. This roadway ran through the thick jungles of Laos and Cambodia, the countries immediately to the west of Vietnam. From 1965 to 1968, American planes bombed the trail every day, using sophisticated detection devices and spy reports to select their targets. But the Communists continued to use the route, making repairs as needed. By 1967, an estimated 20,000 NVA troops used the trail to enter South Vietnam each month, despite the heavy bombing.

U.S. forces also became frustrated with the way their enemy waged war. The American soldiers wanted to engage the Viet Cong and NVA forces in open battle, where they could take full advantage of their superiority in firepower and mobility. But for the most part, the Communists avoided open confrontation with the American forces. Instead, they used sniper attacks, booby traps, and ambushes to terrorize the American troops. When the U.S. units chased after them, they often disappeared into the jungle or hid among village populations. This style of fighting—called guerrilla warfare—angered and discouraged American foot soldiers and generals alike.

The Americans also found it very difficult to remove Viet Cong forces from rural areas permanently. The U.S. forces repeatedly chased the

U.S. Marine carrying blindfolded Viet Cong suspect.
Reproduced by permission of Corbis-Bettman.

enemy out of villages or strategic jungle areas. The military made heavy use of ground troops in these efforts, but their biggest weapon was air power. They targeted many suspected Communist strongholds with bombings of explosives or napalm, a gasoline-based chemical that sent large sections of forest up in flames. But as soon as the American forces left the area, the Communists would creep back and resume their guerrilla operations.

One prime example of this trend was an American military campaign known as Operation Cedar Falls. In January 1967, U.S. military leaders decided to clear the Viet Cong out of a region northwest of Saigon called the "Iron Triangle." They believed that the Communists were using this area as their base for guerrilla activities in nearby villages and terrorist activities in Saigon.

Using both ground and helicopter assault forces, the Americans swept into the Iron Triangle. They killed or captured about 1,000 Viet Cong and seized large amounts of supplies, while suffering far fewer casualties themselves. The U.S. offensive succeeded in chasing the Communists out of the area. But as time passed and American military attention turned elsewhere, Viet Cong forces quietly slipped back into the Iron Triangle to resume their activities. This sequence of events happened time after time across South Vietnam.

Rural Vietnamese trapped in warfare

As the war between the Communists and the Americans intensified, South Vietnam's large peasant population became caught in the middle. On one side, Communist guerrillas struck fear into the hearts of many peasants. Some villagers joined the Viet Cong willingly. They believed the Communist argument that the war was actually a fight for Vietnamese independence from foreign control. But in many other instances, the Viet Cong forced rural villagers to assist them in their war effort. "The first Marines who came to Vietnam learned quickly that the Vietnamese peasant was tired of war, hungry for a little tranquility [peace], and terrified of the Viet Cong guerrillas who . . . murdered their village mayors, extracted rice and tribute [payments to avoid punishment], labor and information . . . and impressed [forced] their chil-

Four "ranch hand" C-123 aircraft spraying a suspected Viet Cong jungle position with defoliation liquid in South Vietnam.
Reproduced by permission of AP/World Wide Photos.

dren into the Viet Cong ranks," recalled one U.S. Marine commander.

As American troops traveled deeper into the countryside, they found that fear of the Viet Cong kept many villagers from cooperating with them. As South Vietnamese General Lu Mong Lan noted in Al Santoli's *To Bear Any Burden,* "in areas close to their sanctuaries in Cambodia, the North Vietnamese were never more than a two-day march from any village. There was always a fear of reprisal [consequences] among people who cooperated with our forces . . . . And there were well-informed VC agents who monitored every villager's activities."

But the peasants also came to resent the American forces marching across their land. They hated and feared U.S. planes, which dropped bombs and defoliants (chemicals designed to kill crops and jungle vegetation in order to deprive Communists of food and cover) all across the South. These bombing campaigns drove hundreds of thousands of peasants from their longtime villages into overcrowded cities. In fact, an estimated four million Vietnamese—about one quarter of the total population—became refugees (people without homes) during the war. Some American strategists applauded this development. They believed that as more villages were abandoned, the Viet Cong and NVA would have greater difficulty obtaining supplies and hiding from U.S. forces.

Rural Vietnamese also suffered because American and South Vietnamese troops could never be sure if the villagers were actually Viet Cong. When these military units entered a village, they often treated the residents roughly as they searched for evidence of Viet Cong membership. After all, they had no way of knowing who was an enemy and who was a friend. Scared and frustrated, American and ARVN troops distrusted every villager they encountered. "At the end of the day, the villagers would be turned loose," recalled one soldier. "Their homes had been wrecked, their chickens killed, their rice confiscated—and if they weren't pro-Vietcong before we got there, they sure as hell were by the time we left." After the war, one South Vietnamese villager compared American efforts to find possible VC fighters in her village to "a raging elephant stomping on red ants too far down in their holes to feel the blows."

As time passed, many of these helpless South Vietnamese families became resigned to the grim situation. Helpless to protect themselves from either side, they simply tried to survive until the war ended. "The villagers were horrified because they couldn't win at all," remembered one U.S. soldier in *To Bear Any Burden.* "If they didn't submit to the Viet Cong and pay their bounty, the chiefs were killed or the young men or women taken away. And then here we come along or the South Vietnamese troops. And they'd have to submit to our will at the same time. So they didn't have a chance. I pitied them."

War settles into a stalemate

By the beginning of 1966, U.S. troop strength in Vietnam was at 250,000. Westmoreland also had substantial South Vietnamese forces under his command. In addition, South Korea, Australia, and New Zealand all sent limited numbers of troops to South Vietnam to help the United States. The size of this military machine enabled America to conduct operations in all corners of South Vietnam, from the coastline to the deep jungles bordering Cambodia.

But as the weeks passed without any major change in the war, Westmoreland and other U.S. officials reluctantly concluded that the United States would have to send additional troops and weaponry to Vietnam. North Vietnam showed no sign of giving up the fight. In fact, the North's leaders continued to insist that peace would not come until the United States left Vietnam and accepted reunification of North and South into one country, as stated in the 1954 Geneva Accords that ended the First Indochina War (1946–54).

Throughout 1966, Westmoreland made repeated requests for additional troops, helicopters, weapons, and other supplies. He and other military leaders told U.S. officials that these extra forces were necessary to break the will of the Communists and force them to give up the fight. The Johnson administration granted most of these requests, hopeful that the new soldiers and guns would finally turn the tide in favor of the Americans. But as the U.S. government steadily increased its spending on the war, Johnson's domestic education and anti-poverty programs became endangered.

Paying for Vietnam

Shortly after Lyndon Johnson became president in 1963, he announced a series of programs designed to battle poverty, racism, pollution, and other American social problems. He hoped to build a "Great Society" by increasing educational and economic opportunities for disadvantaged people throughout the United States. Johnson believed in these programs so deeply that he refused to cut funding for them, even as the price of waging war in Vietnam kept rising.

As a result, the Johnson administration maintained its support for both the war and its social programs, even though it did not have enough money to pay for both. This decision placed a great strain on the U.S. economy. Within months, an economic trend known as inflation developed. During periods of inflation, the cost of food, clothing, and other goods and services rise sharply, making them less affordable. Johnson eventually called for tax increases so that the government could cover its spending. This move failed to calm the country's economic troubles and angered many Americans.

As the U.S. economy stumbled, growing numbers of people blamed the turmoil on the war in Vietnam. "The inspiration and commitment of the Great Society have disappeared," charged Senator William Fulbright (1905–1995), an antiwar Democrat from Arkansas. "In concrete terms, the President simply cannot think about implementing the Great Society at home while he is supervising bombing missions over North Vietnam. There is a kind of madness in the facile [casual] assumption that we can raise the many billions of dollars necessary to rebuild our schools and cities and public transport and eliminate the pollution of air and water while also spending tens of billions to finance an 'open-ended' war in Asia."

Rise of the antiwar movement

During the mid-1960s, President Johnson and his administration were also rocked by growing American opposition to the war on moral grounds. When Johnson first sent American combat troops to Vietnam in March 1965, most Americans supported his decision. But as U.S. casualties (dead and wounded soldiers) mounted and Americans learned more about the war, this support faded. Organized protests against American involvement in Vietnam erupted all across the country in 1966 and 1967. The antiwar movement was especially strong on college campuses, where student activists charged that the United States was waging an immoral and horribly destructive war against the Vietnamese people (see Chapter 8, "The American Antiwar Movement").

As opposition to the war increased on American campuses and city streets, greater numbers of political leaders began questioning U.S. policy as well. They no longer trusted the administration's claims that victory was within reach. Instead, they began to feel that the United States was sacrificing thousands of young men to a war that looked to them like a bloody and wasteful stalemate.

Yet even as the antiwar movement gathered strength, the Johnson administration also faced tremendous pressure to

Thousands of antiwar protesters at the United Nations Plaza, 1967.

Reproduced by permission of AP/World Wide Photos.

maintain or even *increase* its commitment to the war. Large segments of the American population resented the antiwar movement and disagreed with its views. They remained firmly supportive of U.S. military involvement in Southeast Asia.

Many American politicians and military leaders also complained that the United States was not using enough military force in Vietnam. For example, they harshly criticized the administration's decision to spare North Vietnamese airfields and petroleum facilities during the Rolling Thunder bombing campaign. They also urged the administration to expand the war into Laos and Cambodia, where the Ho Chi Minh Trail and countless Communist hideouts were located (see box titled "'Secret War' in Laos" in Chapter 3, "Early American Involvement in Vietnam"). These critics claimed that the Communists would soon be crushed if the United States expanded its military operations and sent additional troops.

"McNamara's War"

As the uproar over American involvement in Vietnam increased from 1965 to 1967, many public officials changed their views on the conflict. The most highly visible member of the Johnson administration to do so was Robert McNamara, the president's secretary of defense.

McNamara had supervised the U.S. military build-up in Vietnam throughout the early and mid-1960s. He was known for his sharp intelligence and reliance on statistics to analyze situations and solve problems. In fact, he was widely credited with improving the management and efficiency of U.S. armed forces in the early 1960s. As the war heated up, he came to be seen as the primary architect of American military strategy in Vietnam. Over time, McNamara became so closely identified with the conflict that some antiwar protestors referred to it as "McNamara's War."

When U.S. combat forces were first sent to Vietnam in early 1965, McNamara was highly confident that his logical approach to problem-solving, combined with superior American resources, would produce a quick victory over the Communists. By late 1965, however, McNamara became convinced that the North would never stop fighting, no matter how much punishment they endured. This realization made him doubt that the United States would ever win the war. Paul Hendrickson, author of *The Living and the Dead: Robert McNamara and Five Lives of a Lost War,* writes that "In essence, what McNamara and a handful of others at the high echelons [levels] of strategy and analysis began to see was this: No matter how many men our side was willing to put in, the enemy would be willing to put in more. They would match us, and up it. They would give a million dead over to their cause. And keep going."

"A Nation at Odds"

As U.S. involvement in the Vietnam War deepened in the mid-1960s, the American public entered a heated debate over the wisdom and morality of these military operations. With each passing month, the divisions widened between people who supported the war and those who opposed it. By 1967, these differences had sparked such great anger and hostility that many Americans worried about the future of the nation. In the following excerpt from "A Nation at Odds," published on July 10, 1967, the editors of *Newsweek* magazine express their concerns about the country's troubled state:

> Cleft [divided] by doubts and tormented by frustration, the nation this Independence Day is haunted by its most corrosive [damaging], ambiguous [vaguely defined] foreign adventure—a bloody, costly jungle war half a world away that has etched the tragedy of Vietnam into the American soul.

> Few scars show on the surface . . . . The casualty lists run inconspicuously [unnoticed] on the inside pages of newspapers; wounded veterans are kept mostly out of sight, remain mostly out of mind. Save on the otherworldly mosaic [images] of the TV screen, the war is almost invisible on the home-front. But, like a slow-spreading blight [disease], it is inexorably [steadily] making its mark on nearly every facet of American life.

> The obvious costs of Vietnam are easy enough to compute: 11,373 American dead, 68,341 wounded, treasure now spent at the rate of $38,052 a minute, swelling the war's price by more than $25 billion in two years. Indeed, never have Americans been subject to such a barrage of military statistics—and never have they been so hopelessly confused by them. There are no statistics to tote up Vietnam's hidden price, but its calculus [result] is clear: a wartime divisiveness all but unknown in America since the Blue bloodied the Gray [in the American Civil War].

> In the new world's citadel [stronghold] of democracy, men now accuse each other of an arrogance of power and of complicity [involvement] in genocide [killing an entire race of people], of cowardice and disloyalty. So incendiary [explosive] have feelings become that close-knit families have had to agree not to disagree about Vietnam at table. Ministers have become alienated from their flocks, parents from their children, teachers from their students and each other, blacks from whites, hawks [supporters of the war] from doves [opponents of the war]. The crisis of conscience has spilled out into the streets—in mammoth antiwar marches like last April's big parade in New York and the "Support our Boys" countermarch a month later . . . .

> The nation has become so committed to seeing Vietnam through to an honorable conclusion that repudiation [rejection] of that commitment would unleash shock waves that would rock the country. Thus, like a neurotic [mentally ill person] clinging desperately to set patterns of behavior, America is likely to submerge its anxieties in a brave show of business-as-usual unless the war dramatically escalates. Deep in their hearts, most Americans cherish the idea that somehow the nightmare will turn out to have a silver lining—that the U.S. will in the end achieve its limited and honorable goals in Vietnam. After all, have Americans ever failed before?

As the war continued in 1966, McNamara privately began pushing for peace negotiations to end the conflict. But all of these diplomatic efforts failed. "My frustration, disenchantment, and anguish deepened" after each failure, McNamara recalls in his memoir *In Retrospect.* "I could see no good way to win—or end—an increasingly costly and destructive war . . . . It became clear then, and I believe it is clear today, that military force—especially when wielded [controlled] by an outside power—just cannot bring order in a country that cannot govern itself."

But even though McNamara became convinced that America could not win in Vietnam, he publicly insisted that the U.S. war effort was going well. In October 1966, for instance, he returned from a trip to Vietnam, his eighth trip to the country in less than five years, and proclaimed that "Today I can tell you that military progress in the past twelve months has exceeded our expectations." But when he delivered his post-trip report to Johnson, he confessed that Communist forces seemed stronger than ever. Many people have criticized McNamara's decision to withhold his doubts from the American public during this time. Journalist David Halberstam, for example, spoke for many when he called it a "crime of silence."

By the summer of 1967, McNamara had privately abandoned all hope that the United States could defeat the Communists in Vietnam. In August, he testified before a Senate committee that was holding hearings on whether the United States should expand its bombing of North Vietnam. The committee was led by Senator John Stennis, a strong supporter of American involvement in Vietnam, and dominated by other senators who supported the war. Dozens of top military officers who testified at the hearing stated that the United States should increase its bombing of the North. But when McNamara testified, he bluntly stated that the Rolling Thunder campaign was a failure and that expanded bombing operations would not change the situation. He admitted that the bombing had put a "high price tag on North Vietnam's continued aggression." But he also said that no amount of bombing could stop North Vietnam from continuing its efforts to win the South, "short, that is, of the virtual annihilation [destruction] of North Vietnam and its people."

Everyone viewed McNamara's testimony as evidence that he no longer believed in the war. President Johnson decided that he had to replace him as secretary of defense. During the last months of 1967, most of McNamara's war responsibilities were given to other officials. In February 1968, he left the administration for a position as head of the World Bank.

State of the war in late 1967

During the final months of 1967, the Johnson administration continued to push forward with the war effort. Boosted by a steady stream of new soldiers, the U.S. force in Vietnam rose to about 485,000 troops. But American casualty figures continued to rise as well. By October 1967, the number of American soldiers killed, wounded, or missing in the war reached the 100,000 mark. From 1966 to 1967, the death rate among American troops in Vietnam doubled to more than 800 a month.

To opponents of the war, these statistics suggested that the war seemed likely to continue for some time, despite America's efforts to crush the enemy. "Air power had not brought the Communists to their knees, neither had General Westmoreland's strategy of attrition [wearing down the enemy with superior troop strength, firepower, and resources]," confirmed Clark Dougan and Stephen Weiss in *The American Experience in Vietnam.* "The commitment of nearly half a million troops had saved South Vietnam from defeat and taken a heavy toll of enemy casualties. U.S. soldiers had fought well under adverse [difficult] conditions, utilizing an enormous advantage in mobility and firepower to drive the Vietcong from even their most secure strongholds. Indeed, whenever American forces actually engaged VC or NVA units, they almost always prevailed. But the primary goal of grinding down the enemy until he hollered 'uncle' was not happening."

Nonetheless, Johnson's generals and military advisors insisted that the war's momentum was shifting in favor of the United States. In addition, the Johnson administration helped South Vietnam hold national elections in late 1967. These elections, which established Nguyen Van Thieu (1923–) and Nguyen Cao Ky (1930–) as the South's leaders, did not improve the performance of the government in meaningful ways. Still,

Johnson hailed the election as a symbol that South Vietnam remained a legitimate nation deserving of protection. He called the election "a milestone along the path toward . . . a free, secure, and peaceful Vietnam."

But the election in South Vietnam did not impress America's growing antiwar movement. In fact, the war had grown into a source of great pain, anger, and conflict in the United States. Many Americans were convinced that the war could still be won if the United States remained firm in its determination to beat the Communists. But many other citizens offered emotional protests against the war. They continued to call for an end to the bombing and withdrawal of U.S. troops from the South. As the debate intensified, each side expressed great bitterness and anger about the beliefs of the other.

In November 1967, General Westmoreland traveled to Washington, D.C., in an attempt to increase congressional and public support for the American war effort. Upon arriving, he told reporters that U.S. efforts to defeat the Viet Cong and NVA were going well. "I have never been more encouraged in my four years in Vietnam," he said. Other administration officials and military experts echoed the general's remarks, arguing that America was slowly but surely winning the war. But even as Westmoreland and other officials offered their assurances, the Communists of Vietnam were preparing a massive military strike for the coming new year. This attack—known as the Tet Offensive—permanently changed the shape of the Vietnam War.

Sources

Berman, Larry. *Planning a Tragedy: The Americanization of the War in Vietnam.* New York: W. W. Norton, 1982.

Caputo, Philip. *A Rumor of War.* New York: Ballantine Books, 1994.

Dougan, Clark, and Stephen Weiss. *The American Experience in Vietnam.* New York: W. W. Norton, 1988.

Hendrickson, Paul. *The Living and the Dead: Robert McNamara and Five Lives of a Lost War.* New York: Alfred A. Knopf, 1996.

Herring, George C. *LBJ and Vietnam: A Different Kind of War.* Austin: University of Texas Press, 1994.

Karnow, Stanley. *Vietnam: A History.* Rev. ed. New York: Penguin Books,

1997.

Kearns, Doris. *Lyndon Johnson & the American Dream*. New York: Harper & Row, 1976.

Kolko, Gabriel. *Anatomy of a War: Vietnam, the United States, and the Modern Historical Experience*. New York: New Press, 1994.

McNamara, Robert, with Brian VanDeMark. *In Retrospect: The Tragedy and Lessons of Vietnam*. New York: Times Books, 1995.

Moore, Harold G., and Joseph L. Galloway. *We Were Soldiers Once . . . And Young*. New York: Random House, 1992.

Santoli, Al. *To Bear Any Burden: The Vietnam War and Its Aftermath in the Words of Americans and Southeast Asians*. Bloomington: Indiana University Press, 1999.

Shandler, Herbert Y. *The Unmaking of a President: Lyndon Johnson and Vietnam*. Princeton, NJ: Princeton University Press, 1977.

Thompson, James Clay. *Rolling Thunder*. Chapel Hill, NC: University of North Carolina Press, 1980.

VanDeMark, Brian. *Into the Quagmire: Lyndon Johnson and the Escalation of the Vietnam War*. New York: Oxford University Press, 1991.

The Tet Offensive (1968)

In late 1967 and early 1968, after three years of bloody war, the U.S. government repeatedly told the American public that the U.S. military was on the verge of victory in Vietnam. But on January 30, 1968, the North Vietnamese Army (NVA) and Viet Cong guerrillas (small groups of fighters who launch surprise attacks) launched the Tet Offensive. This massive surprise attack hit targets all across South Vietnam, astonishing U.S. forces and shocking the American people.

U.S. and South Vietnamese troops eventually pushed back the Communist assault, delivering heavy casualties to NVA and Viet Cong units in the process. But the huge size of the offensive convinced many Americans that the Johnson administration could not be trusted to tell the truth about the war. As William Turley writes in *The Second Indochina War,* "The official optimism of years past suddenly seemed proof of incompetence or deception." Indeed, Tet convinced large segments of the U.S. population that the war might only be won by sacrificing thousands more lives to the conflict.

Tired and disillusioned after Tet, Lyndon Johnson (1908–1973; president 1963–1969) decided not to seek a sec-

Words to Know

ARVN The South Vietnamese army, officially known as the Army of the Republic of South Vietnam. The ARVN fought on the same side as U.S. troops during the Vietnam War.

Communism A political system in which the government controls all resources and means of producing wealth. By eliminating private property, this system is designed to create an equal society with no social classes. However, Communist governments in practice often limit personal freedom and individual rights.

North Vietnam The Geneva Accords of 1954, which ended the First Indochina War (1946–54), divided the nation of Vietnam into two sections. The northern section, which was led by a Communist government under Ho Chi Minh, was officially known as the Democratic Republic of Vietnam, but was usually called North Vietnam.

NVA The North Vietnamese Army, which assisted the Viet Cong guerilla fighters in trying to conquer South Vietnam. These forces opposed the United States in the Vietnam War.

Offensive A sudden, aggressive attack by one side during a war.

South Vietnam Created under the Geneva Accords of 1954, the southern section of Vietnam was known as the Republic of South Vietnam. It was led by a U.S.-supported government.

Viet Cong Vietnamese Communist guerilla fighters who worked with the North Vietnamese Army to conquer South Vietnam.

ond term as president in the upcoming November 1968 elections. He also took steps to begin peace negotiations with North Vietnam. But the war continued, and the debate over Vietnam reached an angry level that sometimes seemed to threaten American society. The explosive situation in U.S. cities and towns became even worse with the assassinations of Martin Luther King Jr. (1929–1968), and Robert F. Kennedy (1925–1968) within the space of a few months. Their deaths, along with the continued bloodshed in Vietnam, made 1968 a tremendously difficult year for the United States and its people.

People to Know

Clark Clifford (1906–) U.S. secretary of defense under President Lyndon Johnson, 1968–1969.

Ho Chi Minh (1890–1969) Vietnamese Communist leader who led Viet Minh forces in opposing French rule and became the first president of North Vietnam in 1954. He also led the North during the Vietnam War until his death.

Hubert H. Humphrey (1911–1978) Vice president of the United States during the Johnson administration, 1964–1968. Became the Democratic presidential nominee in 1968 after Johnson decided not to run for re-election but lost to Richard M. Nixon.

Lyndon B. Johnson (1908–1973) After serving as vice president under John Kennedy, he became the 36th president of the United States after Kennedy was assassinated in 1963. Johnson sent U.S. combat troops to Vietnam. Opposition to his policies convinced him not to seek re-election in 1968.

Robert F. Kennedy (1925–1968) Attorney general under his brother President John Kennedy's administration and until 1965 under President Lyndon Johnson's administration. After being elected U.S. senator from New York, Kennedy became a leading critic of Johnson's policies during the Vietnam War. Became a Democratic candidate for president in 1968, but was assassinated during his campaign.

Martin Luther King Jr. (1929–1968) African American leader of the civil rights movement who opposed the Vietnam War. Worked to link the civil rights and antiwar movements before he was assassinated in 1968.

Richard M. Nixon (1913–1994) Elected as the 37th president of the United States in 1969, at the height of the Vietnam War. Resigned from office during the Watergate scandal in 1974.

William Westmoreland (1914–) Commander of American military forces in Vietnam, 1964–1968.

Defending Khe Sanh

The year-long plunge in American support for the war began in mid-January. At this time, the North Vietnamese Army launched a major attack against Khe Sanh, a U.S. Marine outpost in the far northwestern corner of South Vietnam. This remote stronghold was an important part of the U.S. defenses against Communist forces based in the jungles of nearby Laos.

The Phoenix Program

The Phoenix Program was one of the most controversial "pacification" operations of the Vietnam War. Pacification was the term used for a wide range of efforts to keep Vietnam's rural population loyal to the South Vietnamese government. Launched in mid-1968, the Phoenix Program was intended to "neutralize"—kill or capture—Viet Cong (VC) agents operating in remote villages throughout the South.

The Phoenix Program, called *Phung Hoang* by South Vietnam, was a joint effort of U.S. and South Vietnamese intelligence agents. Under the program, American and South Vietnamese officials worked together to gather information about suspected Viet Cong agents who lived in rural communities. These suspects were then arrested and questioned about their roles in local VC activities. U.S. and South Vietnamese military officials hoped that by removing the Viet Cong threat from the countryside, they could turn the South's peasant population into an asset in the war.

Several problems arose during the first few months that the Phoenix Program went into effect. Many South Vietnamese officials involved in the operation performed poorly. Some refused to cooperate with other officials because of petty power struggles, while others accepted bribes to let suspected VC go free. Other members of the Phoenix operation tortured or murdered suspected Viet Cong guerrillas, despite the objections of American advisors. Worst of all, some innocent villagers were swept up in the operation. These men and women were

U.S. General William Westmoreland (1914–) first learned that Khe Sanh might be targeted for a Communist assault in December 1967. He received intelligence reports indicating that large numbers of NVA troops were moving into the area. These movements reminded him that the Communists had chased the French out of Vietnam a decade earlier by capturing an outpost— Dien Bien Phu—that was in many ways similar to Khe Sanh. The U.S. base was located in the same region of South Vietnam as Dien Bien Phu. It also was similar to Dien Bien Phu in that it was far away from other friendly bases and could only receive supplies by air. Westmoreland's concern that the Communists might try to duplicate their Dien Bien Phu victory convinced him to send reinforcements to the remote marine stronghold.

jailed and tortured solely on the word of officials or neighbors who disliked them for one reason or another. When news of such incidents reached the United States, the American antiwar movement seized on the Phoenix operation as another example of the war's cruel and mindless bloodshed.

Nonetheless, many historians believe that the program did strike a punishing blow against Viet Cong operations in the South. U.S. officials claimed that the program resulted in the "neutralization" of more than 81,000 suspected Viet Cong by 1972. Sadly, some of these people were innocent of charges. After the war, Communist leaders admitted that the program had a devastating impact on their roster of VC agents in the South. They indicated that Phoenix crippled many of their secret networks and made it more difficult for them to maintain control over rural villages.

The Phoenix Program, coupled with the heavy Viet Cong losses during the Tet Offensive, forced the North to rely on its regular army to carry on the war. The Phoenix Program slowly faded away as the VC became less of a threat to rural communities. "Despite the combination of shortcomings and success, the Phoenix program was simply left behind by the changing nature of the war," writes Dale Andradé in *Ashes to Ashes: The Phoenix Program and the Vietnam War.* "By 1970 Hanoi [the North Vietnamese government] had dropped the facade [mask] of internal insurrection [rebellion] and concentrated on building toward a conventional invasion of the South."

By mid-January, an estimated 40,000 NVA troops had surrounded Khe Sanh. They launched their attack on January 21, hitting the base with a heavy rain of rifle fire and artillery and rocket attacks. When the assault was pushed back, the North Vietnamese force settled in for a long siege of the outpost (a siege is a military strategy in which an army attempts to capture a city or military base by surrounding and blockading it).

The Tet Offensive

The developing siege at Khe Sanh concerned American policymakers and military leaders. Nonetheless, most of them remained publicly optimistic about the war effort. In fact, President Lyndon Johnson, General Westmoreland, and many other U.S. officials continued to express confidence that the Vietnam War was finally turning in favor of the United States. Encouraged by battlefield statistics and intelligence reports, they stated that the Communists did not have the strength to carry on the fight much longer.

In late January, the United States agreed to a temporary truce with North Vietnam so that Vietnamese people in both the North and South could celebrate the Tet holiday. Tet, which begins each January 30, is the Vietnamese New Year. Celebrated with festivals, feasts, and family gift-exchanges, Tet is regarded as the most important holiday in Vietnamese culture.

Early in the morning of January 31, however, North Vietnam broke the cease-fire agreement in spectacular fashion. More than 80,000 Viet Cong and NVA troops mounted simultaneous assaults on more than 100 cities, towns, and hamlets across the South. The leading planner of the strategy, North Vietnamese General Vo Nguyen Giap (1911–), hoped that this surprise offensive would spark a popular uprising against the South Vietnam government and sweep Communist leader Ho Chi Minh (1890–1969) to power.

News of the invasion stunned the American public. Over the next several days, televised images of the war flickered in living rooms all across the country. By this time, American viewers had grown familiar with the grim newspaper reports and television footage of the war. But the Tet Offensive gave the American people some particularly dark glimpses into the bloody struggle taking place halfway around the world.

On February 3, for example, the NBC Evening News showed shocking footage of South Vietnamese police commander General Nguyen Ngoc Loan as he executed a captured Viet Cong fighter on a Saigon street. On another occasion, a U.S. military officer gave reporters a tour of Ben Tre, a small town that American helicopter gun ships had demolished in their efforts to reclaim it from the Viet Cong. "It became necessary to destroy the town in order to save it," the officer said.

These and other images convinced countless Americans that the war effort in Vietnam had gone seriously wrong. "The six o'clock news had become the living-room war," writes

Michael Maclear in the *The Ten Thousand Day War*. "The faces on the 'box' [television] did not just haunt from 9000 miles away: they were the boys from next door, and sometimes one's own son. The faces, so youthful, trustful, scarred, scared or brave, peered from every newspaper and every magazine."

Struggle for the South

In the first few days of the Tet Offensive, Viet Cong and NVA units stormed military installations, government buildings, and other strategic targets all across the South. In the capital city of Saigon, for example, Communist forces attacked military bases, the presidential palace, the airport, and the government radio station. They even seized temporary control of the American embassy in Saigon. But these victories in Saigon and elsewhere failed to generate a popular revolt. The South Vietnamese people remained on the sidelines, unwilling to join the Communists.

The North Vietnamese bombing of the grounds of the Eighth Division in the Cholon area of Saigon, 1968.
Reproduced by permission of Corbis-Bettman.

As a result, momentum quickly shifted all across the South. American and South Vietnamese forces launched a massive counterattack that drove the Communists back. Within a matter of days, Viet Cong and NVA units were forced to retreat from nearly all of their positions. A week or so after the Tet Offensive began, the only major city still in Communist hands was Hue, Vietnam's most beautiful city.

North Vietnamese troops seized control of Hue on January 31, the first day of Tet. Upon entering the city, the Communists rounded up thousands of citizens that they considered enemies of their cause. Their targets included government officials, military officers, Roman Catholic priests, policemen, and teachers. The invaders then executed these people in brutal fashion—some were bludgeoned to death or buried alive—and buried them in mass graves. It is believed that a total of about 3,000 people were murdered by the NVA in this sweep.

The battle for Hue

For the next ten days or so, the NVA terrorized the residents of Hue. Meanwhile, U.S. military leaders gathered reinforcements to recapture the city. On February 10, a combined force of U.S. Marines, U.S. Army Cavalry (helicopter units), and South Vietnamese troops launched a counterassault to reclaim Hue. But the Communists mounted a stubborn defense of the city. As the two armies clashed, Hue's streets quickly turned into a gory battlefield.

Over the next two weeks, the fight for control of Hue became one of the most vicious and bloody struggles of the entire Vietnam War. The fierce Communist resistance forced the marine-led American units to take control of the city one street at a time. Braving heavy sniper fire and facing battle-hardened NVA units, the marines slowly advanced through the city, suffering heavy casualties in the process. According to some estimates, one marine was killed or wounded for every three feet of ground gained during the first week of fighting.

As the savage battle continued, Hue itself suffered enormous damage. North Vietnamese rockets and American bombs destroyed entire neighborhoods. The streets became choked with rubble and the dead bodies of soldiers and civilians (people not involved in the military, including women and children). Even its lovely Imperial Palace—an ancient section of the city also known as the Citadel—was reduced to ruins in the fighting. "The battling turned the once beautiful city into a nightmare," reported *Time* magazine.

The Communists finally retreated from Hue on February 24. But the bloodshed did not end there. South Vietnamese troops rushed into the devastated city, where they reportedly murdered hundreds of civilians they believed were sympathetic to the NVA. All in all, an estimated 10,000 people were killed in the battle for Hue, including approximately 5,000 Communist fighters. Casualties on the American side included 1,580 U.S. casualties (526 killed, 1,364 wounded) and 2,214 South Vietnamese casualties (384 killed, 1,830 wounded). In addition, more than three-quarters of the population of Hue was left homeless by the struggle. "The mind reels at the carnage [destruction], cost, and ruthlessness of it all," said one veteran war journalist.

Tet: American victory or defeat?

In the days and weeks following the failed Communist offensive, a great debate arose in America over Tet. Many military leaders and other supporters of American involvement in Vietnam claimed that the attack had resulted in a major defeat for North Vietnam and its Viet Cong allies. After all, the Communists failed to hold any of the cities or towns they had targeted in the invasion. Moreover, the joint American-South Vietnamese response to the invasion had resulted in a punishing counterattack that produced extremely heavy casualties. In fact, an estimated 45,000 NVA and Viet Cong troops were killed during Tet, and another 6,000 were captured.

The Tet campaign also crippled the deadly Viet Cong network that had caused so much trouble in the South in previous years. Indeed, Viet Cong activity declined dramatically from 1968 onward, for the simple reason that many VC units had been destroyed. "The Viet Cong lost the best of a generation of resistance fighters, and after Tet increasing numbers of North Vietnamese had to be sent south to fill the ranks," confirmed Don Oberdorfer in *Tet!*

Finally, the Tet Offensive failed to spark a general rebellion among the South Vietnamese people. Their refusal to join the Communists not only helped U.S. forces beat back the enemy invasion, but also cast a shadow on North Vietnam's claims that it had the support of the average South Vietnamese citizen. "Because the people of the cities did not rise up against the foreigners [Americans] and puppets [leaders in Saigon] at Tet—indeed they gave little support to the attack force—the

Communist claim to moral and political authority in South Vietnam suffered a serious blow," states Oberdorfer.

But while the Tet Offensive produced a decisive military victory for the United States and South Vietnam, it destroyed support for the war on the American homefront. In the weeks before Tet, Johnson and other U.S. officials had repeatedly told the war-weary American public that victory was near. As Oberdorfer notes in *The Bad War: An Oral History,* President Johnson kept telling people that "'We're about to win. Just wait a little while longer. Your patience will be rewarded.' And at that point the Tet Offensive absolutely shattered the waning [decreasing] patience and confidence of the American people."

Indeed, the size and strength of the Communist invasion made it clear that North Vietnam remained a dangerous and determined enemy. Disillusioned and angry, many Americans decided that victory over the North was still years away, and that it could only be attained by sacrificing thousands of American lives and billions of American dollars. They agreed with television journalist Walter Cronkite (1916–), who declared at the height of Tet that "it seems now more certain than ever that the bloody experience of Vietnam is to end in a stalemate." With victory appearing unlikely and antiwar protests causing problems at home, millions of Americans became convinced that the United States should end its involvement in the war. In this way, Tet became a major turning point in how the Vietnam War was viewed and how it was conducted.

Today, many people believe that America's policymakers and military leadership lied about the situation in Vietnam in late 1967 and early 1968 in order to shore up slipping public support for the war. Others believe that these leaders simply underestimated the strength and resolve of the Viet Cong and the North Vietnamese. For their part, many U.S. officials claim that they honestly thought that American forces were on the path to victory in the weeks prior to Tet. "We were not engaging in deception," insisted U.S. General Robert Komer in *The Bad War.* "We genuinely believed at the end of 1967 that we were getting on top . . . . This wasn't public relations, this wasn't Lyndon Johnson telling us to put a face on it [be falsely optimistic]. We genuinely thought we were making it [drawing close to victory]. And then boom, forty towns get attacked, and [the American people] didn't believe us anymore."

The Hills of Khe Sanh

In his book *Dispatches,* American journalist Michael Herr relates his experiences as a reporter in Vietnam. His book provides a firsthand account of the siege of Khe Sanh. The following excerpt from *Dispatches* describes how the countryside around Khe Sanh was destroyed during the siege. It also discusses the emotional toll that the siege took on the U.S. marines stationed there:

> Often you'd hear Marines talking about how beautiful those hills must have been, but that spring they were not beautiful. Once they had been the royal hunting grounds of the Annamese emperors [ancient rulers of Vietnam]. Tigers, deer and flying squirrels had lived in them. I used to imagine what a royal hunt must have been like, but I could only see it as an Oriental children's story . . . . And even now you could hear Marines comparing these hills with the hills around their homes, talking about what a pleasure it would be to hunt in them for anything other than men.

> But mostly, I think, the Marines hated those hills; not from time to time, the way many of us hated them, but constantly, like a curse . . . . So when we decimated [destroyed] them, broke them, burned parts of them so that nothing would ever live on them again, it must have given a lot of Marines a good feeling, an intimation [sense] of power. They had humped those hills until their legs were in an agony, they'd been ambushed in them and blown apart on their trails, trapped on their barren ridges, lain under fire clutching the foliage that grew on them, wept alone in fear and exhaustion and shame just knowing the kind of terror that night always brought to them, and now, in April, something like revenge had been achieved.

> We never announced a scorched-earth policy [a military policy of destroying all land and buildings]; we never announced any policy at all, apart from finding and destroying the enemy, and we proceeded in the most obvious way. We used what was at hand, dropping the greatest volume of explosives in the history of warfare over all the terrain within the thirty-mile sector which fanned out from Khe Sanh. Employing saturation-bombing techniques, we delivered more than 110,000 tons of bombs to those hills during the eleven-week containment of Khe Sanh. The smaller foothills were often quite literally turned inside out, the steeper of them were made faceless and drawless, and the bigger hills were left with scars and craters of [tremendous] proportions . . . .

The siege of Khe Sanh

As the Tet Offensive sent shock waves through South Vietnam and America, the siege of Khe Sanh continued. Each day, the NVA troops surrounding Khe Sanh slammed the base with heavy fire. The trapped marines returned fire as best they could from their heavy fortifications. The primary U.S. weapon in the defense of Khe Sanh, however, was an air bombing campaign known as Operation Niagara. This unrelenting aerial assault dropped an estimated 70,000 to 100,000 tons of bombs and large amounts of napalm (a gasoline-based chemical that burns up trees and other vegetation) on the area around Khe Sanh. Operation Niagara killed an estimated 10,000 NVA troops and transformed the jungle hillsides around the outpost into a barren desert.

Despite the heavy bombardment from American planes, the North Vietnamese maintained their siege. They blasted the base with rocket attacks and positioned snipers all through the hills overlooking the base. At the same time, the NVA dug a system of deep trenches that brought them ever closer to the marines. At night, the marines defending Khe Sanh could hear the Communists digging as they advanced. Meanwhile, heavy NVA artillery and fierce monsoons (heavy tropical rainstorms) sometimes forced the United States to use parachute drops to resupply the battered base.

As the weeks dragged on, conditions inside Khe Sanh deteriorated sharply. Trapped inside sagging trenches and sandbag fortifications by enemy sniper fire, the marines learned to sleep with blankets over their heads to protect their faces from the huge rats that prowled the base. When they awoke, it was to the sound of incoming rockets and bomb-dropping war planes.

Finally, after seventy-seven days, General Giap withdrew his NVA forces from the area surrounding Khe Sanh. This mid-April withdrawal brought one of the most famous struggles of the entire war to a strangely quiet close. Initially, the U.S. military expressed great satisfaction about its successful defense of the region. "The amount of firepower put on that piece of real estate exceeded anything that has ever been seen before in history by any foe," said Westmoreland. "The enemy was hurt, his back was broken, by airpower." The marines voluntarily abandoned Khe Sanh only a few months later, setting fire to the base as they left so that it could not be used by the Communists.

Clifford evaluates the war effort

The Tet Offensive forced the Johnson administration to reassess U.S. progress in Vietnam. On March 1, 1968, Westmoreland requested approval for another 206,000 American troops to be transferred to Vietnam. In the past, Johnson had approved such requests. But in the wake of Tet, the president asked Clark Clifford (1906–), who had recently replaced Robert McNamara (1916–) as secretary of defense, to study the request.

Clifford had supported U.S. involvement in Vietnam over the previous few years. But as he talked with U.S. military leaders and analysts, he changed his mind. "Clifford was astounded to discover that U.S. military leaders had no clear plan to win the war," writes Tom Wells in *The War Within*. "He became convinced U.S. military victory was impossible."

Clifford later admitted that his feelings about the war changed dramatically in the weeks following Tet. His review convinced him that "the military course we were pursuing was not only endless, but hopeless" (Clifford, *Foreign Affairs*). "A further substantial increase in American forces could only increase the devastation and the Americanization [South Vietnamese reliance on American military power] of the war, and thus leave us even further from our goal of a peace that would permit the people of South Vietnam to fashion their own political and economic institutions."

Clifford decided that approval of Westmoreland's request for more soldiers would continue a pattern of sending "more troops, more guns, more planes, more ships . . . without accomplishing our purpose." He also thought that sending new troops would trigger another outburst of turmoil and protest across America. "I was more conscious each day of domestic unrest in our own country," he admitted in *Counsel to the President*. "Draft-card burnings, marches in the streets, problems on school campuses, bitterness and divisiveness [angry disagreement between groups] were rampant."

Johnson and the Wise Men

After finishing his review, Clifford counseled Johnson not to grant Westmoreland's request. Clifford's recommendation surprised the president. Johnson called a meeting of his closest advisors—commonly known as the "Wise Men"—to see if they felt any differently. But one by one, they reluctantly agreed with Clifford's view that the United States should stop increasing its military presence in Vietnam and look for a way to withdraw from the war. Former Secretary of State Dean Acheson (1893–1971) offered a particularly grim perspective on the war. A former supporter of Johnson's war policies, he bluntly stated that an American victory in Vietnam would take at least five more years and require huge new infusions of soldiers and money. The Wise Men agreed that the American public would never allow the war to continue under those circumstances.

The gloomy opinions of the Wise Men stunned and angered Johnson, who worried that Vietnam was destroying his presidency. After all the sacrifices that America had made over the previous few years in Vietnam, Johnson desperately wanted to believe that the United States could still win the war with one final push. But as he listened to his advisors and watched antiwar demonstrations unfold across the country, he began to feel like his dreams of victory were doomed.

General Creighton W. Abrams replaced Westmoreland as commander of the U.S. military forces in Vietnam in 1968.
Courtesy of the U.S. Army Photographic Agency.

Meanwhile, the *New York Times* learned about Westmoreland's request for additional troops and reported it in its March 12 editions. This news sparked a new wave of outrage against the Johnson administration. If the Tet Offensive had been such a disaster for the Communists, asked critics, why did the military need tens of thousands of new troops in Vietnam?

Johnson makes a surprise announcement

As criticism of the Johnson administration's policies in Vietnam continued to increase, the president received a political blow in New Hampshire. On March 12, Senator Eugene McCarthy (1916–) came within a few votes of upsetting Johnson in New Hampshire's primary (a primary is a state election that political parties use to choose their candidate for the presidency). The results of the New Hampshire vote—the first primary in the national race for the Democratic nomination for the presidency—showed that the controversy over Vietnam had greatly weakened Johnson's political position. Four days later, Robert F. Kennedy—the brother of former President John F. Kennedy—announced his intention to challenge Johnson for the Democratic nomination. A harsh critic of Johnson's Vietnam policies who vowed to end the war if elected, Kennedy was widely viewed as a serious challenger for the Democratic nomination.

In the final days of March, Johnson reacted to recent developments in Vietnam and the United States with a series of announcements. First, he announced that Westmoreland, who had commanded the U.S. war effort in Vietnam for the past four years, had been transferred to Washington to serve as chief of staff to the U.S. Army (Westmoreland was replaced in Vietnam by Creighton Abrams). Johnson also decided to send only 13,000 additional troops to Vietnam, far fewer than the U.S. military had requested after Tet.

Finally, on March 31, Johnson addressed the nation on television. During this historic speech, he announced a major cutback in the bombing of North Vietnam. He also called for negotiations with the North to end the Vietnam War. Johnson then concluded his speech with the shocking news that "I shall not seek, and I will not accept, the nomination of my party for another term as your president."

"By the end of March 1968, Lyndon Johnson was a weary man," explains Clark Dougan and Stephen Weiss in *The American Experience in Vietnam.* "The war in Vietnam had taken a heavy toll on him. It had cost him his credibility, and it had eroded his political authority to the point where he could no longer govern effectively. All that remained to be salvaged was what mattered most to him—the respect of his 'fellow Americans.' By withdrawing from the presidential race, Johnson hoped to underscore the sincerity of his desire for peace. More than that, he sought to restore unity to a nation divided by a war he had chosen to fight."

King and Kennedy assassinated

The months immediately following Johnson's surprise announcement were very difficult ones for the American people. On April 4, 1968, civil rights leader Martin Luther King Jr. was assassinated at a motel in Memphis, Tennessee. His violent death outraged blacks across the country and triggered a flurry of riots in American cities. By the time the riots ended, 39 people had been killed and another 2,500 injured.

King's death proved to be only the first in a series of blows that rocked the United States. Two months later, Robert Kennedy was assassinated in Los Angeles after winning the California primary. News of Kennedy's murder triggered another wave of national grief and mourning. A few weeks later, an ugly and vicious clash broke out between antiwar demonstrators and Chicago police outside the Democratic Convention Center, where Vice President Hubert Humphrey (1911–1978) received the Democratic nomination for the presidency. Finally, the war continued to rage in Vietnam, even after peace negotiations opened between U.S. and North Vietnamese representatives in May. These events—combined with deep internal divisions over the war, civil rights, and other domestic issues—led many Americans to believe that the entire country was spinning out of control.

Hubert Horatio Humphrey was defeated by Richard Nixon in the race for the U.S. presidency in 1968. *Reproduced by permission of the Library of Congress.*

Nixon wins the presidency

The 1968 presidential campaign pitted Humphrey against Republican nominee Richard M. Nixon (1913–1994) and Alabama Governor George Wallace (1919–1998), a former Democrat who ran as the nominee of the American Independent Party because of his opposition to Democratic efforts to end segregation. Humphrey campaigned for the presidency on a platform of peace. But many voters associated him with Johnson, and the vice president was unable to convince the American public that he would handle the war differently. On

October 31, one week before the presidential election, Johnson announced a complete bombing halt in North Vietnam. But this decision failed to lift Humphrey to victory. Instead, Nixon narrowly defeated him for the White House.

"Americans had voted for what they perceived as a solid law and order Republican candidate who also promised peace in Vietnam," writes Elizabeth Becker in *America's Vietnam War: A Narrative History.* "After a year that had brought the Tet Offensive, two assassinations, inner-city riots following the King murder, and the Chicago convention, the public wanted an end to the war and to the strife at home." As Nixon prepared to take office, Americans all across the country hoped that he would be able to guide the nation out of Vietnam and heal the divisions that had wracked so many communities.

Sources

Andradé, Dale. *Ashes to Ashes: The Phoenix Program and the Vietnam War.* Lexington, MA: Lexington Books, 1990.

Becker, Elizabeth. *America's Vietnam War: A Narrative History.* New York: Clarion Books, 1992.

Braestrup Peter. *Big Story: How the American Press and Television Reported and Interpreted the Crisis of Tet 1968 in Vietnam and Washington.* Boulder, CO: Westview Press, 1977.

Caute, David. *The Year of the Barricades: A Journey Through 1968.* New York: Harper & Row, 1988.

Clifford, Clark M. *Counsel to the President: A Memoir.* New York: Random House, 1991.

Clifford, Clark M. "A Vietnam Reappraisal" in *Foreign Affairs,* July 1969.

Dougan, Clark, and Stephen Weiss. *The American Experience in Vietnam.* Boston: Boston Publishing, 1988.

Dougan, Clark, and Stephen Weiss. *The Vietnam Experience: Nineteen Sixty-Eight.* Boston: Boston Publishing, 1985.

Gitlin, Todd. *The Sixties: Years of Hope, Days of Rage.* New York: Bantam, 1987.

Herr, Michael. *Dispatches.* New York: Alfred A. Knopf, 1977.

Herring, George C. *LBJ and Vietnam: A Different Kind of War.* Austin: University of Texas Press, 1994.

Johnson, Lyndon B. *The Vantage Point: Perspectives of the Presidency, 1963–1969.* New York: Holt, Rinehart and Winston, 1971.

Maclear, Michael. *The Ten Thousand Day War: Vietnam, 1945–1975*. New York: Avon Books, 1981.

Oberdorfer, Don. *Tet!* New York: Doubleday, 1971.

Prados, John, and Ray Stubbe. *Valley of Decision: The Siege of Khe Sanh*. New York: Houghton Mifflin, 1991.

Spector, Ronald H. *After Tet: The Bloodiest Year in Vietnam*. New York: Free Press, 1993.

Turley, William S. *The Second Indochina War: A Short Political and Military History, 1954–1975*. Boulder, CO: Westview Press, 1986.

Wells, Tom. *The War Within: America's Battle over Vietnam*. Berkeley: University of California Press, 1994.

Westmoreland, William. *A Soldier Reports*. New York: Doubleday, 1976.

The American Antiwar Movement

8

The Vietnam War divided the American people more than any other event since the American Civil War (1861–65). In the early years of U.S. involvement, most people supported the government's policies. But as the war dragged on and more American soldiers were killed or wounded, increasing numbers of Americans began to oppose the war. During the late 1960s and early 1970s, the antiwar movement gained strength and people opposed to the war became more vocal in their protests.

"Opposition began among pacifists [individuals who believe that disputes can be solved peacefully] in the political fringe . . . but then spread to students, academics, artists, intellectuals, clergy, civil rights activists, writers, politicians, journalists, and entertainers," Randy Roberts and James S. Olson explain in the *Encyclopedia of the Vietnam War*. "Some demanded an end to the war because they felt it was immoral, others because it was poorly conceived and unwinnable, and still others because the United States refused to employ the full range of its military power to achieve a military victory. By the early 1970s, opposition to the Vietnam War was endemic

Words to Know

Communism A political system in which the government controls all resources and means of producing wealth. By eliminating private property, this system is designed to create an equal society with no social classes. However, Communist governments in practice often limit personal freedom and individual rights.

North Vietnam The Geneva Accords of 1954, which ended the First Indochina War (1946–54), divided the nation of Vietnam into two sections. The northern section, which was led by a Communist government under Ho Chi Minh, was officially known as the Democratic Republic of Vietnam, but was usually called North Vietnam.

Silent Majority A term used by U.S. President Richard Nixon to describe the large number of American people he believed quietly supported his Vietnam War policies. In contrast, Nixon referred to the antiwar movement in the United States as a vocal minority.

South Vietnam Created under the Geneva Accords of 1954, the southern section of Vietnam was known as the Republic of South Vietnam. It was led by a U.S.-supported government.

Viet Cong Vietnamese Communist guerilla fighters who worked with the North Vietnamese Army to conquer South Vietnam.

Vietnamization A policy proposed by U.S. President Richard Nixon that involved returning responsibility for the war to the South Vietnamese. It was intended to allow the United States to reduce its military involvement without allowing the country to fall to communism.

[native] to American political culture, affecting almost every segment of American society."

During the Vietnam War, disagreements arose among the various groups involved in the antiwar movement. Some groups favored radical and violent forms of protest, while others felt that nonviolent resistance was the best option. These disagreements reduced the movement's effectiveness as well as its popularity among the American people. As the United States gradually reduced its military presence in Vietnam in the mid–1970s, the antiwar movement faded away. But there is little doubt that it had a lasting impact on American society.

Ho Chi Minh (1890–1969) Vietnamese Communist leader who led Viet Minh forces in opposing French rule and became the first president of North Vietnam in 1954. He also led the North during the Vietnam War until his death.

Lyndon B. Johnson (1908–1973) After serving as vice president under John Kennedy, he became the 36th president of the United States after Kennedy was assassinated in 1963. Johnson sent U.S. combat troops to Vietnam. Opposition to his policies convinced him not to seek re-election in 1968.

John F. Kennedy (1917–1963) Served as the 35th president of the United States from 1960 until he was assassinated in 1963.

Martin Luther King Jr. (1929–1968) African American leader of the civil rights movement who opposed the Vietnam War. Worked to link the civil rights and antiwar movements before he was assassinated in 1968.

Ngo Dinh Diem (1901–1963) Vietnamese political leader who became president of South Vietnam in 1954. He gradually lost the support of the United States and was killed following the overthrow of his government in 1963.

Richard M. Nixon (1913–1994) Elected as the 37th president of the United States in 1969, at the height of the Vietnam War. Resigned from office during the Watergate scandal in 1974.

Scattered voices protest early U.S. involvement

During the Eisenhower and Kennedy administrations of the 1950s and early 1960s, most American citizens supported the government's decision to provide economic aid and military advisors to South Vietnam. The American people worried about the spread of communism around the world. For this reason, they believed that the U.S. government was attempting to prevent South Vietnam from coming under the control of Communist-led forces from North Vietnam. But U.S. military involvement in Vietnam grew steadily in the early 1960s, and so did the number of people who spoke out against it.

When the United States first became involved in Vietnam, the people who opposed the government's policies primarily represented traditional pacifist groups. These groups—which

Hawks vs. Doves

The terms "hawks" and "doves" were used to describe different government officials based on their views of the Vietnam War. In general, hawks supported the U.S. government's reasons for sending troops to Vietnam, and they were willing to take whatever steps were necessary to win the war. Prominent hawks included Secretary of State Dean Rusk (1909–1994) and National Security Advisor Walt Rostow (1916–).

In contrast, doves opposed U.S. military involvement. Some questioned the importance of Vietnam to U.S. interests, while others did not believe the United States could win the war. Doves pressured government leaders to end the bombing of North Vietnam, negotiate a settlement, and bring the American troops home. Some of the most prominent doves included Senator George McGovern (1922–) and Senator William Fulbright (1905–1995).

tended to oppose all war on moral or religious grounds—included members of the Quaker religion (also known as the Society of Friends), the Fellowship of Reconciliation (FOR), and the War Resisters League (WRL). These groups spoke out against the Vietnam War in the early 1960s, just as they had spoken out against World War II (1939–45) and the Korean War (1950– 53). They protested against the growing numbers of American military advisors being sent to Vietnam, and they asked the U.S. government to try to negotiate a settlement between North and South Vietnam.

Most leaders within the U.S. government favored taking a strong stand against communism. They believed that America's future depended on supporting democratic principles and governments around the world. But there were a few key government officials who questioned the wisdom of becoming involved in a war in Vietnam. Some officials believed that the revolution taking place in Vietnam was a struggle for independence after many years of foreign rule. They knew that the leader of North Vietnam, Ho Chi Minh (1890–1969), held Communist beliefs. But they thought he was unlikely to align himself with other Communist governments, like the Soviet Union, after fighting so long for Vietnamese independence. Other American officials felt uncomfortable supporting the South Vietnamese government because its leader, President Ngo Dinh Diem (1901–1963), was not willing to make democratic reforms.

One of the earliest opponents of U.S. involvement was George Ball, who served as undersecretary of state in the Kennedy administration. When President Kennedy (1917–1963; president 1960–1963) decided to send an 8,000-man task force to South Vietnam in 1961, Ball warned that the United States might be drawn into a war it could never win. "Once large numbers of U.S. troops are committed to direct combat, they will begin to take heavy casualties in a war they are ill-equipped to fight in a non-cooperative if not downright hostile countryside," Ball wrote in a memo. "Once we suffer large casualties, we will have started a [nearly] irreversible process. Our involvement will be so great that we cannot—without national humil-iation—stop short of achieving our com-plete objectives. Of the two possibilities I think humiliation would be more likely than the achievement of our objectives—even after we have paid terrible costs."

In addition to pacifist groups and a few government advisors, some members of the media criticized early U.S. involvement in Vietnam. Govern-ment leaders depended on the press to give the American people its official view of the conflict. But a few reporters who covered Vietnam in the early 1960s—such as David Halberstam of the *New York Times,* Neil Sheehan of United Press International, Peter Arnett of Associated Press, and Stanley Karnow of *Time*—presented a less positive view of the situation. They noted that Diem's government was corrupt and unpopu-lar, and warned that Communist gueril-las (guerrillas are small groups of fight-ers who launch surprise attacks) known as the Viet Cong (VC) controlled large areas of the South Vietnamese countryside.

George W. Ball was one of the earliest opponents of U.S. involvement in the Vietnam War.
Reproduced by permission of the Library of Congress.

Opposition grows after U.S. sends combat troops

After President Kennedy was assassinated, Lyndon B. Johnson (1908–1973; president 1963–1969) became president of the United States in November 1963. In early 1965, Johnson increased U.S. involvement in Vietnam by starting bombing raids and sending combat troops. Before this time, Americans had acted only as military advisors to the South Vietnamese forces.

At first, most American citizens supported the president's decision to expand the U.S. role in Vietnam. They expected that the American troops, with their superior weapons and training, would quickly drive the Viet Cong forces out of South Vietnam. But before long, people started to feel the effects of the war. More than 180,000 American troops had been sent to Vietnam by the end of 1965, and Johnson planned to send 160,000 more in 1966. As more American troops saw combat, more reports of casualties (dead and wounded soldiers) came back to the United States. Young men across the country began to worry that they might be selected for military service in the draft.

Opposition to the war started to grow after Johnson sent American troops to Vietnam. One of the traditional pacifist groups, the WRL, organized the first nationwide demonstration against the war. A group of religious leaders formed a new organization, called Clergy and Laity Concerned About Vietnam (CALCAV), that opposed the war on moral grounds. More than thirty other antiwar organizations formed during 1965, as more and more Americans began to disagree with Johnson's policies. Many of these antiwar groups joined together under the National Coordinating Committee to End the War in Vietnam.

The involvement of the United States in the Vietnam War became particularly unpopular on college campuses. One factor in the campus unrest was that college students were the right age to be drafted into the military. In addition, college professors and other well-educated Americans tended to follow politics more closely than other segments of society. These factors led both professors and students to question the government's policies. In March 1965, a group of faculty at the University of Michigan organized a "teach-in" about the Vietnam War. With 3,500 students in attendance, they discussed the causes of the war and the effects of U.S. policies. Before long, antiwar teach-ins were occurring on a number of other college campuses.

One of the most prominent antiwar groups was Students for a Democratic Society (SDS). This group, which was largely composed of college students, had been active in seeking equal rights and opportunities for African Americans during the civil rights movement. Once President Johnson sent combat troops into Vietnam, SDS changed its focus to protesting against the war. "We feel that the war is immoral at its root, that it is fought alongside a regime with no claim to represent its people, and that it is foreclosing the hope of making America a decent and truly democratic society," declared the SDS mission statement. In April 1965, SDS held a rally in Washington, D.C., that attracted 20,000 protesters.

Opposition to the war also grew within the civil rights movement. Many black leaders had initially supported the U.S. government's decision to send troops to Vietnam. Some black leaders were reluctant to criticize President Johnson because they believed he supported their call for civil rights. But before long, many civil rights leaders began to change

Civil rights leader Martin Luther King, Jr., became an outspoken opponent of the Vietnam War.
Reproduced by permission of the Library of Congress.

their minds about Vietnam. They noticed that the war drew government attention and resources away from programs designed to reduce discrimination and poverty. They also grew concerned about the high number of African American casualties in the war. Black men were more likely to be drafted than whites, and they were more likely to be assigned to dangerous combat duty. As a result, black soldiers accounted for twenty-five percent of Americans killed in Vietnam in 1965 and 1966, even though they made up only thirteen to fourteen percent of all U.S. forces.

Civil rights leader Martin Luther King Jr. (1929–1968) began speaking out against the war in July 1965. As it became clear that the African American community was bearing more than its share of the losses in Vietnam, several civil rights groups joined the antiwar movement. In 1966, heavyweight boxing champion Muhammad Ali (1942–) announced that he would refuse to serve in the army if he was drafted. He followed up on this promise by ignoring his draft notice the following year. Although Ali was stripped of his title and his boxing license, he became a prominent symbol of resistance to the war.

March on the Pentagon

The size of U.S. forces stationed in Vietnam continued to grow in 1966 and 1967, eventually reaching more than 500,000 troops. But these forces did not seem to be gaining much ground against the Viet Cong. Disturbed by the ever-growing number of American soldiers killed and wounded, some government leaders began questioning U.S. policy. Several prominent Republican members of Congress—including Senator George Aiken (1892–1984) of Vermont, Senator Clifford Case (1904–1982) of New Jersey, and Senator Mark Hatfield (1922–) of Oregon—spoke out against the war. Of course, President Johnson, a Democrat, expected to receive criticism from members of the opposing political party. But then several prominent Democrats began to express their doubts about the war as well. Democratic leaders who withdrew their support from the president included Senator Mike Mansfield (1903–) of Montana, Senator Robert Kennedy (1925–1968) of New York, and Senator Eugene McCarthy (1916–) of Minnesota.

A majority of American citizens also began to question the country's involvement in Vietnam during this time. Public opinion polls showed that support for Johnson's policies had dropped from 61 percent in 1965 to 50 percent in 1966, and then continued falling to 44 percent in 1967. This dissatisfaction could be seen at the antiwar rallies and protests, which became more frequent and involved larger numbers of people. In April 1967, for example, 130,000 people attended the Spring Mobilization antiwar demonstration in New York City, and another 70,000 participated in related events in San Francisco.

As the antiwar movement gained strength, the media increased its coverage of protests and other events. As a result, the movement became more visible and influential. One of the largest antiwar demonstrations took place in Washington, D.C., in October 1967. More than 100,000 people marched through the streets of the city and listened to speeches and protest songs near the Washington Monument. Later, many of these demonstrators marched across a bridge to Arlington, Virginia, where they continued their protest at the Pentagon, an enormous building that served as the headquarters for the U.S. Department of Defense.

This demonstration, known as the March on the Pentagon, became a huge media event. U.S. Army troops were called out to prevent protesters from entering the building, and news crews took pictures of hippies (usually refers to young people who oppose conventional standards and customs) placing flowers in the barrels of the soldiers' guns. Many well-known singers, writers, poets, and artists showed up and performed for the cameras. Although the protests began peacefully, they grew more confrontational over time. As night fell, some protesters got into a riot with police and were arrested.

The March on the Pentagon showed the world that opposition to the Vietnam War was growing in the United States. Afterward, some people expressed concern that such large-scale protests might encourage the Viet Cong and put American troops in danger. President Johnson even asked the Central Intelligence Agency (CIA) to investigate some of the protest leaders. He felt that the antiwar movement would lose public support if he could link some of its leaders to communism.

Trouble within the movement

Despite its growing size and influence, however, the antiwar movement still struggled to find a unified voice during these years. After all, the movement was made up of many different groups with different protest goals. This situation sometimes created tension within the antiwar movement. For example, civil rights leader Martin Luther King Jr. urged antiwar demonstrators to use nonviolent forms of protest. But more militant black leaders, like Stokely Carmichael (1941–1998) of the Student National Coordinating Committee (SNCC), argued that violence was acceptable and even necessary to achieve their goals.

By the late 1960s, polls showed that the majority of Americans opposed the U.S. military involvement in Vietnam. But even among people who were against the war, few could agree on what action the government should take. "Political diversity proved to be a double-edged sword," Tom Wells explains in *The War Within: America's Battle over Vietnam.* "Although it compounded the movement's numbers, it engendered [caused] fierce and enduring disputes among protesters that tore peace organizations apart. Often, participants at antiwar meetings could agree on little more than their opposition to U.S. intervention."

At this point, some radical antiwar groups began resorting to violent confrontation in order to stand out from the rest of the movement. Such groups engaged in riots, broke into or destroyed buildings, burned the American flag, or called for the overthrow of the U.S. government. Some people even displayed the North Vietnamese flag and expressed their support for the Viet Cong. The behavior of the radical members of the antiwar movement disgusted and frightened many Americans, including some who opposed the war. In fact, some experts claim that more people might have protested against the war except that they did not want to be associated with this sort of behavior. "The fringe of the antiwar movement engaging in violence attracted more attention than the hundreds of thousands of ordinary people who occasionally marched, went to vigils, or wrote members of Congress," Robert D. Schulzinger writes in *A Time for War.* "The tumult [chaos] within the antiwar movement turned away as many people as it recruited."

Democratic presidential convention of 1968

The same type of debate that took place within the antiwar movement also occurred within the Democratic Party. Some Democratic leaders pushed President Johnson to commit more troops and win the war in Vietnam. But many others wanted him to withdraw troops and negotiate a settlement. Senator Eugene McCarthy, a prominent Democrat who opposed Johnson's policies, announced his intention to run against Johnson in hopes of becoming the Democratic candidate for president in 1968. Throughout this political turmoil, Johnson and his advisors continued to tell the American people that his strategy was working. They claimed that the American bombing of North Vietnam, along with the U.S. troop movements in South Vietnam, was slowly but surely defeating the Viet Cong.

In January 1968, however, North Vietnamese forces launched a major offensive attack into the South. This military action became known as the Tet Offensive (see Chapter 7, "The Tet Offensive (1968)"). American and South Vietnamese forces managed to turn back the attack, and the Viet Cong suffered significant losses. But the size and strength of the attack stunned the American people. Many had believed the president when he assured them that North Vietnam was losing the war. After the Tet Offensive, they lost faith in Johnson's leadership and worried that the war might continue for many more years. People on all sides of the issue started to become weary of the war. As a result, antiwar protests grew larger and more violent. In one incident, members of SDS seized several campus buildings at Columbia University in New York City and pressured the school to stop doing military research.

As public opinion toward Johnson became increasingly negative after the Tet Offensive, Senator Robert F. Kennedy announced that he would seek the Democratic nomination for president as well. With so many of his former supporters lining up against him, President Johnson decided not to run for re-election. At this point, Vice President Hubert Humphrey (1911–1978) also joined the race.

The Democratic Party formally nominated Humphrey for president at a convention in Chicago during the summer of 1968 (Kennedy had appeared likely to receive the nomination,

Richard Nixon puppet, held by war protester in 1973.
Reproduced by permission of Corbis-Bettman.

but he was assassinated shortly before the convention). Inside the convention hall, the Democrats struggled to agree on the Vietnam policy they would present in their campaign. Meanwhile, the streets of Chicago outside the convention hall became the site of a raucous antiwar protest. Well-known antiwar activists from a wide variety of groups showed up to add their voices to the demonstrations, including Tom Hayden (1939–) of SDS, David Dellinger (1915–) of the National Mobilization to End the War in Vietnam (MOBE), Bobby Seale (1936–) of the Black Panthers, and Jerry Rubin (1938–1994) and Abbie Hoffman (1936– 1989) of the Youth International Party (YIPPIE).

Chicago Mayor Richard Daley (1902–1976) sent his police force to control the protesters, and the situation quickly turned into a riot. Scenes of fights between antiwar activists and police officers dominated television newscasts and overshadowed the convention. Some people claimed that the police used excessive force against the protesters. More than one thousand protesters and two hundred police officers were injured in the fighting. A year later, seven of the main organizers of the protest—known as the Chicago Seven—were put on trial for conspiracy to cause a riot. But the antiwar activists refused to cooperate. Instead, they used their appearance in court as an opportunity to present their political views. They even draped a Viet Cong flag over the table where they sat. Although several of the protesters were convicted, the decision was later overturned.

Nixon and Vietnamization

The controversy surrounding the Democratic convention made many voters wonder whether the Democrats could lead the country out of the situation in Vietnam. These doubts helped Republican candidate Richard M. Nixon (1913–1994; president 1969–1974) defeat Humphrey in the 1968 election to become president of the United States. One of Nixon's main campaign promises was to find a way to end the war.

Upon taking office in January 1969, Nixon announced a new policy he called Vietnamization. He explained that Johnson had "Americanized" the war by sending U.S. combat troops to Vietnam. Now, Nixon planned to return responsibility for fighting the war to South Vietnam. He promised to withdraw U.S. troops gradually, while also building up the South Vietnamese army and government. In this way, the United States could end its military involvement without allowing the country to fall to communism.

Many Americans were pleased that Nixon seemed committed to ending the war. But most people in the antiwar movement felt that he was not moving quickly enough. After all, more than 7,000 American soldiers died between the time he took office and August 1969, when he removed the first U.S. troops from Vietnam. Antiwar rallies and demonstrations continued, as protesters tried to force the president to move faster. In October 1969, an activist named Sam Brown organized the first Moratorium Day demonstrations. Various antiwar groups encouraged their members to take a day off from work or school in order to protest the war. Millions of people participated in Moratorium Day events across the United States. In Vietnam, thousands of American soldiers wore black arm bands to show their support for ending the war.

On November 3, Nixon responded to the widespread protests with what became known as his Silent Majority speech. In this speech, Nixon claimed that the antiwar activists were a "vocal minority" within American society. He also criticized the protesters for behaving in ways that embarrassed the United States. He said that the antiwar demonstrations made it more difficult for him to put policies in place to end the war. Nixon then appealed to the "silent majority" of patriotic Americans who did not participate in antiwar protests. He asked these people to support his efforts to forge a "just and lasting peace" in Vietnam. He said that he wanted to withdraw the American troops from Vietnam, but he wanted to do it in a way that would preserve the honor of the United

States. He claimed that an immediate withdrawal would lead to "a collapse of confidence in American leadership, not only in Asia but throughout the world."

Kent State tragedy

At first, Nixon's speech seemed to have the opposite effect than he intended. Instead of calming protests and increasing support for his policies, it appeared to make the antiwar movement more vocal than ever. In fact, a second Moratorium Day took place on November 15 and attracted even more participants than the first one. Then, in April 1970, Nixon ordered U.S. troops to invade Cambodia, the Asian nation on Vietnam's western border. He claimed that the Viet Cong had established bases and supply stations in Cambodia, and that fighting in Cambodia was the only way to defeat the Communists. But many Americans saw Nixon's decision to invade Cambodia as an escalation of the war. They felt that the president had gone back on his promise to end the war and bring the troops home.

The antiwar movement reacted to the invasion of Cambodia by launching protests across the country. Many of these antiwar demonstrations took place on college campuses, including the campus of Kent State University in Ohio. Beginning on May 1, hundreds of Kent State students gathered to protest the invasion of Cambodia. Some of the demonstrations turned violent. On May 2, the protesters burned down a campus building that had been used for military training of the Reserve Officers Training Corps (ROTC). In response, Ohio Governor James Rhodes called out the National Guard to restore order. But the demonstrations continued, resulting in several angry confrontations between students and guardsmen. During one of these confrontations on May 4, members of the National Guard fired their guns into a crowd of demonstrators, killing four students and injuring nine others.

Many Americans were shocked and outraged at the tragedy that had taken place on the Kent State campus. Angry demonstrations against the killing of the students broke out on many other college campuses. In fact, many colleges decided to close for the year and send students home early in order to prevent violent protests. But some people had grown

so tired of the unrest in American society—and felt so much resentment toward the antiwar movement—that they claimed the Kent State protesters had gotten what they deserved.

The protests over the invasion of Cambodia and the events at Kent State marked the strongest point of the antiwar movement. Over the next few years, the movement gradually lost members and became less visible. Part of the reason for the decline was disagreements between the various antiwar groups. Some groups, like SDS, became more radical and violent in their protests, which reduced support for the overall movement among average American citizens. But the main reason for the decline in the antiwar movement was that Nixon eventually followed through with his Vietnamization plan. The number of U.S. troops in Vietnam dropped from 475,000 in 1969 to 335,000 in 1970, and fell to 157,000 by the end of 1971. Many people began to believe that the war was finally coming to an end.

Students react after viewing others shot to death during a confrontation with the Ohio National Guard on the Kent State University campus in Ohio.
Reproduced by permission of Corbis-Bettman.

United States ends involvement

As President Nixon continued withdrawing U.S. troops from Vietnam, the number of American soldiers killed in combat also declined. In 1969, 9,400 Americans lost their lives in Vietnam. But this number fell to 1,400 in 1971 and 300 in 1972. These statistics gave the American people hope that the president's plan was working. At this point, a strong majority of U.S. citizens wanted the war to end, although many still wanted it to happen in a way that would preserve American dignity.

With another presidential election coming in 1972, Nixon tried to negotiate a peace treaty with North Vietnam. His Democratic opponent, Senator George McGovern (1922–) of South Dakota, promised to withdraw all American troops immediately if he became president. In March 1972, North Vietnam launched another offensive attack into South Vietnam, which became known as the Easter Offensive. In response, Nixon ordered large-scale strategic bombing of the North. After losing 100,000 troops in these conflicts, North Vietnam returned to the negotiating table in the fall. The two sides reached a tentative agreement to end the war in October 1972.

In November, Nixon was re-elected as president. Voters appreciated the fact that he had ended U.S. involvement in Vietnam. In addition, many people had found McGovern's views to be too extreme. By early 1973, the North Vietnamese had returned American prisoners of war (POWs), and only 20,000 American troops remained in Vietnam as advisors to the South Vietnamese army. Despite the peace agreement, however, many government leaders remained concerned about the situation in Vietnam. They worried that the North would break the peace agreement and attack the South, and they believed that the South could not defend itself without American help. Since U.S. involvement had become so unpopular among the American people, some officials thought that Nixon might secretly try to provide assistance.

In July 1973, the U.S. Congress took steps to prevent Nixon from sending American troops back to Vietnam. They passed the War Powers Resolution, which required the president to ask permission of Congress before he committed any troops to combat. This congressional action made Nixon very angry. He felt that Congress was trying to take away some of his powers as president. But by the fall of that year, Nixon had

other worries. Specifically, he was trapped in a scandal known as Watergate. Reporters discovered that Republican agents associated with Nixon's re-election campaign had broken into the Democratic Party headquarters, stolen documents, and set up wiretaps prior to the 1972 presidential election. As investigators pursued the case, it became clear that the president had learned about the burglary and then tried to prevent that information from becoming public. As a result of the scandal, Nixon lost the respect of the American people, and he resigned as president in August 1974.

By this time, North Vietnam was threatening to take over South Vietnam once again. President Gerald Ford (1913–; president 1974–1977) requested emergency aid for the South, but the U.S. Congress refused to provide it. As a result, North Vietnamese forces captured the South Vietnamese capital of Saigon on May 1, 1975. This event reunited the country under Communist rule and brought an end to the war. South Vietnam finally fell to communism, despite everything that the

Antiwar protesters outside the U.S. Capitol, blocking the main entrance to the House of Representatives, in 1971.
Reproduced by permission of Corbis-Bettman.

Conscientious Objectors

A conscientious objector (CO) is someone who is opposed to war for religious or moral reasons. During the height of the Vietnam War, when U.S. troops suffered large numbers of casualties (killed and wounded soldiers), many young men became desperate to avoid being drafted and sent into combat. But the United States had strict laws that required qualified men to report for military service when their names were selected in the draft. As a result, more and more American men tried to claim CO status in order to avoid being drafted into the U.S. military (sometimes the government makes conscientious objectors exempt from military service or allows them to serve in a non-combat capacity).

There were some legal ways to avoid or delay military service. For example, young men who had physical problems, were enrolled in college, worked in an industry that was vital to the war effort, were needed at home to support a family, or joined the National Guard might be allowed to defer or postpone their military service. Almost 600,000 young men who could not obtain legal deferments chose illegal ways to avoid military service during the Vietnam years. About 50,000 fled to Canada, while 20,000 others assumed false identities or went into hiding in the United States.

Nearly 200,000 Americans were formally accused of draft law violations.

Avoiding military service was a high priority among members of the antiwar movement. Many protesters felt that they should not have to fight in Vietnam because they did not support the U.S. government's actions there. In fact, many antiwar activists encouraged other people to resist the draft. Some antiwar groups set up counseling centers to inform young men about their options if they were drafted.

Many people who opposed the war tried to avoid military service by claiming conscientious objector status. At first, government rules required people to prove that they opposed all war on specific religious grounds in order to receive a CO deferment. As opposition to the war grew, however, the rules became more liberal. Instead of specific religious grounds, COs were allowed to base their opposition to the Vietnam War on moral or ethical grounds. As a result, the number of people granted CO status rose from 6 out of every 100 draftees in 1966 to 25 out of every 100 in 1970. Overall, an estimated 170,000 Americans received conscientious objector deferments during the Vietnam War, although 300,000 others had their requests denied.

U.S. government had done for more than twenty years to prevent it. Yet most Americans seemed willing to accept the defeat. Few people wanted the United States to become involved in Vietnam again.

Impact of the antiwar movement

Ever since the end of the Vietnam War, people have debated about the effectiveness and long-term impact of the American antiwar movement. Many historians believe that the antiwar movement caused lasting changes in American society. According to Schulzinger, "The antiwar movement did not end the war in Vietnam, but it did alter, almost irrevocably, the perceptions of ordinary citizens of their society and their government It also altered the perceptions of leaders toward the public." The American people tended to view institutions differently after Vietnam, including universities, the

Veterans Join the Fight against the War

As the strength of the antiwar movement began to decline in the early 1970s, a powerful new voice emerged to challenge U.S. involvement in Vietnam. A group of former soldiers who had fought in Vietnam founded an antiwar group called Vietnam Veterans Against the War (VVAW) in 1967. They started out by protesting against the terrible conditions in Veterans Administration hospitals, where many wounded Vietnam veterans were treated. By 1970, VVAW had become one of the most respected and influential of the American antiwar groups.

Many veterans continued to support the war effort after they returned home to the United States. But many other soldiers questioned the U.S. government's policies upon returning home. In fact, some veterans became vocal opponents of the war. Since they had firsthand knowledge of the situation, their protests gained instant credibility in the eyes of antiwar activists and government officials alike. In fact, when VVAW members echoed the comments of other protesters, some people took the whole antiwar movement more seriously.

In February 1971, the VVAW organized an event called the Winter Soldier Investigation in Detroit, Michigan. At this point, the news was full of stories about atrocities (extremely brutal or cruel acts) committed by American soldiers in Vietnam. One of the most publicized incidents was the My Lai massacre, in which U.S. troops had entered a Vietnamese village in search of enemy forces and proceeded to murder hundreds of unarmed civilians, including elderly people, women, and children (see box titled "The My Lai Massacre" in Chapter 12, "Nixon's War (1969–1970)").

military, the media, and the government. For example, the antiwar movement shed light on several instances when the president or other officials had misled the public. As a result, many people found it more difficult to trust the government.

Many people also believe that the antiwar movement had a strong effect on government policies, both during the Vietnam years and afterward. "The U.S. government took the antiwar movement quite seriously," Wells notes. "[Officials in the Johnson and Nixon administrations] considered the movement a nagging sign of domestic dissatisfaction with the war, a threat to their base of domestic support, a menace to American

The U.S. government claimed that the My Lai massacre was an isolated incident. Military officials issued statements declaring that American troops never committed atrocities. But at the Winter Soldier Investigation, dozens of veterans showed up and said that atrocities were common. In fact, several of the veterans admitted that they had personally witnessed or participated in the killing of innocent civilians in Vietnam. These reports convinced many people that the American forces in Vietnam were out of control, and gave added strength to the antiwar movement.

In April 1971, VVAW members organized another protest in Washington, D.C. About 1,000 veterans held a memorial service at the Tomb of the Unknown Soldier in Arlington National Cemetery. But they were not allowed to lay wreaths on the graves of soldiers who had been killed in Vietnam. Angry at this turn of events, a number of veterans—some of them in wheelchairs due to wounds they received in Vietnam—went to the Capitol building and threw their military service medals on the steps.

One positive impact of the VVAW was to improve relations between veterans and antiwar protesters. Some antiwar activists tended to blame soldiers for the situation in Vietnam. But as more veterans began speaking out against the war, they were able to convince the protesters that they had a lot in common. As VVAW founder Jan Barry explains in *The War Within*, "When we would meet other people in the peace movement we constantly said to them, 'Stop screaming at the GIs! Talk to them. Listen to them. They might really agree with you.' That's exactly what happened."

social stability, and a source of encouragement to the Vietnamese army." Both Johnson and Nixon watched news reports of protests and collected information about some of the most prominent antiwar activists. At times, the threat of public opposition may have convinced them to change their policies. "The movement kept Nixon at crucial junctures from ratcheting up the war," former antiwar activist Todd Gitlin writes in the foreword to *The War Within*. "It functioned as a veto force."

On the other hand, some historians believe that the antiwar movement was not as effective as it might have been. "Antiwar activists contributed to the growth of public disaffection with the war and helped give it focus, but they were unable to harness it," Charles DeBenedetti and Charles Chatfield write in *An American Ordeal: The Antiwar Movement of the Vietnam Era*. Disagreements within the antiwar movement reduced its effectiveness. So did the extreme protests and violence used by some radical members of the movement. "The war might have been somewhat more unpopular had the protest not existed [since] the Vietnam protest movement generated negative feelings among the American people," John Mueller is quoted as saying in the *Historical Atlas of the Vietnam War*. "Opposition to the war became associated with violent disruption, stink bombs, desecration [violation] of the flag, profanity, and contempt for American values."

Perhaps the biggest mistake of the antiwar movement was its treatment of American soldiers and veterans (see Chapter 10, "Coming Home: Vietnam Veterans in American Society"). Some protesters tended to blame U.S. soldiers for the tragic situation in Vietnam, instead of blaming the government leaders who had sent them there. In some instances, antiwar activists spit on returning veterans and called them babykillers. "What I found in the antiwar movement," Stephen E. Ambrose writes in his introduction to *Telltale Hearts: The Origins and Impact of the Vietnam Antiwar Movement*, "was not an understanding that the Army had been given an impossible job to do by the civilian leadership, but rather a hatred for the Army and its personnel. This was a terrible thing." Not surprisingly, many soldiers and veterans felt great anger and resentment toward the antiwar movement because of this treatment.

Some historians have even claimed that the American antiwar movement prolonged the conflict in Vietnam. They contend that the vocal opposition limited the options of U.S. government leaders and made it more difficult for them to end the war. As President Johnson once said, "The weakest link in our armor is American public opinion." Some historians also argue that the unrest in the United States helped the Vietnamese Communists win. They claim that the widespread protests against American involvement convinced the Viet Cong and North Vietnamese that they just needed to hold on until the U.S. government was forced to withdraw.

But other historians see the antiwar movement as a prime example of democracy at work. Although there were problems within the movement and some protesters went too far, the fact that such large numbers of Americans were able to band together, express their opinions, and influence the government to end the war makes the Vietnam protests an important part of the nation's history.

Sources

DeBenedetti, Charles, and Charles Chatfield. *An American Ordeal: The Antiwar Movement of the Vietnam Era.* Syracuse, NY: Syracuse University Press, 1990.

Garfinkle, Adam. *Telltale Hearts: The Origins and Impact of the Vietnam Antiwar Movement.* New York: St. Martin's Press, 1995.

Kutler, Stanley I., ed. *Encyclopedia of the Vietnam War.* New York: Scribner's, 1996.

Levy, David W. *The Debate over Vietnam.* 2d ed. Baltimore: Johns Hopkins University Press, 1995.

Schulzinger, Robert D. *A Time for War: The United States and Vietnam, 1941–1975.* New York: Oxford University Press, 1997.

Summers, Harry G., Jr. *Historical Atlas of the Vietnam War.* Boston: Houghton Mifflin, 1995.

Wells, Tom. *The War Within: America's Battle over Vietnam.* Berkeley: University of California Press, 1994.

Zaroulis, Nancy, and Gerald Sullivan. *Who Spoke Up? American Protest against the War in Vietnam, 1963–1975.* Garden City, NY: Doubleday, 1984.

The American Soldier in Vietnam

9

More than 2.5 million American men served in Vietnam during the war. Some of these men were career military officers. But many others were poor or working-class teenagers who enlisted or were drafted into the military right out of high school. A large proportion of the U.S. troops consisted of African American men from the inner cities, the sons of immigrants from factory towns, and boys from rural farming communities.

Upon arriving in Vietnam, American soldiers found themselves in a strange land of watery fields and dense jungles. This unfamiliar environment made their jobs more difficult and unpleasant. Their feelings of vulnerability were increased by strained relations with Vietnam's rural communities. In the early years of the war, some U.S. soldiers expected the South Vietnamese people to greet them as heroes. Instead, the local farmers and villagers usually viewed the Americans with distrust or even hostility. In fact, some South Vietnamese civilians (people not involved in the military, including women and children) actively helped the Viet Cong guerillas (small groups of fighters who launch surprise attacks) that the Americans were fighting against.

Words to Know

Communism A political system in which the government controls all resources and means of producing wealth. By eliminating private property, this system is designed to create an equal society with no social classes. However, Communist governments in practice often limit personal freedom and individual rights.

North Vietnam The Geneva Accords of 1954, which ended the First Indochina War (1946–54), divided the nation of Vietnam into two sections. The northern section, which was led by a Communist government under Ho Chi Minh, was officially known as the Democratic Republic of Vietnam, but was usually called North Vietnam.

NVA The North Vietnamese Army, which assisted the Viet Cong guerilla fighters in trying to conquer South Vietnam. These forces opposed the United States in the Vietnam War.

South Vietnam Created under the Geneva Accords of 1954, the southern section of Vietnam was known as the Republic of South Vietnam. It was led by a U.S.-supported government.

Viet Cong Vietnamese Communist guerilla fighters who worked with the North Vietnamese Army to conquer South Vietnam.

Never knowing who to trust, the U.S. combat troops experienced constant fear and anxiety during their frequent patrols of the villages and countryside. They knew that the enemy was all around them, but their main form of contact came through traps or ambushes rather than large-scale battles. As a result, many American soldiers became increasingly frustrated with the war and the U.S. strategy. "How can you defeat an enemy who knows the land intimately, who has every reason to regard it as his own backyard, and who has fought for decades, even centuries, to rid it of foreign invaders?" Christian Appy writes in his book *Working-Class War.*

The tense atmosphere and frustrating nature of the war eventually caused a significant decline in the motivation and performance of American forces in Vietnam. Some American soldiers reacted to their situation by lashing out violently against the Vietnamese, while others took out their anger on U.S. military leaders. Some used drugs or alcohol to help them cope with their experiences. As the overall situation for American troops became worse, race relations within the U.S. military also deteriorated.

The draft

Since 1973, when U.S. troops withdrew from Vietnam, Americans who have served in the U.S. military have done so voluntarily. During the Vietnam War, however, at least one-third of the American troops were selected for military service through an involuntary process known as the draft. A government agency called the Selective Service collected the names of all American men between the ages of eighteen and twenty-six. When a man's name was drawn, he was required to report to his local draft board for evaluation. There, he would either qualify for a deferment (an official delay of military service), or he would be inducted into the armed forces. In this way, many young men ended up serving in Vietnam whether they wanted to or not.

There were some legal ways to avoid or delay military service. For example, young men who had physical problems, were enrolled in college, worked in an industry that was vital to the war effort, were needed at home to support a family, or joined the National Guard might be granted deferments. Altogether, 27 million American men came of draft age during the Vietnam War years. About 60 percent, or 16 million, of these draftable men avoided service in legal ways. Of the 40 percent that did serve in the military in the late 1960s and early 1970s, only about 2.5 million went to Vietnam. The rest remained in the United States or served on bases in Europe.

The ten percent of the draft-age generation that ended up serving in Vietnam consisted of three groups of relatively equal size. One-third were volunteers who had chosen to join the military. Many of these men were career soldiers or recent graduates of military academies. Another third were drafted into the military. The final third enlisted because they expected to be drafted soon. In some cases, men who entered the service by enlisting rather than being drafted received better duty assignments.

A "working-class war"

Since the draft officially ended in 1973, many people have studied the role it played in determining the racial, ethnic, and social class makeup of the American troops in Vietnam. These studies have concluded that the average U.S. soldier was a 19-year-old man from a poor or working-class family who had not attended college. Such findings have confirmed the widespread belief that U.S. draft policies unfairly targeted the segments of American society with the least political power. "Vietnam was a place where the elite went as reporters, not as soldiers," reporter David Halberstam noted. "Almost as

Military Dogs in Vietnam

About 4,000 dogs served with the American military in Vietnam during the war. Some of these animals were pets that were donated to the armed forces by American owners. As military dogs, they were trained to sniff out booby traps, land mines, tunnels, snipers, and hidden stashes of weapons and other supplies. The dogs also served as sentries at U.S. bases and helped drag wounded American soldiers to safety in medical units. The dogs were so effective in helping the American soldiers avoid enemy traps that the North Vietnamese placed a high value on killing them. Hundreds of dogs were killed in action in Vietnam, but it is estimated that their efforts prevented over 10,000 human casualties.

Charlie Cargo, an American soldier who served as a dog handler in Vietnam, remembered an occasion when his dog, Wolf, saved his life: "He latched onto my hand. He gave me a friendly nip on the hand and looked at me. Wolf absolutely would not let me go by him. I looked straight ahead and not more than two feet away was a tripwire [a trigger for a hidden explosive device]. And I would have died right there with him if he wouldn't have found that wire."

Sadly, only 200 of the American military dogs returned to the United States at the end of the Vietnam War. Official U.S. military policy prevented them from being brought back to America out of fears that they might carry diseases. Instead, the dogs were classified as "surplus armaments" (extra military equipment) and either put to sleep or left with the South Vietnamese army when the U.S. troops were withdrawn in 1973.

many people from Harvard won Pulitzer Prizes [a prestigious award for journalism] in Vietnam as died there."

Many of the ways in which draft-age men received deferments favored those who were wealthy and well-educated. For example, wealthy young men could afford to remain in college full-time—and even pursue advanced degrees following graduation—in order to qualify for student deferments. But these deferments were not available to students who had to work their way through college on a part-time basis. In addition, wealthy young men could obtain deferments for physical problems more easily than poor or working-class men. Rather than trying to convince a draft board that they were physically unable to serve in the military, these men could get a note

"Charlie," looking over sights of .50 Caliber machine gun, mounted atop an tank in Vietnam, 1966. *Reproduced by permission of AP/World Wide Photos.*

Many American veterans, as well as citizens who had donated their pets, were angry and disgusted at the treatment the military dogs received. After all, these dogs had served their country as loyal soldiers, and many of them were considered heroes for saving men's lives. "That's just unheard of to do that to a four-footed soldier," U.S. Army dog handler John Burnam stated.

Since then, the contribution of American military dogs has been recognized in several books and documentary films. On February 21, 2000, a memorial was dedicated in Riverside, California, to honor the American military dogs who served in Vietnam and other wars. In addition, the U.S. government agreed to change its policy so that war dogs would no longer be left behind when American troops were withdrawn from a conflict.

from their family doctors. Finally, wealthy and educated young men were more likely to be aware of all the ways they might avoid military service. In fact, antiwar organizations often held meetings on college campuses to inform potential draftees about their options.

Appy estimates that the American forces in Vietnam consisted of twenty-five percent poor, fifty-five percent working-class, and twenty percent middle-class men. Very few U.S. soldiers came from upper-class families. Many of the men who served in Vietnam were minorities from the nation's inner cities. African Americans accounted for about fourteen percent of the American forces. Many other U.S. soldiers came from small rural towns or farming communities. According to

Soldier and scout dog in South Vietnamese jungle searching for entrenched North Vietnamese.
Reproduced by permission of AP/World Wide Photos.

Appy, about two percent of Americans lived in towns with populations smaller than 1,000 in the 1960s. But about eight percent of the U.S. soldiers who died in Vietnam came from towns that size.

Although the draft did tend to target men from working-class homes, there were other factors that led these men to fight in Vietnam in greater numbers than other groups. For example, many of these men inherited strong family traditions of military service and felt it was their duty to join the armed forces. "My father had served, everyone in our community had served. My two brothers served over in Vietnam," veteran Dave Christian told Michael Maclear in *The Ten Thousand Day War*. "I hailed from a steel community and we handed out 29,000 boys from my county alone."

In addition, men from poor families tended to have fewer job options in civilian [non-military] society. Some of them considered the military a good place to receive training.

"The Marines provided them with a guaranteed annual income, free medical care, free clothing, and something else, less tangible but just as valuable—self-respect," former U.S. Marine Philip Caputo explains in *A Rumor of War*. "The man who wore that uniform was somebody. He had passed a test few others could. He was not some down-on-his-luck loser pumping gas or washing cars for a dollar-fifty an hour, but somebody, a Marine."

The men who served in Vietnam also tended to be younger than the U.S. soldiers who had fought in previous wars. The average age of American troops in Vietnam was nineteen, compared to an average age of twenty-six for U.S. soldiers in World War II (1939–45). During most of the Vietnam War, nineteen-year-olds were not even allowed to vote. The voting age in the United States changed from twenty-one to eighteen in 1971.

Partly due to their young age and working-class backgrounds, the U.S. soldiers in Vietnam did not tend to be well-educated. As of 1967, eighty percent of the American troops had a high school education or less, and only six percent had completed four years of college. In comparison, forty-five percent of the generation that reached draft age during the Vietnam War attended college. Many people criticized the government policies that selected mainly young, uneducated men from the nation's less-affluent families to serve in Vietnam. "Where were the sons of all the big shots who supported the war? Not in my platoon," veteran Steve Harper noted in *No Victory Parades*. "If the war was so important, why didn't our leaders put everyone's son in there, why only us?"

The combat soldier's experience in Vietnam

When American soldiers arrived in Vietnam, they entered a land, climate, and culture that was very different from the United States. For example, the weather in Vietnam tended to be very hot and humid. During the spring "monsoon" season it would rain nonstop for days at a time. The fertile river valleys tended to be flat and fairly open, but also extremely wet. Vietnamese peasants grew rice in these lowland

The Land Becomes an Enemy

To some American combat soldiers in Vietnam, mines and booby traps turned the land into an enemy more frightening and deadly than the Viet Cong. In the following passage from his book *A Rumor of War,* former Marine Philip Caputo describes the emotional toll these hidden explosive devices took on the troops:

> The foot soldier has a special feeling for the ground. He walks on it, fights on it, sleeps and eats on it; the ground shelters him under fire; he digs his home in it. But mines and booby traps transform that friendly, familiar earth into a thing of menace, a thing to be feared as much as machine guns or mortar shells. The infantryman knows that any moment the ground he is walking on can erupt and kill him; kill him if he's lucky. If he's unlucky, he will be turned into a blind, deaf, emasculated [changed so that he is no longer a man], legless shell . . . . Walking down the trails, waiting for those things to explode, we had begun to feel more like victims than soldiers.

areas in wet fields known as paddies. The valleys were surrounded by steep hills and rugged mountains that were covered by a thick jungle of trees and tropical plants.

Combat troops spent much of their time patrolling the countryside in small groups, searching for Viet Cong guerilla fighters or North Vietnamese Army (NVA) forces. Sometimes they would set out on foot from a U.S. base camp. Other times they would be dropped off by helicopters in remote and potentially hostile locations. They would march for days or weeks at a time, carrying heavy packs full of food, clothing, weapons, and ammunition. During the time they spent on patrol, they rarely had an opportunity to bathe or enjoy a hot meal.

No matter where in Vietnam these American units patrolled, the landscape made travel difficult. In the rice paddies, the U.S. soldiers often slogged through water and mud that came up to their waists. When they got back on dry land, they had to check their skin for blood-sucking leeches. In the jungles, they often had to hack their way through dense vegetation. Sometimes it would take an entire day to move two miles. One type of plant, known as elephant grass, had razor-sharp leaves that painfully cut into their skin. They also had to deal with swarms of mosquitoes. In the mountains, they exhausted themselves by marching up and down steep hillsides. Many soldiers became ill from drinking dirty water or developed painful sores on their feet.

These tiring and unpleasant patrols made up much of an average U.S. combat soldier's experience in Vietnam. "Perhaps the best single image with which to synthesize [combine different ideas into one] the physical experience of the American combat soldier in Vietnam would be that of a column of men spaced about five yards apart; burdened with 80-pound packs; wearing thick armored vests called flak jackets; carrying rifles, mortars, hundreds of rounds of ammunition, and three or four canteens; and patrolling on foot through jungles, mountains, or rice paddies," Appy writes. "Among the infantrymen, the 'grunts,' this was known as 'humping the boonies.'"

Hours of boredom and seconds of terror

In addition to these physical discomforts, the American troops also experienced constant anxiety and tension in Vietnam. As they marched through the rice paddies and jungles, U.S. combat units never knew when enemy forces would suddenly appear. They spent long periods of time searching the countryside without ever finding Viet Cong or NVA forces. In 1968, for example, American patrols encountered the enemy on only one out of every hundred missions. When the two sides did meet, they rarely fought large-scale battles that allowed the United States to use its superior firepower. Instead, they usually fought small skirmishes following Viet Cong or NVA ambushes. "You go out on patrol maybe 20 times or more and nothin', just nothin'," a soldier told *Time* magazine in 1965. "Then, the 21st time, zap, zap, zap, you get hit—and Victor Charlie [the Viet Cong, or VC] fades into the jungle before you can close with him. "

Viet Cong guerillas liked to launch surprise attacks at night or during bad weather in order to gain an advantage over the Americans and their powerful weapons. They also hid in villages or dense jungles and fired upon U.S. troops as they passed by on patrol. NVA troops controlled the time and place of most of their battles with American forces. They usually started firefights by ambushing U.S. combat patrols. After a while, some U.S. soldiers began to feel like the purpose of their endless patrolling was to serve as bait for attacks by enemy forces. After all, such attacks gave American military leaders information about the size and location of NVA troops. They needed this information to pinpoint their bombing raids.

Even though U.S. combat patrols encountered Viet Cong guerillas and NVA soldiers only rarely, they often found

American soldier, cleaning missile launcher in Vietnam.
Reproduced by permission of the Library of Congress.

evidence of enemy activities. For example, enemy forces buried land mines and set booby traps throughout the countryside of South Vietnam. These carefully hidden explosive devices caused a great deal of death and suffering among the American troops. In fact, mines and booby traps accounted for between twenty and twenty-five percent of U.S. casualties (killed and wounded soldiers) during the Vietnam War.

American combat soldiers had to remain alert at all times, even when they were exhausted from many hours of patrolling. Besides looking for enemy troops, they had to watch out for tiny trip wires that caused hidden hand grenades to explode, and for signs of digging that might indicate a land mine or a dangerous pit. The constant threat of triggering a hidden explosive caused some soldiers to become paralyzed with fear and indecision. After all, every spot where they stepped or sat might lead to injury or death. This tense atmosphere took a heavy emotional toll on the U.S. troops.

Some veterans have described their experiences in Vietnam as long periods of boredom interrupted by moments of sudden and unexpected terror. "Looking at your watch, counting the days, marking off the days you have left in Vietnam on a little calendar drawn on your helmet," veteran Tim O'Brien remembered of his time on combat patrol. "It is monotony punctuated by moments of sheer terror, just horrible stuff. And after the war is over you don't remember the monotony and the boredom and the mosquitoes and the heat. You remember those few moments of real terror."

U.S. soldiers' feelings about the Vietnamese

As they traveled through the countryside looking for enemy forces, American combat patrols routinely entered and searched South Vietnamese villages for hidden weapons, extra supplies of food, young men of military age, and other possible signs of Viet Cong activity. The combat patrols rarely found any strong evidence linking the villages to the Viet Cong. But somehow they knew that the enemy had been there. O'Brien compared searching South Vietnamese villages to hunting a hummingbird (a tiny bird that flies very quickly with a darting motion): "You would get to one village: nothing there. Another village—and nothing there. The enemy, the hummingbird that we were after, was just buzzing around. You secure a village, you search it, and you leave, and the village reverts [goes back] to the enemy."

One reason that many U.S. soldiers suspected that the South Vietnamese villagers cooperated with the Viet Cong was that the villagers never seemed to trip land mines. The Viet Cong did not want to blow up villagers, because they depended on the local people for supplies and other support. So they trained the villagers to recognize subtle signs of a mine or booby trap. For example, the Viet Cong might tie a piece of grass into a knot, with the loop end pointing toward the hidden explosive. "Here's a woman of twenty-two or twenty-three. She is pregnant, and she tells an interrogator that her husband works in Danang and isn't a Viet Cong," former marine E. J. Banks recalled to Stanley Karnow in *Vietnam: A History.* "But she watches your men walk down a trail and get

Soldiers Feel Strong Emotions

For some American combat soldiers, the constant anxiety and tension of their time in Vietnam served to heighten their senses and emotions. In the following excerpt from a *New York Times Magazine* article, Tim O'Brien recalls the deep love he felt during the war:

Vietnam was more than terror. For me, at least, Vietnam was partly love. With each step, each light-year of a second, a foot soldier is always almost dead, or so it feels, and in such circumstances you can't help but love. You love your mom and dad, the Vikings, hamburgers on the grill, your pulse, your future—everything that might be lost or never come to be. Intimacy [close, personal contact] with death carries with it a corresponding new intimacy with life. Jokes are funnier, green is greener. You love the musty morning air. You love the miracle of your own enduring capacity for love. You love your friends in Alpha Company—a kid named Chip, my buddy. He wrote letters to my sister, I wrote letters to his sister. In the rear [non-combat support areas], back at Gator, Chip and I would go our separate ways, by color, both of us ashamed but knowing it had to be that way. In the bush, though, nothing kept us apart. "Black and White," we were called. In May of 1969, Chip was blown high into a hedge of bamboo. Many pieces. I loved the guy, he loved me. I'm alive. He's dead. An old story, I guess.

killed or wounded by a booby trap. She knows the booby trap is there, but she doesn't warn them. Maybe she planted it herself."

Over time, as mines and booby traps killed and injured more American soldiers, U.S. combat patrols grew angry that the villagers did not warn them of nearby dangers. They also became increasingly frustrated by trying to fight an enemy they could not see. Some soldiers reacted to their fear, anger, and frustration by treating the villagers very harshly. In some instances, they beat up women, children, or elderly men who refused to give them information. Other times, they burned down huts and destroyed food supplies.

The South Vietnamese people were very poor, and they suffered great hardships during the war. Thousands of villages were destroyed by U.S. bombing missions or American combat patrols. This destruction left many Vietnamese people homeless and forced them to live as refugees. Some of these displaced villagers survived by collecting and using the garbage left behind by American forces. For example, some refugees sorted through dumps near U.S. military bases and carefully saved scraps of food, metal, or wood. Others begged for handouts from passing soldiers.

At first, many U.S. soldiers felt sympathy for the South Vietnamese people. Some gave candy to the children and tried to help in other ways. Over time, however, American troops' view of the Vietnamese began to change. Some soldiers began to resent their constant demands for food and money. Others grew angry that the South Vietnamese did not seem to appreciate American efforts to save their country from a Communist takeover.

Part of the problem was that most American soldiers did not understand the South Vietnamese people and culture. "My time in Vietnam is the memory of ignorance," O'Brien wrote. "I didn't know the language. I knew nothing about the culture, nothing about the religion, nothing about the village community. I knew nothing about the aims of the people— whether they were for the war or against the war . . . . The final effect was of a moron wandering through a foreign land, or a blind man wandering through a foreign land."

Atrocities

In the early 1970s, the American public was shocked by a series of news reports about atrocities (acts of extreme cruelty or brutality) committed by U.S. soldiers in Vietnam. Many factors combined to cause American combat troops to lash out violently against Vietnamese civilians. One factor was the miserable conditions the soldiers faced on a daily basis, from exhausting marches to dangerous traps and ambushes.

Another factor was the frustration and uncertainty the U.S. soldiers felt toward the Vietnamese people. Many American troops felt that they could not trust anyone Vietnamese— including peasants, farmers, bar girls, old women, and children—because they might be agents of the Viet Cong. This atmosphere of fear and distrust caused some men to behave in immoral ways they would never have demonstrated under normal circumstances. "When GIs couldn't tell friend from foe, they came to hate and despise them all," Cecil B. Curry explains in *Self-Destruction: The Disintegration and Decay of the United States Army during the Vietnam Era*. "Viewing all Vietnamese as less than human released American boys from their own humanity."

Some experts claim that U.S. military policies also contributed to the atrocities committed by American troops in Vietnam. One of the main U.S. strategies for winning the war was to kill as many Viet Cong and NVA forces as possible. Rather than trying to capture and hold territory as they had in previous wars, American military leaders hoped to use bombing attacks and combat forces to break the enemy's ability and willingness to fight.

For troops in the field, this strategy placed a strong emphasis on "body counts," or the number of enemy soldiers killed. In fact, many U.S. combat units measured their progress by how many Vietnamese Communists they had killed. But since it was often difficult to tell friends from enemies, the emphasis on body counts led to many civilian deaths. "The military mission became to inflict casualties and the primary reason for existence became to minimize your own casualties. And you were sort of walking that tightrope the whole time," veteran James Webb recalled in *Working-Class War.* "Ethical confusion is the only word that I can use. It just sort of mounts."

There is no doubt that some American soldiers committed atrocities during the Vietnam War. In the My Lai massacre of 1968, for example, U.S. troops raided a South Vietnamese village and killed between 300 and 400 innocent civilians (see box titled "The My Lai Massacre" in Chapter 12, "Nixon's War (1969–1970)"). But many other American soldiers conducted themselves honorably throughout their time in Vietnam. Unfortunately, the poor treatment the South Vietnamese people received from some American soldiers led to greater support for the Viet Cong and NVA. "Why didn't they get behind us? Why didn't they care that we were dying for them?" veteran Tobias Wolff asked in *Time.* "Every time we slapped someone around, or trashed a village, or shouted curses from a jeep, we defined ourselves as the enemy and thereby handed more power and legitimacy to the people we had to beat."

Decline in U.S. morale and performance

During the early years of the war, many American servicemen supported the U.S. government's decision to become involved in Vietnam. They believed it was important to stop the spread of communism in Southeast Asia. As a result, the morale of American troops was fairly high—at first. By the late 1960s and early 1970s, however, both the morale and performance of the U.S. forces declined rapidly. As the number of American casualties increased, some soldiers were overcome by fear. Others grew frustrated with the U.S. military strategy, which seemed to risk their lives on endless patrols without any clear purpose.

Another reason for declining morale and performance was the one-year tour-of-duty rotation schedule used in Vietnam. In previous wars, U.S. troops were required to serve for the duration of the conflict. But during the Vietnam War, individual combat soldiers were rotated into and out of the country on a one-year schedule. Rather than following orders and trying to achieve military goals, some soldiers focused only on staying alive for those 365 days. They tried to avoid combat whenever possible and did not form close relationships with other members of their military units.

Some historians blame the American antiwar movement for the decline in the motivation and performance of U.S. troops in Vietnam (see Chapter 8, "The American Antiwar Movement"). As the war dragged on, opposition to it became more widespread and vocal. American soldiers knew that the war was unpopular at home. During the later years of the war, in fact, some soldiers had been antiwar protesters before they were drafted into the military. The atmosphere back in the United States caused many American soldiers to question their involvement in Vietnam, and to resist the orders of U.S. military leaders.

Desertions, fraggings, and drug use

The decline in morale among U.S. troops contributed to a number of significant problems, including atrocities, desertions (when a soldier leaves the military illegally before his term of service has ended), violence toward officers, drug use, and strained race relations. Desertions became a major problem during the Vietnam War. The number of U.S. soldiers who left their units for more than 30 days without permission increased from 15 per 1,000 in 1966 to 70 per 1,000 in 1972. About 100,000 U.S. soldiers were discharged from the military for such offenses. Antiwar groups claimed that the increasing numbers of desertions proved that the American combat troops opposed the war. In reality, few soldiers left their units during combat patrols of South Vietnam—partly because it was even more dangerous to travel through the countryside alone.

As American soldiers grew more frustrated with the war and how it was being conducted, some began to take out their frustrations on officers. Many officers who commanded U.S. troops in Vietnam were good leaders who earned the respect of their men. But some officers seemed to place their own desire for glory and promotions ahead of the safety and welfare of their units. For example, U.S. soldiers resented officers who directed dangerous field combat from the safety of high-flying helicopters or distant command posts. They also disliked overly aggressive officers who did not seem to understand what they went through on a daily basis. Soldiers who resented or distrusted their officers sometimes refused to follow orders or even resorted to violence.

The intentional use of violence toward unpopular officers was common enough in Vietnam that a new word was invented to describe it. "Fragging" initially referred to the practice of using a fragmentation weapon (an explosive device, such as a hand grenade) to murder an officer. But the term was later used in reference to any deliberate act of violence toward a higher-ranking person. For example, disgruntled soldiers might sabotage a helicopter or shoot an officer during combat with enemy forces. The U.S. military reported 730 fragging incidents between 1969 and 1971, which resulted in 83 officer deaths. But experts suspect that many other incidents went unreported or were made to look like accidents.

Another problem associated with the decline in morale of U.S. soldiers was increased drug use. Drugs were inexpensive and easy to obtain in Vietnam. Many soldiers used them to escape from the boredom of their daily lives or to rebel against military authority. Others resorted to drugs when they could not cope with the violence they witnessed. "Drugs became the main expression of discontent—in effect, an inoculation [form of protection] against 'Nam,'" Michael Maclear explains in *The Ten Thousand Day War*. Drug use was especially common on military bases and in support units. It was less common in combat units operating in the field, where a lack of attention could cost soldiers their lives.

Drug use became a severe problem between 1969 and 1971, when the U.S. government was beginning to withdraw American troops from Vietnam. Marijuana use peaked at 58 percent of U.S. forces during this period, while heroin use increased from 2 percent of American soldiers to 22 percent. The hard drugs American soldiers used in Vietnam were much more powerful and addictive than the versions available in the United States. As a result, as many as 500,000 U.S. soldiers became addicted to drugs. In 1971, for example, 5,000 American soldiers were hospitalized for combat wounds, while 20,500 were treated for drug abuse.

Strained race relations

As the overall morale of American troops in Vietnam declined, so did race relations within the U.S. military. In the early years of the war, many African American men viewed military service as a positive thing. They believed that the military offered opportunities for training and career advancement that were not available to them in civilian society. But such attitudes began to change as black soldiers faced discrimination in Vietnam.

For example, black soldiers often found themselves passed over for promotions. Only two percent of officers in the U.S. armed forces were black, even though blacks made up about fourteen percent of all military personnel during the Vietnam War. In addition, black soldiers often received less desirable housing and duty assignments than white soldiers in the same unit. They tended to be assigned to dangerous combat duty more often than white soldiers. As a result, African Americans made up twenty-five percent of the U.S. soldiers killed in Vietnam during 1965 and 1966.

For the most part, race relations remained positive in American combat units. Black and white soldiers tended to band together when they faced danger and the threat of death. But race relations deteriorated significantly in non-combat support units and base camps during the late 1960s. In some cases, African American soldiers intentionally segregated themselves from the rest of their unit. They stuck together and often refused to associate with whites. At the same time, some white soldiers in base camps made racist comments or displayed racially insensitive symbols, like the Confederate flag (the symbol of the slaveholding South during the American Civil War). In some cases, racial tensions exploded into violence. Such incidents contributed to the overall decline in the performance of American troops in Vietnam.

Sources

Appy, Christian. *Working-Class War: American Combat Soldiers and Vietnam.* Chapel Hill: University of North Carolina Press, 1993.

Baskir, Lawrence M., and William A. Strauss. *Chance and Circumstance: The Draft, the War, and the Vietnam Generation.* New York: Knopf, 1978.

Caputo, Philip. *A Rumor of War.* New York: Ballantine Books, 1994.

Curry, Cecil B. (as Cincinnatus). *Self-Destruction: The Disintegration and Decay of the U.S. Army in Vietnam.* New York: W. W. Norton, 1981.

Ebert, James R. *A Life in a Year: The American Infantryman in Vietnam, 1965–1972.* Novato, CA: Presidio, 1986.

Helmer, John. *Bringing the War Home: The American Soldier in Vietnam and After.* New York: Free Press, 1974.

Karnow, Stanley. *Vietnam: A History.* Rev. ed. New York: Penguin Books, 1997.

Lewy, Gunter. *America in Vietnam.* New York: Oxford University Press, 1978.

Maclear, Michael. *The Ten Thousand Day War: Vietnam, 1945–1975.* New York: Avon Books, 1981.

MacPherson, Myra. *Long Time Passing: Vietnam and the Haunted Generation.* Garden City, NY: Doubleday, 1984.

Polner, Murray. *No Victory Parades: The Return of the Vietnam Veteran.* New York: Holt, Rinehart and Winston, 1971.

Starr, Paul. *The Discarded Army.* New York: Charterhouse, 1974.

Coming Home: Vietnam Veterans in American Society

10

When the American soldiers returned home from World War II in 1945, they were greeted as heroes in the United States. Cities and towns across the country held parades to honor the returning veterans and recognize the sacrifices they had made. But the homecoming was very different for most Vietnam veterans. They came back to find the United States torn apart by debate over the Vietnam War. There were no victory parades or welcome-home rallies. Instead, most Vietnam veterans returned to a society that did not seem to care about them, or that seemed to view them with distrust and anger.

"Men who fought in World War II or Korea might be just as haunted by what they had personally seen and done in combat," Arnold R. Isaacs writes in *Vietnam Shadows: The War, Its Ghosts, and Its Legacy.* "But they did not come home, as the Vietnam vets did, to a country torn and full of doubt about why those wars were fought and whether they had been worthwhile. Nor did they return as symbols of a great national failure."

Many of the young men who fought in Vietnam had a great deal of difficulty readjusting to life in the United States.

Words to Know

Post-Traumatic Stress Syndrome (PTSS)
A set of psychological problems that are caused by exposure to a dangerous or disturbing situation, such as combat. People who suffer from PTSS may have symptoms such as depression, flashbacks, nightmares, and angry outbursts. The condition is also known as Post-Traumatic Stress Disorder (PTSD).

Veteran A former member of the armed forces; sometimes called a "vet" for short.

Veterans Administration A U.S. government agency responsible for providing medical care, insurance, pensions, and other benefits to American veterans of Vietnam and other wars.

Some struggled to overcome physical injuries, emotional problems, or drug addictions from their time in Vietnam. Others had trouble feeling accepted by their friends and families. Some returning soldiers blamed their situation on the antiwar movement and developed a deep resentment toward antiwar protesters. But many other veterans began to question the war and their own actions in it.

A chilly reception

Some people who opposed American involvement in the Vietnam War treated U.S. soldiers and veterans poorly. They tended to blame American troops for the tragic situation in Vietnam, instead of blaming the government leaders who had sent them there. "Some protesters simply did not make a clear distinction between the war and those who fought it, and they regarded American soldiers as ready and willing killers or ignorant dupes," Christian G. Appy explains in his book *Working-Class War: American Combat Soldiers and Vietnam.* In some instances, antiwar protesters reportedly spit on returning veterans and called them baby-killers. Although such incidents were rare, the stories were often repeated among U.S. soldiers in Vietnam. These stories added to the soldiers' resentment of the antiwar movement.

Rather than being greeted with anger and hostility, however, most Vietnam veterans received very little reaction when they returned home. They mainly noticed that people seemed uncomfortable around them and did not appear interested in hearing about their wartime experiences. "Society as a whole was certainly unable and unwilling to receive these men with the support and understanding they needed," Appy writes. "The most common experiences of rejection were not

American Prisoners of War (POWs)

There was one group of Vietnam veterans who received a warm greeting from fellow Americans upon returning home—those who had been held captive as prisoners of war (POWs). Since most of the fighting in the Vietnam War took place in South Vietnam, few American combat soldiers were captured and taken prisoner by North Vietnamese Army (NVA) forces. Most of the nearly 600 Americans who became POWs were pilots whose planes were shot down during bombing missions over North Vietnam.

Beginning in 1964, the NVA held American POWs in several prison camps in North Vietnam. Many of these men were held captive for years. Most of the POWs were treated badly. They were kept in miserable living conditions and often endured torture at the hands of the North Vietnamese. Their captors used brainwashing and brutal force to try to get them to sign confessions or make statements against the U.S. government or in favor of North Vietnamese Communists.

Although the American people were bitterly divided over the Vietnam War, everyone seemed greatly concerned over the welfare of the POWs. It was one of the few issues on which supporters and opponents of the war could agree. When the POWs were released in early 1973 with the signing of a peace agreement, they were greeted as heroes across the United States. Television footage showed tearful family reunions as former POWs stepped off airplanes. The men appeared at numerous rallies and ceremonies attended by top government officials.

The POWs became one of the few sources of American pride in the aftermath of the Vietnam War. "The heroes' welcome given to the 591 men freed in early 1973 was made into a kind of strange substitute for the victory parade Americans would never have," Arnold R. Isaacs writes in *Vietnam Shadows: The War, Its Ghosts, and Its Legacy.* "The prisoners' goal had been to survive and protect their honor under brutal torture; if the nation's goals hadn't been achieved in Vietnam, then the POWs' record of bravery and endurance would have to do."

explicit acts of hostility but quieter, sometimes more devastating forms of withdrawal, suspicion, and indifference."

John Kerry, a Vietnam veteran who later became a U.S. senator, remembered how he felt shortly after returning home from the war: "There I was, a week out of the jungle, flying from San Francisco to New York. I fell asleep and woke up yelling,

Vietnam veteran passing through the arrival gate at Oakland Army Base. *Reproduced by permission of AP/World Wide*

probably a nightmare. The other passengers moved away from me—a reaction I noticed more and more in the months ahead. The country didn't give a [care] about the guys coming back, or what they'd gone through. The feeling toward them was, 'Stay away—don't contaminate us with whatever you've brought back from Vietnam.'" This type of reaction made many veterans feel alone and isolated from the rest of American society.

Even people who supported American military involvement in Vietnam did not always support the returning veterans. Some Vietnam veterans thought that Americans who had fought in earlier wars might be more helpful than other people. After all, veterans of World War II (1939–45) and the Korean War (1950–53) understood what combat was like. But many veterans of earlier wars seemed to look down on Vietnam veterans because they did not win the Vietnam War.

Confronted with reactions of indifference, fear, or anger, some veterans kept their wartime experiences to themselves. They refused to discuss Vietnam with anyone but other veterans, because no one else seemed to understand or care. "There has really never been anyone who has asked me: 'What happened to you over there? What was it like?' It's like having a whole year of your life that didn't exist," veteran Jamie Bryant told Isaacs in *Vietnam Shadows*. "When you first get back, you don't think about it much. Then you begin to wonder why no one asks the questions. Then you begin to feel like maybe it isn't something you should talk about."

Veterans' views of the antiwar movement

Many Vietnam veterans blamed the antiwar movement for the chilly reception they got upon returning to the United States. They believed that it was not fair for antiwar protesters to question their actions during the war. After all, most protesters had not been to Vietnam. In the eyes of the veterans, these protesters could not understand what the war had been like. In addition, many veterans thought that the antiwar movement should blame the government officials who had sent them to Vietnam, because as soldiers they had only followed orders.

Probably the biggest reason many Vietnam veterans felt anger and resentment toward the antiwar protesters was that they came from different social classes. The majority of men who served in Vietnam came from poor or working-class backgrounds. In contrast, many of the antiwar protesters were college students who came from middle- or upper-class families. Many of the deferments (official postponements of military service) granted to young men to avoid serving in Vietnam favored those who were wealthy and well-educated. For example, wealthy young men could afford to remain in college full-time—and even pursue advanced degrees following graduation—in order to qualify for student deferments. But these deferments were not available to students who had to work their way through college on a part-time basis.

Working-class men who were drafted often resented the student protesters, who used their social standing to avoid serving and then led rallies against the war from the safety of the United States. "To many veterans," Appy writes, "all protest seemed like yet another class privilege enjoyed by wealthier peers, and even moderate objections to the war, if made by draft-immune college students, were often read as personal attacks.

Student protests put into bold relief the contrast between the experiences of the two groups. Watching protest marches reminded some veterans of their own marches in Vietnam—those endless, exhausting, and dangerous humps. While they were enduring the hardship and danger of the war, college students were—in the eyes of many soldiers—frolicking on campus in a blissful round of sex, drugs, and rock n' roll *and* getting the credentials necessary to gain high-paying jobs."

Most veterans felt proud of their service to their country in Vietnam, yet many also had some doubts about the war and their own actions in it. In fact, some veterans protested against the war once they returned to the United States. But these antiwar veterans felt that they had earned the right to question the government's policies, while the student protesters had not. "For every guy who resists the draft one of us gotta go and he gets sent out into the boonies to get his backside shot at," veteran Steve Harper recalled after running into antiwar protesters in Chicago. "One of their signs read, 'We've already given enough.' And I thought, 'What *have* they given?'"

Difficulties readjusting to American society

Many Vietnam veterans built successful lives after they returned home from the war. They finished their educations, established good careers, and had families. But many other veterans had a tough time readjusting to life in the United States after they completed their military service. "I had the distinct feeling (common among returning veterans, I think) that this was not my country, not my time," veteran Larry Heinemann recalls in *Vietnam Shadows*. The cold reception the veterans got from many Americans left them feeling different and alone.

In addition, many veterans went from the jungles of Vietnam to their hometowns so quickly that they did not have time to adjust. Unlike previous wars, when it usually took weeks for soldiers to be discharged and transported home, U.S. soldiers often returned from Vietnam within two days. Return-

POW Robert L. Stirm, greeting his family at Travis Air Force Base, after returning from the Vietnam War, 1973. *Reproduced by permission of AP/World Wide Photos.*

ing to the safety and comfort of home so quickly made it more difficult for them to make sense of the danger and misery they experienced in Vietnam.

Some veterans returned from Vietnam with severe physical disabilities or emotional problems. The Vietnam War had a much higher ratio of wounded to killed soldiers than any previous war. Faster evacuation of wounded soldiers from battlefields and advances in medical treatment meant that more men survived combat injuries. But it also meant that more veterans came home with serious, crippling injuries, such as amputated limbs and paralysis. In addition, many American soldiers used hard drugs during their service in Vietnam. Drugs such as marijuana, opium, and heroin were cheap and easy to obtain. Drug addiction continued to be a problem among veterans when they returned home.

Since most of the soldiers who served in Vietnam were very young and came from working-class families, they did not have access to private health care in the United States. Instead, they had to depend on the U.S. government to provide them with treatment and rehabilitation. Unfortunately, the government agency charged with caring for veterans, called the Veterans Administration (VA), did not do a good job of helping the Vietnam veterans. Many of the VA hospitals where they received treatment were dirty, understaffed, and unable to provide what veterans needed.

Post-traumatic stress syndrome

To make matters worse, the U.S. government at first denied that some of the veterans' health problems were related to their service in Vietnam. For example, many veterans developed mental and emotional problems as they struggled to cope with their feelings about the war. They suffered from symptoms including depression, guilt, flashbacks, nightmares, mood swings, angry outbursts, anxiety, and paranoia. Doctors eventually gave this condition a name, Post-Traumatic Stress Syndrome (PTSS), and recognized it as a real psychological illness.

Studies have estimated that as many as 800,000 Vietnam veterans suffered from PTSS. Probably just as many others had mild forms of PTSS that were not diagnosed. But the VA did not admit that PTSS existed until 1979, six years after the last American soldiers returned from Vietnam. In addition, VA hospitals and doctors did not do well in treating veterans with PTSS. Unable to find relief from their physical pain and mental anguish, some Vietnam veterans decided to end their own lives. In fact, some experts believe that the number of veterans who committed suicide after returning home from Vietnam was at least as great as the 58,000 Americans who died in the war.

Many Vietnam veterans also had trouble earning money and supporting themselves upon returning to the United States. Following World War II, the U.S. government had established a generous benefit program for veterans. This program paid veterans' living expenses plus offered them full college tuition. But the government was not so generous with Vietnam veterans. Partly because it had spent so much money conducting the war, the government offered veterans only $200 per month. This amount was barely enough to cover living expenses, let alone enable the veterans to continue their educations.

As it turned out, about 250,000 Vietnam veterans were unable to find jobs when their military service ended. Most of these men did not have a college degree. Some desperate veterans turned to crime or drugs to earn money. In fact, 25 percent of the American soldiers who saw combat in Vietnam were arrested on criminal charges within ten years of coming home, most for drug-related offenses.

Doubts about service

After returning to the United States, many veterans continued to support American military involvement in Vietnam. Even though they had not accomplished all of the U.S. goals, they still felt proud of their service to their country. They believed that they had done their duty and fought bravely for a good cause. They blamed America's political and military leaders for not coming up with a strategy that would allow them to win, or the American public for its lack of support.

But some other veterans developed grave doubts about the war and their own actions as soldiers. They questioned the reasons for U.S. involvement in Vietnam, and they felt deep

Agent Orange

The U.S. military used a wide range of chemicals to aid troops in combat during the Vietnam War. These chemicals included tear gas, smoke screens, napalm (a highly flammable form of jellied gasoline), and herbicides (chemicals used to kill plants or prevent their growth).

The U.S. military sprayed herbicides over large areas of the Vietnamese countryside during the war. Military leaders wanted to clear thick stands of jungle and forest where they believed enemy forces might be hiding. They also wanted to kill rice and other crops that might be used to supply enemy troops. In 1967 alone, American planes sprayed 4.8 million gallons of herbicide and destroyed 1.2 million acres of forests and farmland.

One of the common herbicides used in Vietnam was called Agent Orange, after the orange stripe on the drums used to transport the chemical. Agent Orange contained several toxic compounds, including dioxin and 2,4,5-T. By 1979, the U.S. Environmental Protection Agency had banned the use of these compounds because of concerns that they were harmful to humans and animals.

Many American soldiers were exposed to Agent Orange and other chemicals during their time in Vietnam. Upon returning home, some of these veterans began to experience health problems that they blamed on their exposure to herbicides. For example, they had high rates of skin rashes, nerve disorders, birth defects, and cancer. "I was exposed to dioxin from the Agent Orange that was sprayed all throughout the delta," Congressional Medal of Honor winner Sam Davis told Clark Dougan and Stephen Weiss in *The American Experience in Vietnam*. "Most of the things that are wrong with me today, except for my back problem, can be attributed to dioxin. Because of my exposure to it, my internal organs work at the rate of a seventy- or seventy-five-year-old man—which is really confusing when you're only forty."

In 1977, Vietnam veterans formed several groups in order to inform the American people about their illnesses and to try to raise money for research and support. The veterans' groups also sued the manufacturers of Agent Orange. In 1984, they received an out-of-court settlement of $180 million from the chemical companies. The following year, the U.S. government agreed to provide another $1 billion for research into the health effects of the wartime chemical use.

regret about the death and destruction the war had caused the Vietnamese people. Such doubts were very hard on veterans, because they made it seem as if their sacrifices in Vietnam had been meaningless.

African American veterans were particularly affected by doubts about their military service. They returned home to communities that had strong antiwar feelings. Black leaders had opposed the Vietnam War from the beginning because they felt it took the country's attention away from the civil rights movement and social programs designed to benefit the poor. "Black people would say there was no reason for a black man to be there," veteran Robert L. Young notes in *Vietnam Shadows*. "It's not his war. His war is here at home."

Some Vietnam veterans became active in the antiwar movement when they returned to the United States. In the later years of the conflict, veterans were among the most effective activists opposing the war. People on both sides respected their views and took them seriously. By 1971—when conflicts within the antiwar movement had reduced its effectiveness—Vietnam Veterans Against the War (VVAW) became one of the most important antiwar groups. (See box titled "Veterans Join the Fight against the War" in Chapter 8, "The American Antiwar Movement.")

Changing American views toward veterans

As waves of Vietnam veterans returned home in the late 1960s and early 1970s, the nation was locked in a bitter debate about the war. The heated arguments within the United States over military involvement in Vietnam kept most people from welcoming the veterans or recognizing their service. "Ignoring the Vietnam vet was just one part of the more general phenomenon of ignoring the nation's entire, shattering, unhappy Vietnam experience in all of its aspects," David Levy writes in *The Debate over Vietnam*.

By the 1980s, however, many Americans began to change their views of Vietnam veterans. They began to see that even if the war was wrong, most of the men who fought it were just ordinary guys doing their jobs. Many people started to feel sympathy and even gratitude toward the veterans. Soldiers who had served in Vietnam finally began receiving recognition and marching in holiday parades across the country. In 1985, *Newsweek* reported that "America's Vietnam veterans, once viewed with a mixture of indifference and outright hostility by their countrymen, are now widely regarded as national heroes."

Sources

Appy, Christian G. *Working-Class War: American Combat Soldiers and Vietnam.* Chapel Hill: University of North Carolina Press, 1993.

Dougan, Clark, and Stephen Weiss, eds. *The American Experience in Vietnam.* New York: W. W. Norton, 1988.

Figley, Charles R., and Seymour Leventman, eds. *Strangers at Home: Vietnam Veterans since the War.* New York: Praeger, 1980.

Helmer, John. *Bringing the War Home: The American Soldier in Vietnam and After.* New York: Free Press, 1974.

Hubbell, John, with Andrew Jones and Kenneth Y. Tomlinson. *P.O.W.: A Definitive History of the American Prisoner-of-War Experience in Vietnam, 1964–1973.* New York: Reader's Digest Press, 1976.

Isaacs, Arnold R. *Vietnam Shadows: The War, Its Ghosts, and Its Legacy.* Baltimore: Johns Hopkins University Press, 1997.

MacPherson, Myra. *Long Time Passing: Vietnam and the Haunted Generation.* Garden City, NY: Doubleday, 1984.

Starr, Paul. *The Discarded Army.* New York: Charterhouse, 1974.

The War's Effect on the Vietnamese Land and People

11

About 58,000 American soldiers were killed during the Vietnam War, and another 304,000 were wounded. Without a doubt, the war took a terrible toll on the United States. But since most of the fighting took place in Vietnam, the Vietnamese land and people paid a much heavier price for the war. An estimated 4 million Vietnamese were killed or wounded on both sides of the conflict, including as many as 1.3 million civilians (people not involved in the military, including women and children) in South Vietnam.

Much of the death and destruction resulted from bombing. The U.S. military used more than 14 million tons of explosives during the Vietnam War, mostly on the South Vietnamese countryside. This meant that American planes dropped more than twice as many bombs as U.S. forces had used during World War II (1939–45)—all on an area about the size of California. The U.S. military also sprayed millions of gallons of defoliants (chemical agents that killed or burned crops, forests, and other vegetation) on the South Vietnamese land during the war.

The widespread destruction of the farms and villages in the South Vietnamese countryside turned huge numbers of

Words to Know

Communism A political system in which the government controls all resources and means of producing wealth. By eliminating private property, this system is designed to create an equal society with no social classes. However, Communist goverments in practice often limit personal freedom and individual rights.

North Vietnam The Geneva Accords of 1954, which ended the First Indochina War (1946–54), divided the nation of Vietnam into two sections. The northern section, which was led by a Communist government under Ho Chi Minh, was officially known as the Democratic Republic of Vietnam, but was usually called North Vietnam.

South Vietnam Created under the Geneva Accords of 1954, the southern section of Vietnam was known as the Republic of South Vietnam. It was led by a U.S.-supported government.

Viet Cong Vietnamese Communist guerilla fighters who worked with the North Vietnamese Army to conquer South Vietnam.

peasants into homeless refugees. Many of these people fled to the cities, where they made a living any way they could—including through illegal activities. The poverty and desperation of the war years—along with the influence of Americans—resulted in major changes to Vietnamese families, culture, and society. "The United States, motivated by the loftiest intentions, did indeed rip South Vietnam's social fabric to shreds," Stanley Karnow comments in *Vietnam: A History.*

U.S. bombing destroys farms and forests

Before the Vietnam War, the South Vietnamese countryside was lush and green. Farmers tended rice paddies (wet fields where rice is grown) in fertile river valleys. The surrounding hillsides were covered with jungles of trees and plants. But when U.S. troops arrived in 1965, they learned that the jungles provided ideal hiding places for the Communist guerilla fighters known as the Viet Cong (guerrillas are small groups of fighters who launch surprise attacks). They also realized that the rice paddies and rural villages were good sources of food and supplies for the Viet Cong. To eliminate these sources of support for the enemy, the U.S. military bombed the South Vietnamese countryside using airplanes and heavy artillery for many years.

Across all of Indochina (the region of Southeast Asia that includes Vietnam, Cambodia, and Laos), the United States used an average of 142 pounds of explosives per acre of land. But most of the bombing was concentrated in South Vietnam, particularly the northern provinces

Three U.S. Air Force planes spraying Agent Orange over a field in South Vietnam, 1966. *Reproduced by permission of AP/World Wide Photos.*

and the area around the capital city of Saigon. The bombing did terrible damage to the land. It destroyed many of the dams and canals that the peasants had installed to irrigate their farmland. It also created huge craters in the rice paddies and hillsides. In fact, by the end of the war there were an estimated 21 million bomb craters in South Vietnam. "From the air some areas in Vietnam looked like photographs of the moon," researchers Arthur H. Westing and E. W. Pfeiffer wrote in *Scientific American*.

Waiting for News of Death

Thousands of Vietnamese soldiers from both the North and the South were killed during the Vietnam War. The deaths of loved ones took a terrible toll on the families left behind. The Communist government of North Vietnam sometimes made such loss even more difficult for the survivors.

North Vietnamese leaders worried that the people would lose their will to fight if they knew the true cost of the war. For this reason, they sometimes withheld information about killed or wounded soldiers from the men's wives or parents. The Communists also discouraged people from talking about their fears or mourning for their loved ones during the war. Instead, they expected people to concentrate their efforts on helping the North win.

In the following passage from David Chanoff's book *Vietnam: A Portrait of Its People at War*, a North Vietnamese woman named Nam Duc Mao remembers the loss of her brother-in-law:

Starting in 1968, they began sending men from our village to the South. If someone didn't want to go, he had his rations cut off. My sister's husband went. In 1970 my mother found out that he had been killed. My mother was an officer of the court, so she found out through friends of hers in the government. She told me, but neither of us was able to tell my sister. It was too risky. Nobody was allowed to talk about deaths or rumors of deaths, not until the official death notification came from the army. Up until then, if you talked about things like this it was considered anti-state [against the government], you were undermining people's morale. You would get into trouble or be sent to jail.

But it was very hard, because sometimes the wives didn't hear officially for years. But news would come indirectly that somebody's husband or son had been killed. It would come from messages sent by friends who were in the army or by other soldiers from the village, or in some other way. So sometimes a woman knew that her husband was dead, but she couldn't mourn out loud or she and the rest of her family would be in trouble with the police.

That's why my mother and I couldn't tell my sister. But I tried to keep her from hoping that he would come back. I especially wanted her to move out of her parents-in-law's house. I tried to persuade her to leave her husband's family and to live as if her husband were dead, even if she didn't know for sure that he was.

But I wasn't successful. My sister told me, "I'll wait for my husband to come home." I'd say, "It could be a terribly long time."

In addition to the widespread bombing, U.S. forces sprayed defoliants and herbicides (harsh chemicals that kill plants) on large sections of South Vietnam. "Air Force planes sprayed 18 million gallons of herbicide containing dioxins [toxic chemicals] on some six million acres—around one-seventh of South Vietnam's total land area, and a much higher proportion of its most fertile cropland and richest forests," James William Gibson reveals in *The Perfect War: The War We Could Not Lose and How We Did.* "An additional 1,200 square miles of territory were bulldozed flat, stripped of all life." Some military observers claim that the once-green land looked like it had been "torn apart by an angry giant" or mashed into a "gray porridge."

The combination of the bombing and the spraying of chemicals destroyed nearly half the crops in South Vietnam. Before the war, the country had been one of the largest exporters of rice in the world. But during the war, the loss of crops forced South Vietnam to import one million tons of rice each year. Much of this rice came from the United States. Despite the U.S. aid, however, hunger and starvation were common among rural people.

Some U.S. officials called for an end to the bombing, claiming that the destruction hurt the South Vietnamese without helping the U.S. cause. "There is nothing in the history of warfare to compare with [what we have done in Indochina]. A 'scorched earth' policy has been a tactic of warfare throughout history, but never before has a land been so massively altered and mutilated that vast areas can never be used again or even inhabited by man or animal," Senator Gaylord Nelson stated in 1972. "Our program of defoliation, carpet bombing with B-52s, and bulldozing . . . did not protect our soldiers or defeat the enemy, and it has done far greater damage to our ally than to the enemy."

South Vietnamese people become refugees

The destruction of the South Vietnamese countryside with bombs and defoliants took a terrible toll on the people who lived there. "For the common people, the war was a dreadful random infliction [cause of suffering] that on any given day or night could disrupt their lives, destroy their homes, wound their loved ones, or kill them outright," Kim Willenson writes in *The Bad War: An Oral History of the Vietnam War.* Many peo-

Kim Phuc, age 9, after ripping off her burning clothes as she and other terrified Vietnamese children try to escape a napalm attack.

Reproduced by permission of AP/World Wide Photos.

ple left the rural villages where their families had lived for generations and became refugees. In fact, as many as four million Vietnamese (one-fourth of the total population of the South) fled to the outskirts of cities and towns, where they hoped to escape the bombing and find a way to make a living.

Some American military leaders believed that destroying rural villages and grouping the South Vietnamese people near cities was a good strategy. They claimed that it would reduce support and supplies for the Viet Cong guerillas in the countryside. After areas were bombed, U.S. troops were sent into villages on "search-and-destroy" missions. The soldiers would question the local people and look for evidence of Viet Cong activity. But it was often difficult for the Americans to tell whether villagers were loyal to the South Vietnamese government or whether they supported the Communists. This uncertainty caused some soldiers to treat the villagers harshly. Even when the U.S. troops managed to clear a village of enemy agents, the Viet Cong usually returned within a short time.

Many South Vietnamese villagers were afraid to cooperate with either the Americans or the Viet Cong. They worried that if they did, the other side would punish them. This created a feeling of hopelessness among many rural South Vietnamese. "Most people didn't even know the difference between communism and democracy," recalled John Kerry, a Vietnam veteran who went on to become a U.S. senator. "They only wanted to work in rice paddies without helicopters strafing them and bombs with napalm burning their villages and tearing their country apart. They wanted everything to do with the war, particularly with this foreign presence of the United States of America, to leave them alone in peace, and they practiced the art of survival by siding with whichever military force was present at a particular time, be it Viet Cong, North Vietnamese, or American."

Stuck in the middle of fights between the Americans and the Viet Cong, and facing the constant threat of bombing, large numbers of South Vietnamese villagers fled to the cities. Before the war, ninety percent of South Vietnam's population had lived in rural villages in the countryside. But during the war, sixty percent of the population lived in urban areas. The cities were not equipped to handle the huge number of refugees. In Saigon, many peasants ended up living in makeshift refugee camps. "There were insufficient housing, sanitation, transportation, social services, and jobs to accommodate the tens of thousands of newcomers who settled in each month," Edward Doyle and Stephen Weiss write in *A Collision of Cultures: Americans in Vietnam, 1957–1973*. "In Saigon this provoked a state of emergency. Huge shantytowns encircled the city's prosperous center."

A Wall with Two Million Vietnamese Names

In 1982, the U.S. government dedicated a memorial to the American soldiers who died during the Vietnam War. The Vietnam Veterans Memorial in Washington, D.C., is a black granite wall nearly 500 feet long. The names of the 58,000 Americans killed in Vietnam are etched onto its face. There is no similar memorial to the estimated two million Vietnamese soldiers and civilians who were killed during the war. But if the names of these people were etched onto a wall, it would have to be 40 times larger than the American memorial—or close to four miles long.

Conditions in the refugee camps were very poor. There was no way to dispose of garbage and human waste, which polluted water supplies and spread disease. Unable to find jobs, many people went hungry or resorted to begging in the streets. Many refugees survived by collecting and recycling the things U.S. troops left behind. For example, some villagers would collect the brass shell casings that fell on the ground after American forces fired on the enemy. They would use the metal to create brass ashtrays to sell on the streets of Saigon.

The destruction of villages also separated families and eliminated the family structure that was so important to Vietnamese culture. By 1972—when the United States was removing its troops from Vietnam— there were an estimated 800,000 orphaned children roaming the streets of Saigon and other cities. "The refugees, uprooted from the devastated land and fearful of renewed offensives, remained in the cities and towns—their disrupted, dispirited families aggravating the instability of South Vietnam's already fragile society," Stanley Karnow writes in *Vietnam: A History.*

Transformation of Saigon

The influx of refugees and the presence of Americans brought vast changes to South Vietnamese cities, especially the capital city of Saigon. The population of Saigon tripled during the Vietnam War to reach three million in 1970. Most of these new people were refugees whose homes in the countryside had been destroyed. But the city also became the central location for thousands of American military leaders, journalists, aid workers, missionaries, businessmen, and construction workers during the war years.

The Americans tended to be quite wealthy compared to the South Vietnamese. They created a new market for luxury goods like cars, motorcycles, televisions, and stereos. The wealth and comfort of the Americans sometimes provided a sad contrast to the poverty and desperation of the local people in Saigon. For example, reporter Stanley Karnow remembers standing on the terrace of the fancy Continental Palace Hotel, "where limbless Vietnamese victims of the war would crawl like crabs across the handsome tile floor to accost [confront and demand money from] American soldiers, construction workers, journalists, and visitors as they chatted and sipped their drinks under the ceiling fans."

Before long, the American influence began to have negative effects on the social structure in Saigon. Thousands of Vietnamese found jobs in service industries that sprang up to cater to the Americans. Some worked in hotels, restaurants, or construction sites, but many others became involved in illegal activities. For example, an estimated 500,000 South Vietnamese women became prostitutes during the war. Many of these women were poor peasants who had no other way of feeding their families. There was also an active drug trade in Saigon during the war. Drugs like marijuana, opium, and heroin were readily available in the city. In fact, they were sometimes sold by children on street corners. Finally, there was an enormous black market for stolen goods in Saigon. Many of the items for sale came from U.S. military shipments.

Many South Vietnamese people found it tempting to become involved in such illegal activities. After all, a young woman who worked as a prostitute could earn more money in a week than her peasant family would ordinarily earn in a year. Some Vietnamese used their newfound wealth to buy luxury goods such as electric rice cookers, bicycles, and televisions. These people formed a new, privileged urban class that turned the structure of Saigon society upside down. Suddenly, construction workers and drug dealers made much more money than policemen and soldiers in the South Vietnamese army.

Over time, people's values changed to reflect the new order in the city. They began to prefer the jobs that would enable them to purchase luxuries, even if these jobs were illegal or immoral. Many of these changes in people's behavior and relationships lasted long after the war ended. Some observers blamed the situation on the American influence. "Saigon was an addicted city, and we were the drug," James Fenton wrote in *Granta*. "The corruption of children, the mutilation of young men, the prostitution of women, the humiliation of the old, the division of the family, the division of the country—it had all been done in our name."

Effects on the North

Despite the fact that South Vietnam was America's ally in the Vietnam War, it suffered severe damage to its land, people, and culture. The war also affected North Vietnam, but not as severely or as permanently as the South. After all, most of the heavy fighting took place in the South. The United States never launched a full-scale invasion of North Vietnam, because U.S. leaders worried that such an action might provoke neighboring China into joining the fight.

Still, the U.S. military dropped one million tons of bombs on North Vietnam during the war. The idea behind the bombing was to break the will of the Communist government, and to destroy their ability to fight and send supplies to the South. For this reason, most of the bombing targeted urban areas of North Vietnam. The U.S. bombing campaigns did severe damage to over 70 percent of the industries in the North, which cut the amount of goods the country was able to produce in half. The bombing also destroyed thousands of buildings, damaged 4,000 villages, and occasionally hit schools, churches, and hospitals.

Another major target was North Vietnam's network of roads and railroad lines. These transportation routes were hit

Vietnamese mother carrying her severely burned child down Route One, after a misdirected napalm attack.
Reproduced by permission of AP/World Wide Photos.

with an average of 24 bombs per kilometer. Author Michael Maclear traveled one highway in North Vietnam for 250 miles in 1969. A journey that would have once taken four hours ended up taking four days. "The awesome bomb craters along the 'highway' interlocked almost end to end, negotiable only by jeep," he recalls in *The Ten Thousand Day War*. "There was just a very rough route stitched from broken-down rock, thousands of loose planks and nerve-wracking bamboo platforms bridging the craters and canals. Wrecked vehicles and twisted rail lines littered the entire route, with rusted metal rising in grotesque shapes from the adjacent rice-lands."

The North Vietnamese government took a number of steps to reduce the impact of the U.S. bombing. For example, they spread some industries out into the countryside, and they built networks of tunnels and shelters to protect people in the cities. Citizens were required to wear camouflage clothing to avoid attracting the attention of American planes. "I remember once driving through an area and to my great astonishment the whole field of maize [corn] suddenly got to its feet and charged across the road," British reporter Wilfred Burchett recalled. The bombing did force the Communists to devote some of their manpower to rebuilding tasks, which reduced the number of people who were available to fight in the South. But most of the roads, buildings, and factories were eventually rebuilt with aid from the Soviet Union and China.

Since most of the bombing in North Vietnam was aimed at urban areas, it did not destroy as much farmland in the North as it did in the South. One study estimated that only 5.6 percent of North Vietnamese farmland suffered severe damage during the war. But since many peasant men were recruited to join the North Vietnamese Army, many of the farming tasks were performed by women during the war years. Women worked in the rice paddies and created new, cooperative systems of growing and irrigation that required fewer people.

Sources

Chanoff, David. *Vietnam: A Portrait of Its People at War*. New York: Tauris/St. Martin's, 1996.

Doyle, Edward, and Stephen Weiss. *A Collision of Cultures: The Americans in Vietnam, 1954–1973*. Boston: Boston Publishing Company, 1984.

Fenton, James. "The Fall of Saigon." *Granta,* no. 15, 1985.

FitzGerald, Frances. *Fire in the Lake: The Vietnamese and the Americans in Vietnam.* Boston: Little, Brown, 1972.

Gibson, James William. *The Perfect War: The War We Couldn't Lose and How We Did.* Boston: Atlantic Monthly Press, 1986.

Hawthorne, Lesleyanne, ed. *Refugee: The Vietnamese Experience.* New York: Oxford University Press, 1982.

Herrington, Stuart A. *Silence Was a Weapon: The Vietnam War in the Villages.* Novato, CA: Presidio Press, 1982.

Karnow, Stanley. *Vietnam: A History.* New York: Viking, 1983.

Maclear, Michael. *The Ten Thousand Day War: Vietnam, 1945–1975.* New York: Avon, 1981.

Schell, Jonathan. *The Real War: The Classic Reporting on the Vietnam War.* New York: Pantheon, 1987.

Westing, Arthur H., and E. W. Pfeiffer. "The Cratering of Indochina." *Scientific American,* May 1972.

Willenson, Kim. *The Bad War: An Oral History of the Vietnam War.* New York: New American Library, 1987.

Nixon's War (1969–70)

12

When Richard M. Nixon (1913–1994; president 1969–1974) became president of the United States in January 1969, he promised to guide America out of the Vietnam War by pursuing a policy of "peace with honor." This meant that the withdrawal of American forces from Vietnam would have to take place in a way that avoided any appearance of defeat.

After assuming office, Nixon and his advisors first considered a strategy of intensified attacks on North Vietnam. But the president reluctantly decided that escalation [increased military operations] would probably not bring about a negotiated peace agreement. Instead, the Nixon administration pursued a plan called "Vietnamization," in which primary responsibility for fighting the North shifted from the U.S. military to South Vietnamese armed forces. As a result of this strategy, American troop commitments in Vietnam began to drop for the first time since 1965.

But events in Indochina continued to produce angry divisions throughout America. Reports of U.S. war crimes surged upward, creating serious questions about the conduct of American soldiers in Vietnam. In addition, American involvement in

Words to Know

ARVN The South Vietnamese army, officially known as the Army of the Republic of South Vietnam. The ARVN fought on the same side as U.S. troops during the Vietnam War.

Cambodia Southeast Asian nation located on the western border of South Vietnam. During the Vietnam War, Cambodia experienced its own civil war between its pro-U.S. government and Communist rebels known as the Khmer Rouge.

Communism A political system in which the government controls all resources and means of producing wealth. By eliminating private property, this system is designed to create an equal society with no social classes. However, Communist goverments in practice often limit personal freedom and individual rights.

Escalation A policy of increasing the size, scope, and intensity of military activity.

Indochina The name sometimes given to the peninsula between India and China in Southeast Asia. The term narrowly refers to Cambodia, Laos, and Vietnam, which were united under the name French Indochina during the colonial period, 1893–1954.

Khmer Rouge Communist-led rebel forces that fought for control of Cambodia during the Vietnam War years. The Khmer Rouge overthrew the U.S.-backed government of Lon Nol in 1975.

North Vietnam The Geneva Accords of 1954, which ended the First Indochina War (1946–54), divided the nation of Vietnam into two sections. The northern section, which was led by a Communist government under Ho Chi

neighboring Cambodia began to increase. This development sparked widespread fears that the Vietnam War might spread beyond its borders. America's domestic turmoil did not peak until mid-1970, when four college students were shot to death on the campus of Kent State University during an antiwar rally.

Frustrating negotiations with the North

Upon assuming office, President Nixon repeatedly told members of his administration that he would not let the Vietnam War ruin his presidency. "I'm not going to end up like

Minh, was officially known as the Democratic Republic of Vietnam, but was usually called North Vietnam.

NVA The North Vietnamese Army, which assisted the Viet Cong guerilla fighters in trying to conquer South Vietnam. These forces opposed the United States in the Vietnam War.

Saigon The capital city of U.S.-supported South Vietnam. Also an unofficial shorthand way of referring to the South Vietnamese government.

Silent Majority A term used by U.S. President Richard Nixon to describe the large number of American people he believed quietly supported his Vietnam War policies. In contrast, Nixon referred to the antiwar movement in the United States as a vocal minority.

South Vietnam Created under the Geneva Accords of 1954, the southern section of Vietnam was known as the Republic of South Vietnam. It was led by a U.S.-supported government.

Tonkin Gulf Resolution Passed by Congress after U.S. Navy ships supposedly came under attack in the Gulf of Tonkin, this resolution gave U.S. President Lyndon Johnson the authority to wage war against North Vietnam.

Viet Cong Vietnamese Communist guerilla fighters who worked with the North Vietnamese Army to conquer South Vietnam.

Vietnamization A policy proposed by U.S. President Richard Nixon that involved returning responsibility for the war to the South Vietnamese. It was intended to allow the United States to reduce its military involvement without allowing the country to fall to communism.

[President] Lyndon Johnson, holed up in the White House, afraid to show my face on the street," said Nixon. "I'm going to end the war in Vietnam. Fast." With this in mind, Nixon indicated that he was willing to end the war if North Vietnam's Communist government would agree to what he called a "fair negotiated settlement that would preserve the independence of South Vietnam." At a minimum, Nixon wanted to negotiate a treaty that would give the South a chance to hold off the North after American troops left the region.

At first, Nixon tried to convince North Vietnam's Communist leaders that the United States might initiate a

People to Know

Ho Chi Minh (1890–1969) Vietnamese Communist leader who led Viet Minh forces in opposing French rule and became the first president of North Vietnam in 1954. He also led the North during the Vietnam War until his death.

Lyndon B. Johnson (1908–1973) After serving as vice president under John Kennedy, he became the 36th president of the United States after Kennedy was assassinated in 1963. Johnson sent U.S. combat troops to Vietnam. Opposition to his policies convinced him not to seek re-election in 1968.

Henry Kissinger (1923–) U.S. national security advisor (1969–1975) and secretary of state (1973–1977) during the Nixon administration. Represented the United States in peace negotiations with North Vietnam

Lon Nol (1913–1985) Cambodian military and political leader who overthrew the government of Prince Norodom Sihanouk in 1970. Despite U.S. military assistance, he was removed from power by Communist Khmer Rouge forces in 1975.

Nguyen Van Thieu (1923–) President of South Vietnam, 1967–1973.

Richard M. Nixon (1913–1994) Elected as the 37th president of the United States in 1969, at the height of the Vietnam War. Resigned from office during the Watergate scandal in 1974.

Prince Norodom Sihanouk (1923–) Member of the royal family that ruled Cambodia, 1941–70. After his government was overthrown by Lon Nol, he supported the Communist Khmer Rouge forces that were trying to take control of Cambodia.

ruthless and punishing military offensive against the North if an acceptable peace agreement was not reached. This strategy was based in part on the president's genuine belief that the United States had used its military ineffectively over the previous few years in Vietnam. "Nixon felt that military pressure had failed thus far because it had been employed in a limited, indecisive manner," writes George C. Herring in *America's Longest War*. The president abandoned plans for a major increase in American military operations only after being persuaded that it would not produce a quick victory.

Still, Nixon, National Security Advisor Henry Kissinger (1923–), and other administration officials continued to discuss options for expanding the war. In addition, they came to see the *threat* of escalation as a weapon that could be used against the Communists. At one point they even resorted to a so-called "madman strategy" in an effort to drag North Vietnam to the negotiating table. In this scheme, Nixon administration officials quietly told reporters that the president was considering the use of nuclear weapons against the North. The administration hoped that rumors of nuclear attack might convince North Vietnam to end the war.

The North did agree to hold peace talks with the United States. For the most part, however, the Communists showed little interest in compromise at the negotiations. The negotiators for the North believed that sooner or later the domestic unrest in the United States would force the Americans to abandon South Vietnam, leaving the Saigon-based government defenseless against the North. This belief gave them the strength to continue the war, even though the conflict had produced great devastation and loss of life in both the North and the South. As North Vietnamese Premier Pham Van Dong said, "Americans do not like long, inconclusive wars—and this is going to be a long, inconclusive war. Thus we are sure to win in the end."

In his first term as president, Richard Nixon carried out a "Vietnamization" policy to remove U.S. troops from Vietnam and replace them by members of the South Vietnamese army. Many U.S. troops remained, however, and the Nixon administration even expanded the war into Cambodia and Laos. *Reproduced by permission of the Library of Congress.*

"Vietnamization"

After rejecting military options that required increased U.S. commitments of troops and weaponry in Vietnam, the Nixon administration turned instead to a strategy called "Vietnamization." Under this new policy, American forces would gradually transfer responsibility for Saigon's defense to the South Vietnamese military, freeing U.S. troops to return home. "The key new element in our strategy was a plan for the complete withdrawal of all American combat forces from Vietnam," Nixon explains in *No More Vietnams*. "Americans needed tangible evidence that we were winding down the war, and the South Vietnamese needed to be given more responsibility for their defense . . . . As South Vietnamese forces became stronger, the rate of American withdrawal could become greater."

Nixon launched this policy in the spring of 1969 without consulting the South Vietnamese government of President Nguyen Van Thieu (1923–). Thieu and many other South Vietnamese reacted bitterly to the decision. They resented the suggestion that the South Vietnamese had been nothing more than bystanders in the war over the previous several years. They also worried that the United States was using Vietnamization as a way to exit the war with its pride intact, without regard for the future of the South. Thieu and other South Vietnamese leaders recognized that when the United States departed, their government would be more vulnerable to the Communist forces of North Vietnam.

Still, Thieu and South Vietnam's military leadership had no choice but to accept Nixon's Vietnamization policy. The Vietnamization process began over the next several months. U.S. military personnel scrambled to prepare the South's armed forces to take on increased responsibilities for the war effort. American advisors strengthened and modernized many aspects of South Vietnam's army, navy, and air force. Their efforts helped improve the performance of South Vietnam's military in several critical areas, although high rates of desertion (soldiers leaving the military illegally before their term of services has ended), corruption in the officer corps, and other problems remained.

In addition, U.S. ships transported huge quantities of rifles, helicopters, planes, ships, grenade launchers, boots, and other supplies to South Vietnam to outfit its armed forces. Finally, U.S. troops launched a series of attacks on North Vietnamese supply lines and military bases in order to keep the enemy from taking advantage of this transition period. By mid-1969, the process of "Vietnamization" was in full swing.

The secret bombing of Cambodia

But even as the Nixon administration moved to reduce America's presence in Vietnam, it expanded its wartime activities into Cambodia, Vietnam's neighbor to the southwest. Ever since the early stages of the Vietnam War, Cambodia had adopted a neutral position in the conflict. But as the war progressed, the jungles of Cambodia became an important base for Communist Vietnamese activity. Many of the North's main supply routes and military roads—including the famous Ho Chi Minh Trail—ran through eastern Cambodia.

In addition, many Viet Cong and North Vietnamese Army (NVA) units used the thick forests of Cambodia for secret bases in their war against the South. Finally, North Vietnam provided significant assistance to Cambodian Communists, who were fighting to overthrow Cambodian leader Prince Norodom Sihanouk (1923–) and his government. By the late 1960s, these Communist rebels—known as the Khmer Rouge—had grown into a major threat to Sihanouk's rule.

In early 1969, Sihanouk appealed to the United States for help in dealing with the Khmer Rouge and their NVA allies. Nixon responded by authorizing a major bombing campaign against North Vietnamese sanctuaries in eastern Cambodia. He and his advisors believed that they could accomplish many goals by targeting key NVA bases in Cambodia. They could disrupt Communist supply routes, prevent the North from taking advantage of future U.S. troop withdrawals, and help Sihanouk fight off the Khmer Rouge. But Nixon knew that the American people would view his decision to bomb Cambodia as an escalation of the war. After all, the U.S. military had not operated in neutral Cambodia in the past. To avoid creating an uproar, the president concealed this bombing campaign from both the U.S. Congress and the American public.

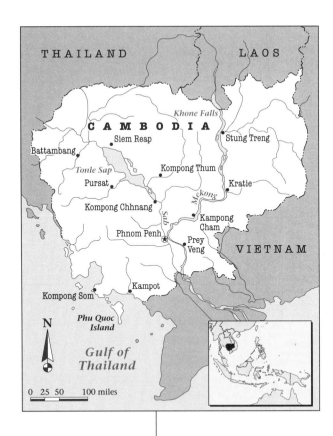

Cambodia and surrounding area.
Map by XNR Productions, Inc. Reproduced by permission of Gale Group.

During the course of the bombing campaign, which lasted from March 1969 to August 1973, American planes dropped an estimated 110,000 tons of bombs on Cambodia. The air strikes continued even after Sihanouk's prime minister, Lon Nol (1913–1985), displaced Sihanouk as the nation's ruler in a 1970 coup (overthrow of the government). After seizing power, Lon Nol tolerated the continued U.S. air strikes because his government was very dependent on American military and economic aid. Many historians, however, believe that the bombing campaign merely pushed the Communists deeper into Cambodian territory, where they became an even greater threat. In the meantime, Sihanouk joined with the Khmer Rouge—his former enemies—in hopes of regaining power.

The death of Ho Chi Minh

On September 2, 1969, longtime North Vietnamese leader Ho Chi Minh (1890–1969) died. His death attracted worldwide attention and triggered a period of national mourning in the North. The government in Hanoi remained strong, however. In fact, veteran revolutionaries like Le Duan, Pham Van Dong, and Vo Nguyen Giap (1911–) had assumed responsibility for many of North Vietnam's domestic and war policies during the mid-1960s. "Like Ho, they regarded the defeat of the United States and its South Vietnamese allies to be a sacred duty," writes Stanley Karnow in *Vietnam: A History*.

Despite the unyielding reputation of North Vietnam's political leadership, some members of the Nixon administration privately expressed hope that the death of Ho—the most famous revolutionary leader in Vietnamese history—might produce a change in North Vietnam's negotiating position. After all, the war had taken a heavy toll on Communist positions throughout the South, as well as the cities and towns of the North, over the previous few years. Moreover, Nixon's decision to approve secret bombing runs in Cambodia showed the North that the United States remained a dangerous enemy that remained willing to use punishing force.

But the North's leadership did not budge from its two longtime conditions for peace: 1) unconditional withdrawal of American troops from Vietnam, and 2) formation of a new government in South Vietnam with Communist representation. The North never wavered from these positions because it continued to believe that it could outlast the United States in the war. In fact, North Vietnamese confidence in an eventual American withdrawal was so great that Northern diplomats admitted that they were willing to sit at the negotiation table "until the chairs rot" before they would compromise on their basic goals.

Moratorium Day

Nixon's promise to begin withdrawing American troops from Vietnam in 1969 quieted some of the antiwar protests that had rocked the United States during the final years of the Johnson administration. In addition, disputes within the antiwar movement over strategy and goals decreased its effectiveness during this time. But the antiwar movement remained a potent force in the United States. As the weeks passed, its membership argued that Nixon was withdrawing American soldiers too slowly. They noted that between the time Nixon took office in January 1969 and the first withdrawal of American troops in August 1969, another 7,000 U.S. soldiers had been killed in Vietnam.

In an effort to push Nixon to end the war more quickly, members of the antiwar movement organized the first of a monthly series of nationwide protests on October 15, 1969. During this protest, which came to be known as Moratorium Day, Americans signaled their antiwar feelings in a variety of ways. Millions of American workers and students took a day off from work or classes to demonstrate against the war. Huge antiwar crowds assembled in New York, Boston, and other large cities, and smaller rallies were held in dozens of other cities and towns across the nation. One of the most publicized of these rallies took place in Washington, D.C., as Coretta King (1927–)—wife of murdered civil rights leader Martin Luther King Jr. (1929–1968)—led 30,000 people in a silent candlelight vigil past the White House.

Nixon's "Silent Majority"

The Moratorium Day demonstrations alarmed and angered the Nixon administration. Some members of the

Nixon White House privately shared the antiwar sentiments of the demonstrators. But most others, including the president himself, viewed the antiwar movement with great hostility. As Jeffrey Kimball writes in *Nixon's Vietnam War*, "the president worried a great deal about the impact of protest on the 'condition of the country' and on his ability to wage the war effectively." As a result, the Nixon administration decided to launch an all-out public relations campaign to reduce the strength of the antiwar movement in the weeks following the Moratorium Day demonstrations.

The first and most important element of the administration's new campaign was a speech delivered by Nixon. This speech—later dubbed his "Silent Majority" speech—proved to be a very effective weapon in the war to win the support of America's confused and war-weary population.

Nixon's speech, delivered to a national television audience on November 3, 1969, was designed to rally public support for his policies in Vietnam. During this speech, the president insisted that the war in Vietnam was of great importance to America's future. "For the United States, the first defeat in our nation's history would result in a collapse of confidence in American leadership, not only in Asia, but throughout the world," he said.

Nixon also defended his strategy for ending the war. He explained his Vietnamization policy in appealing terms, describing it as a plan that would reduce American casualties and eventually end U.S. involvement in the conflict, while also preserving American pride. In addition, he tried to enlist the support of average Americans by describing the war as a patriotic struggle to defend American ideals. He assured listeners that he could bring the war to a satisfactory conclusion with the support of the nation's patriotic "Silent Majority." Finally, he denounced the antiwar movement as a noisy minority intent on leading the nation down the path of ruin. Nixon urged the American public to resist the demonstrators. "North Vietnam cannot humiliate the United States," he declared. "Only Americans can do that."

In the days following Nixon's "Silent Majority" speech, the White House followed up with a series of demonstrations, speeches, and other activities meant to generate additional support for the president and his Vietnam policies. "Primarily targeted at energizing the Silent Majority, the campaign's major themes were support for the war, the president, the country, veterans, and POWs," writes Kimball. "The icon [symbol] of the effort was the American flag, which was waved, raised, reproduced on automobile bumper stickers, and worn as a political button or lapel pin. Associating his Vietnam policies with the flag, America's only universal symbol of patriotism, Nixon identified the opponents of the war as unpatriotic scoundrels."

The Nixon administration's attacks on the American antiwar movement proved effective in some ways. The "Silent Majority" speech and other actions produced greater support for Nixon's policies in Vietnam. The campaign also succeeded in increasing negative public opinion of antiwar demonstrators. But the administration's efforts failed to silence the movement or erase the doubts that millions of other Americans continued to hold about the war.

Nixon approves invasion of Cambodia

In March 1970, Nixon delighted the American public by announcing his intention to withdraw 150,000 U.S. soldiers in Vietnam by the end of year. To many Americans, his announcement seemed to be the surest sign yet that U.S. involvement in the nightmarish war was finally drawing to a close. Even veteran antiwar activists reacted favorably to Nixon's withdrawal notice. But one month later, on April 30, Nixon told the American people that he had authorized a major military operation into Cambodia, Vietnam's neighbor to the west. This decision stunned the war-weary American public.

The move into eastern Cambodia was undertaken by a joint U.S. and South Vietnamese force. During the invasion (or "incursion," as Nixon called it), American and South Vietnamese units targeted enemy bases throughout the country's remote eastern forests. Their tanks, helicopters, and infantry forces roamed through the region for two months before withdrawing back into Vietnam.

Nixon claimed that he authorized the April advance into Cambodia because of a growing Communist threat within its borders. "A Communist-dominated Cambodia would have placed South Vietnam in an untenable [impossible] military situation and would have endangered the lives of thousands of United States troops," Nixon explains in *No More Vietnams*. "I therefore decided the time had come to take action against the Communist sanctuaries in Cambodia, both to relieve the pressure on Phnom Penh [the capital of Cambodia] and to reduce the threat these North Vietnamese bases posed to South Vietnam."

After the operation was over, the Nixon administration described it as a big success. In fact, Nixon later says in *No More Vietnams* that the incursion into Cambodia "was the most successful military operation of the entire Vietnam War." He claimed that the incursion saved Cambodia from falling under Communist control and that it significantly damaged North Vietnam's military operations in the region. Many historians agree with Nixon's view. "From a military point of view, the incursion was a success," writes Harry G. Summers Jr., in *Historical Atlas of the Vietnam War*. "The pressure on Lon Nol had been relieved and the NVA offensive had been set back for two years, lessening the dangers to the U.S. withdrawal. As President Nixon said on June 30, 'We have bought time for the South Vietnamese to strengthen themselves against the enemy.'"

But other historians claim that Nixon's invasion of Cambodia did not significantly change the situation in Vietnam. They also believe that American involvement in the country helped usher in a horrible civil war that killed millions of Cambodians during the 1970s. "The effect [of the invasion] on the war in Vietnam was nil [zero]," claims Marilyn B. Young, author of *The Vietnam Wars: 1945–1990*. "The effect on Cambodia was devastating."

Young and other critics charge that the invasion of Cambodia, combined with the U.S. bombing campaign that remained in effect, only drove the NVA deeper into Cambodian territory. They also claim that Nixon's 1970 invasion led North Vietnam to increase its support for the Khmer Rouge Communist rebels who were fighting to overthrow Lon Nol's U.S.-supported regime. "In the particularly brutal civil war that followed [between Lon Nol and the Khmer Rouge], the United States lavishly supported the Cambodian government and unleashed thousands of tons of bombs on Cambodia," states Young. "The ultimate tragedy was that from beginning to end, the Nixon administration viewed its new ally as little more than a pawn to be used to help salvage the U.S. position in Vietnam, showing scant [little] regard for the consequences for Cambodia and its people."

Nationwide protests against Nixon

Nixon's decision to invade Cambodia enraged the antiwar movement and shocked the general public. Only days earlier, the general feeling among the American people was that Nixon was gradually guiding the United States out of Vietnam, just as he had promised. For this reason, the president's decision to charge into Cambodia sparked anger and disillusionment among many Americans. They suddenly became worried that the Vietnam War might spread throughout all of Indochina.

Massive antiwar protests broke out at hundreds of college campuses all across the country in the days following the invasion of Cambodia. Rallies against the war were also organized in dozens of other communities nationwide. These protests triggered angry reactions from Nixon, who referred to the protestors as "bums," as well as millions of Americans who supported the president's Vietnam policies.

The turmoil on American college campuses came to a shocking climax on May 4, 1970. A National Guard unit stationed at Kent State University in Ohio fired into a crowd of student protestors, killing four students and wounding nine others. Two days later, two more student protestors were killed at Jackson State College in Mississippi. The deaths of these students sparked a new explosion of demonstrations at universities and colleges from California to New England. More than 500 campuses were temporarily shut down as a result of the demonstrations, and 51 were closed for the remainder of the academic year.

Anger in Congress

Nixon's decision to send troops into Cambodia also aroused considerable anger in Congress, where antiwar sentiment was growing steadily stronger. In fact, "the Cambodian incursion . . . provoked the most serious congressional challenge to presidential authority since the beginning of the war," writes George Herring in *America's Longest War*. "The president

The My Lai Massacre

The My Lai Massacre was one of the most horrible events of the entire Vietnam War. It took place on March 16, 1968, in My Lai, a small hamlet located in northern South Vietnam. On that day, a squad of U.S. soldiers commanded by Lt. William Calley entered the village. Charged with searching for enemy forces, the soldiers quickly determined that the hamlet and its civilian population—primarily women, children, and elderly people—posed no danger to them.

But rather than move on, the soldiers abruptly went on a murderous killing spree, massacring between 300 and 500 unarmed villagers over a period of several hours. During this time, the soldiers torched houses, raped dozens of women and children, and shot or stabbed terrified villagers who tried to escape. The American troops executed most of the villagers by lining them up in ditches and shooting them in heavy bursts of rifle fire.

The slaughter ended when U.S. helicopter pilot Hugh C. Thompson flew over My Lai during a reconnaissance (information gathering) mission. Alarmed by the scene below, he quickly landed his helicopter in the village. Once he landed, the pilot realized that Calley and his platoon intended to wipe out the entire village. Thompson knew that he could not stop the slaughter by himself. But he immediately loaded a large group of terrified villagers onto his helicopter to evacuate them, instructing his door gunner to shoot Calley if he interfered.

After the slaughter was over, Calley's commander, Captain Ernest L. Medina, covered up the incident in his reports. Thompson submitted his own report on the atrocities (extremely cruel or brutal acts) committed at My Lai, but his account was ignored until March 1969. At that time, an American ex-soldier named Ronald Ridenhour heard rumors about the massacre and sent a series of letters to military authorities. Ridenhour's letters triggered an investigation headed by Lieutenant General William R. Peers.

The investigation was kept quiet until November 1969, when *New York Times* reporter Seymour Hersh learned of the incident. His report on the massacre, which appeared in the *New York Times* and other newspapers across the country on

had consulted with only a handful of legislators [before approving the operation], all of them sympathetic. Many, including Senate Minority Leader Hugh Scott, were outraged at having been kept in the dark, and others were infuriated by Nixon's broadening of the war."

Lt. William Calley (far right).
Reproduced by permission of the
Columbus Ledger–Enquirer.

November 13, shocked an already war-weary American public.

Over the next few months, Calley, Medina, and two dozen other American soldiers received military trials on a variety of charges, from murder to covering up evidence of the atrocity. Calley alone was charged with 102 counts of murder. In the meantime, the U.S. Congress and the American public engaged in a fierce debate over the massacre and Calley's role in it. Many people—including many American soldiers and officials—were horrified by the incident and wanted to see Calley and the others punished for their war crimes. But many other people actually defended Calley as a pawn in the larger debate over the war. "To supporters of the war, Calley was being railroaded by the antiwar protestors [for doing his duty]," explains Harry G. Summers Jr., in *Historical Atlas of the Vietnam War*. "To the latter, he was being unfairly singled out, for they believed that such atrocities were commonplace, and were condoned [accepted] and even encouraged by the Army itself."

Calley was sentenced to life in prison for the murder of 22 Vietnamese civilians on March 29, 1971. All the other soldiers brought to trial were acquitted (found not guilty) of the charges. But many Americans expressed anger at the sentence imposed on Calley. In August, Calley's sentence was reduced to ten years by Secretary of the Army Howard Calloway. On November 9, 1974, President Nixon ordered Calley released from prison with a dishonorable discharge from the Army.

On June 26, 1970, the Senate voted to repeal (abolish) the Tonkin Gulf Resolution. This 1964 resolution had given presidents Lyndon Johnson (1908–1973; president 1963–1969) and Nixon authority to "take all necessary measures" against Communist forces in Indochina. Both presidents had

Honor guards in front of a memorial to the My Lai Massacre, where 504 people died.
Reproduced by permission of AP/World Wide Photos.

used the broad authority of the resolution to take whatever actions they wanted in Vietnam, without asking the permission of Congress. In December, the House of Representatives voted to repeal the measure as well.

The congressional repeal of the resolution did not strip Nixon of his power to conduct the war as he wanted. After the repeal, he used his constitutional authority as commander in chief to pursue his military goals in Vietnam. But the congressional decision to revoke the resolution did symbolize the nation's deep unhappiness with the war. It was widely interpreted as a way of punishing Nixon for his actions in Cambodia.

The My Lai Massacre revealed

In November 1970, the war-weary American public received yet another shock that increased calls for a swift withdrawal of all U.S. troops from Vietnam. The *New York Times* revealed that in March 1968, a platoon of U.S. soldiers had murdered hundreds of unarmed Vietnamese civilians—mostly women and children—in the hamlet of My Lai. The newspaper also reported that army investigators had known of the massacre for eighteen months but covered it up.

News of the My Lai incident and the army cover-up triggered strong emotions of shame, disgust, and anger among millions of ordinary Americans. They were joined by antiwar activists, who saw the My Lai massacre as a horrible symbol of an immoral and vicious war. They claimed that the incident showed that the war was turning young American men into monsters. But millions of Americans refused to believe that the incident had even taken place. They could not imagine U.S. soldiers taking part in such a terrible slaughter of innocent people.

Sources

Ambrose, Stephen E. *Nixon*. 3 vols. New York: Simon and Schuster, 1987–1991.

Garfinkle, Adam. *Telltale Hearts: The Origins and Impact of the Vietnam Antiwar Movement*. New York: St. Martin's Press, 1995.

Gibson, James W. *The Perfect War: The War We Couldn't Lose and How We Did*. New York: Atlantic Monthly Press, 1986.

Herring, George C. *America's Longest War: The United States and Vietnam, 1950–1975*. New York: McGraw-Hill, 1979.

Kimball, Jeffrey. *Nixon's Vietnam War*. Lawrence, KS: University Press of Kansas, 1998.

Levy, David. *The Debate Over Vietnam*. Baltimore: Johns Hopkins University Press, 1991.

Nixon, Richard. *No More Vietnams*. New York: Arbor House, 1985.

Schulzinger, Robert D. *A Time for War: The United States and Vietnam, 1941–1975*. New York: Oxford University Press, 1997.

Shawcross, William. *Sideshow: Kissinger, Nixon, and the Destruction of Cambodia*. New York: Simon and Schuster, 1979.

Summers, Harry Jr. *Historical Atlas of the Vietnam War*. Boston: Houghton Mifflin, 1995.

Wicker, Tom. *One of Us: Richard Nixon and the American Dream*. New York: Random House, 1991.

Young, Marilyn B. *The Vietnam Wars, 1945–1990*. New York: HarperCollins, 1991.

America Withdraws from Vietnam (1971–73)

13

The United States continued to withdraw its troops from Vietnam throughout the early 1970s. At the same time, America transferred its many military responsibilities over to the South Vietnamese Army (ARVN) as part of its "Vietnamization" strategy. But even as the size of the U.S. ground forces steadily declined, South Vietnam remained heavily dependent on American air power. In fact, U.S. bombers, helicopter gun ships, and other aircraft were essential to the South, both offensively and defensively. U.S. air power was particularly important in turning back North Vietnam's 1972 Easter Offensive.

In late 1972, the endless peace negotiations between the United States and North Vietnam finally took a promising turn. When the negotiations faltered once again in December, President Richard Nixon (1913–1994; president 1969–1974) approved the so-called "Christmas Bombing" of North Vietnam. Talks resumed a short time later, and in January 1973 the two sides reached agreement on a treaty that finally ended U.S. military involvement in Vietnam. South Vietnam's President Nguyen Van Thieu (1923–) bitterly opposed the deal, for he

Words to Know

ARVN The South Vietnamese army, officially known as the Army of the Republic of South Vietnam. The ARVN fought on the same side as U.S. troops during the Vietnam War.

Cambodia Southeast Asian nation located on the western border of South Vietnam. During the Vietnam War, Cambodia experienced its own civil war between its pro-U.S. government and Communist rebels known as the Khmer Rouge.

Hanoi The capital city of Communist North Vietnam. Also an unofficial shorthand way of referring to the North Vietnamese government.

Indochina The name sometimes given to the peninsula between India and China in Southeast Asia. The term narrowly refers to Cambodia, Laos, and Vietnam, which were united under the name French Indochina during the colonial period, 1893–1954.

Khmer Rouge Communist-led rebel forces that fought for control of Cambodia during the Vietnam War years. The Khmer Rouge overthrew the U.S.-backed government of Lon Nol in 1975.

Laos A Southeast Asian nation located on the western border of North Vietnam. During the Vietnam War, Laos experienced its own civil war between U.S.-backed forces and Communist rebels known as the Pathet Lao.

North Vietnam The Geneva Accords of 1954, which ended the First Indochina War (1946–54), divided the nation of Vietnam into two sections. The northern section, which was led by a Communist government under Ho Chi Minh, was officially known as the Democratic Republic of Vietnam, but was usually called North Vietnam.

NVA The North Vietnamese Army, which assisted the Viet Cong guerilla fighters in trying to conquer South Vietnam. These forces opposed the United States in the Vietnam War.

Pentagon Papers A set of secret U.S. Department of Defense documents that explained American military policy toward Vietnam from 1945 to 1968. They created a controversy when they were leaked to the national media in 1971.

Saigon The capital city of U.S.-supported South Vietnam. Also an unofficial shorthand way of referring to the South Vietnamese government.

South Vietnam Created under the Geneva Accords of 1954, the southern section of Vietnam was known as the Republic of South Vietnam. It was led by a U.S.-supported government.

Vietnamization A policy proposed by U.S. President Richard Nixon that involved returning responsibility for the war to the South Vietnamese.

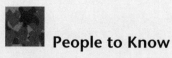

People to Know

Lyndon B. Johnson (1908–1973) After serving as vice president under John Kennedy, he became the 36th president of the United States after Kennedy was assassinated in 1963. Johnson sent U.S. combat troops to Vietnam. Opposition to his policies convinced him not to seek re-election in 1968.

Henry Kissinger (1923–) U.S. national security advisor (1969–1975) and secretary of state (1973–1977) during the Nixon administration. Represented the United States in peace negotiations with North Vietnam

Le Duc Tho (1911–1990) North Vietnamese Communist leader who represented North Vietnam in peace negotiations with the United States.

Lon Nol (1913–1985) Cambodian military and political leader who overthrew the government of Prince Norodom Sihanouk in 1970. Despite U.S. military assistance, he was removed from power by Communist Khmer Rouge forces in 1975.

George McGovern (1922–) U.S. senator from South Dakota who opposed the Vietnam War. Became the Democratic presidential nominee in 1972 but lost the election to Richard M. Nixon.

Nguyen Van Thieu (1923–) President of South Vietnam, 1967–1973.

Richard M. Nixon (1913–1994) Elected as the 37th president of the United States in 1969, at the height of the Vietnam War. Resigned from office during the Watergate scandal in 1974.

feared that the treaty's terms placed his government in jeopardy. But when it became clear that the United States was prepared to abandon him if he resisted, Thieu reluctantly prepared for life without U.S. military protection.

U.S. military performance declines

The U.S. strategy of "Vietnamization"—a policy in which U.S. military forces transferred their war responsibilities to the South Vietnamese military so that American troops could be sent home—proceeded rapidly in the early 1970s. At the beginning of 1970, 450,000 American troops were stationed in Vietnam. By the end of 1971, only 157,000 remained. As American soldiers departed, South Vietnamese forces assumed control of American bases and other installations scattered throughout the country. The duties of the remaining American troops, meanwhile, shifted from "search and destroy" missions deep into remote areas to patrols of southern towns and other security operations.

To many observers, the U.S. withdrawal of ground forces from Vietnam was taking place in the nick of time. In the years immediately following the arrival of U.S. combat troops in 1965, many American units had performed at a very high level. Most soldiers fought bravely and conducted themselves honorably, despite being tangled in a confusing and frightening war. In the late 1960s and early 1970s, however, U.S. military performance in Vietnam underwent a dramatic decline. Some soldiers who served at this time continued to fulfill their duties well. But the discipline and performance of American troops as a whole deteriorated badly.

By mid-1971, U.S. military performance in Vietnam had declined so sharply that some observers warned that America's armed forces were on the verge of total collapse. This drop in performance took many forms. Some soldiers avoided combat or disobeyed orders. Others threatened or even murdered their commanding officers. Drug abuse and racial tensions took a heavy toll on many military units as well. Finally, reports of American brutality toward Vietnamese civilians (people not involved in the military, including women and children) rose dramatically during this period. "These [offenses] ranged from shooting water buffaloes for sport to running cyclists off the road, from throwing C-ration cans [heavy metal food cans] at Vietnamese children to using peasants for target practice," write Clark Dougan and Stephen Weiss in *The American Experience in Vietnam*. "As large numbers of U.S. troops withdrew into heavily populated rear areas, public drunkenness, disorderly conduct, and theft became more common. In the countryside, a deadly combination of too much frustration and too little discipline led to a substantial increase in formal allegations of war crimes."

There were many reasons for this downturn in conduct and performance. Some of the factors cited include the frustrating and frightening nature of the conflict, dramatic changes in American society and culture, poor military leader-

ship, depression over the war's unpopularity in the United States, and resentments that the war was being fought primarily by sons from America's minority and working-class families. But the single biggest factor in the drop in U.S. military performance may have been the average soldier's feeling that he was trapped in the middle of a pointless war. This feeling, according to Dougan and Weiss, "left most soldiers with little sense of mission other than personal survival." The gradual

Vietnamese woman carrying wounded daughter, trying to flee heavy fighting.
Reproduced by permission of AP/World Wide Photos.

withdrawal of American troops from Vietnam further intensi-fied this feeling, for no one wanted to be the last U.S. soldier killed in Vietnam.

Heavy losses in Laos

The growing crisis within the U.S. military was one factor in Nixon's decision to proceed with his policy of Viet-namization in 1971. The other major factor was continued strong opposition to the war among the American public. But while Vietnamization enabled Nixon to speed up the with-drawal of U.S. combat troops, his administration continued to provide significant air support to the South Vietnamese government.

One region of Indochina in which America's awesome air power was most strongly felt was Laos, Vietnam's neighbor to the northwest. Throughout the 1960s, this small nation had been torn by warfare. The Communist North Vietnamese Army (NVA) used Laos as a base for guerrilla (guerrillas are small groups of fighters who launch surprise attacks) activity into South Viet-nam. In addition, a large section of the Ho Chi Minh Trail—the North's main supply and communications route into South Viet-nam—ran through Laos. Finally, Laos had been wracked by an ongoing civil war that pitted the Laotian government against the Pathet Lao, a Communist rebel organization that wanted to seize power for itself. Not surprisingly, the heavy Communist activity in Laos attracted a number of U.S. air bombing campaigns and other military activities over the course of the decade (see box titled, "'Secret War' in Laos" in Chapter 3, "Early American Involvement in Vietnam (1954–1962)").

In February 1971, the battle for control of Laos took center stage in the Vietnam War. Eager to show that South Vietnamese forces were capable of handling the war without the assistance of U.S. ground troops, Nixon approved a major incursion (raid) into Laos in order to destroy Communist bases and disrupt the Ho Chi Minh Trail. Seventeen thousand South Vietnamese troops, transported by U.S. helicopters and sup-ported by U.S. artillery and airpower, crossed into Laos to attack NVA positions. U.S. ground troops were not part of the raid. In fact, they were forbidden from taking part in the offen-sive, code-named Lam Son 719. The U.S. Congress had imposed restrictions on the use of U.S. troops after Nixon's 1970 invasion of Cambodia. Under these new rules, American ground forces were no longer allowed to fight outside of Vietnam's borders.

Upon moving into Laos, the ARVN forces confronted a far greater number of North Vietnamese troops than they anticipated. Approximately 20,000 NVA troops rushed to meet the invasion force, and reinforcements soon increased the size of the Communist defenses to 40,000 troops. The South Vietnamese army continued to move forward, supported by hundreds of American helicopters and bombers, but the North Vietnamese held strong.

The battle in Laos continued throughout late February and the month of March. South Vietnamese troops absorbed the worst of the NVA attacks, but U.S. airplane and helicopter pilots also came under heavy fire from artillery and other anti-aircraft weaponry. "For four weeks now, American helicopter pilots have flown through some of the heaviest flak in the history of the Indochinese war," reported *Newsweek* on March 15, 1971. "The customary bravado of the American chopper pilot [is] beginning to wear a bit thin."

After six weeks of bloody fighting, the battered South Vietnamese army called a ragged retreat. As the ARVN troops straggled back toward South Vietnam, the enemy gave chase. Both the White House and the South Vietnamese government insisted that the ARVN withdrawal was an "orderly retreat." But when television audiences saw film clips of terrified South Vietnamese soldiers clinging to the sides of helicopters in desperate attempts to get home, many viewers dismissed these statements as yet another attempt to mislead the American public. In fact, only massive U.S. air strikes saved the ARVN from suffering a disastrous defeat.

Laos.
Map by XNR Productions, Inc. Reproduced by permission of Gale Group.

As it was, the raid proved to be a total failure. The South Vietnamese invasion force lost almost half of its troops during the operation. The United States, meanwhile, suffered 1,400 casualties (killed and wounded soldiers) and significant damage to its helicopter fleet (108 helicopters were lost during the raid, and another 618 were damaged). Finally, the invasion failed to meet any of its military goals.

Nixon's frustrations grow

The defeat in Laos confirmed major American concerns about the state of South Vietnam's military. In fact, U.S. military experts warned the Nixon administration that the ARVN continued to suffer from a wide range of problems, including poor morale, high rates of desertion (soldiers leaving the military illegally before their terms of service have ended), lack of trained personnel, and a corrupt and inexperienced officer corps. They also complained that the South's military units continued to rely too heavily on American artillery and air support.

These reports greatly concerned Nixon, who continued to pursue a political settlement to the war. In May 1971, the United States and North Vietnam entered into secret negotiations to end the war. Unlike previous meetings held in earlier years, both sides showed a greater willingness to compromise at these sessions. For a while, Nixon held out hope that an acceptable treaty might be reached by the end of the summer. But the talks broke down when the North refused to budge from its longtime demand that South Vietnam President Nguyen Van Thieu be removed from office as part of any agreement.

Thieu, meanwhile, won re-election as South Vietnam's president in September after forcing his two leading opponents out of the race. Thieu's efforts to manipulate the election in his favor were tolerated—and perhaps assisted—by American officials because the Nixon administration viewed Thieu as a strong ally. But the rigged elections drew harsh criticism from congressional opponents of the war and triggered renewed complaints about Nixon's Vietnam policies from antiwar activists.

The Pentagon Papers

Another source of frustration for Nixon during the summer of 1971 was the publication of the so-called Pentagon Papers by the *New York Times*. This massive collection of secret defense department documents traced the history of U.S. policy in Vietnam from the end of World War II (1939–45) to the final months of Lyndon B. Johnson's presidency. Formally known as the *History of U.S. Decision-making Process on Vietnam, 1945–1967,* the so-called Pentagon Papers had been given to the *Times* by U.S. official Daniel Ellsberg, a former war supporter who became a strong opponent of American involvement in Vietnam.

Nixon was enraged when the *New York Times* began publishing excerpts from the Pentagon Papers on June 13, 1971. Convinced that their release would hinder his own ability to wage war in Vietnam, he tried to stop their publication in court. But other newspapers soon began publishing excerpts as well. On June 30 the U.S. Supreme Court ruled that the *Times* had the constitutional right to publish the documents.

As the Pentagon Papers were published over the next several weeks, many sectors of the American public expressed anger and disappointment at what the documents revealed. To many Americans, the Pentagon Papers indicated that the Johnson administration and other U.S. officials had repeatedly deceived Congress and the general public over the years in order to justify and expand U.S. involvement in Vietnam. Leaders of the antiwar movement, meanwhile, expressed outright fury at the information contained in the papers. They charged that the documents proved that America's long and bloody involvement in the Vietnam War was based on a foundation of lies.

The controversy over the Pentagon Papers also worsened the already terrible relations between Nixon and America's antiwar movement. In fact, Nixon's hatred of the protestors became so great that he approved a variety of illegal activities designed to intimidate or spy on antiwar leaders. For example, the White House created a secret group known as the "plumbers" to gather information against opponents of the war and other people thought to be enemies of the administration. This group's activities came to light only after they broke into the Democratic Party's campaign headquarters at

Washington, D.C.'s Watergate Hotel in June 1972. The Nixon administration's later efforts to cover up the burglary created the so-called "Watergate" scandal that forced Nixon to resign from office in August 1974.

Peace talks continue

In late 1971, Nixon's primary negotiator, National Security Advisor Henry Kissinger (1923–), resumed peace talks with North Vietnam and its chief representative, Le Duc Tho. These discussions were serious. But as with previous peace talks, they failed to produce an agreement to end the war. "They eventually broke down for the same reasons earlier efforts had failed," explains George Herring in *America's Longest War.* "Having invested so much blood, treasure, and prestige in a struggle of more than ten years' duration, neither side was yet willing to make the sorts of concessions necessary for peace. Perhaps more important, each side still felt that it could get what it wanted by means other than compromise."

Nixon was disappointed when Kissinger returned without an agreement in hand. The president knew that the American public's opposition to the war was rising to its highest levels yet. In fact, one poll conducted in late 1971 showed that seventy-one percent of the people believed that America should never have entered Vietnam. Another fifty-eight percent called the war "immoral." The president recognized that if the war continued deep into 1972, when presidential elections would be held, it might cost him a second term in office.

Nonetheless, Nixon refused to agree to North Vietnam's demands of an immediate American withdrawal from Vietnam and the removal of Thieu. He took this stand partly because he continued to believe that the United States could eventually negotiate a better deal for itself and South Vietnam. But Nixon also realized that as U.S. troops were being withdrawn from Vietnam, the American public's interest in the war was waning. The majority of Americans opposed U.S. involvement in the conflict. But with few U.S. combat troops left in Vietnam, their opposition became overshadowed by a general relief that American soldiers were no longer being sacrificed to the war effort.

The Easter Offensive

By early 1972, almost all U.S. ground forces had been withdrawn from Vietnam. Of the 95,000 U.S. military personnel remaining in the country, only 6,000 were combat troops. This decline in U.S. troop strength prompted North Vietnam to launch a massive invasion—called the Easter Offensive—into South Vietnam in the spring of 1972 in hopes of winning the war once and for all.

When the North Vietnamese Communists launched their invasion on March 30, they were confident that they would roll to victory. After all, they had been conserving their strength for the past two years in preparation for such an operation. In addition, they believed that the South Vietnamese military would not fight well without the support of U.S. troops. Finally, the leaders of the North thought that antiwar sentiment within the United States would prevent the Nixon administration from responding to the attack with a massive military operation of its own. As the invasion developed, however, it became clear that the North had underestimated the response of both the United States and South Vietnam.

In its early stages, the Easter Offensive looked like it might produce a quick victory for the Communists. A total of 125,000 NVA troops surged into South Vietnam in three main forces, supported by large numbers of tanks and heavy artillery. They overwhelmed ARVN forces in a series of clashes, driving toward the South's major population centers along the coast. But the South Vietnamese military showed surprising grit as the battle wore on, and they halted the Communist advance. By May, the invasion had stalled and turned into a vicious toe-to-toe battle.

U.S. air power smashes advance

Nixon, meanwhile, reacted angrily to the Easter Offensive. The North Vietnamese "have never been bombed like they're going to be bombed this time," Nixon stated when he heard about the invasion. On April 4, he authorized U.S. air strikes and artillery fire against Communist targets from U.S. warships located in the South China Sea. This U.S. air campaign also included targets in North Vietnam. These strikes marked

The Montagnard Tribes of Vietnam

The montagnards, or "mountain people," of Vietnam are a distinct ethnic group who live in remote mountain areas of central Vietnam. Historically, the montagnard tribespeople kept a great distance between themselves and the Vietnamese people who competed for control of the rest of the nation. The proud and independent montagnards maintained a primitive society deep in Vietnam's interior, resisting all Vietnamese efforts to impose authority over them.

When the Vietnam War expanded in the early 1960s, however, the montagnards found it impossible to avoid becoming entangled in the conflict. Military forces from Vietnam's warring North and South both tried to enlist the support of the tribespeople in hopes of using them for military advantage. After all, the montagnard homeland was viewed as an important strategic area. It offered both a potential invasion route into the heart of South Vietnam and an ideal launching area for raids against Communist camps in Laos and Cambodia.

Over time, the United States succeeded in recruiting a number of montagnard tribes to the side of the South. American officials convinced the montagnards that their way of life would be in danger if the North succeeded in its efforts to capture control of the South.

During the early 1960s, American Green Beret units (elite, specially trained members of the U.S. Marines) and other U.S. intelligence personnel organized the montagnards into military units that guarded their mountain homes against Northern invasion. The Americans also sometimes used the montagnards in guerrilla raids into Communist-controlled areas. The bravery and toughness of the montagnards deeply impressed many U.S. troops, and Green Beret units and other American forces expressed great affection and sympathy for the montagnards as the war dragged on.

By the mid-1960s, however, many montagnards refused to aid the South because of mistreatment at the hands of

the first bombings of the North since 1968, when Operation Rolling Thunder came to an end (see Chapter 6, "Vietnam Becomes an American War (1965–1967)"). In May, Nixon ordered the mining of several North Vietnamese harbors and a further expansion of air strikes against North Vietnam. This campaign of sustained bombing took a heavy toll on Northern factories, airfields, bridges, highways, and other targets.

Montagnard tribesmen wearing battle gear.
Reproduced by permission of Corbis-Bettman.

In the late 1960s, the montagnard units were transferred from U.S. supervision to the Army of South Vietnam as part of the "Vietnamization" process. This change failed miserably, however, because of the hostility and distrust that dominated montagnard-Vietnamese relations. By late 1971, most montagnards left the South's military forces. Disillusioned and angry, they either returned home or took up arms against the South.

According to official estimates, approximately 200,000 montagnards were killed during the Vietnam War. In addition, 80 percent or more of the tribespeople were forced to abandon their homes during the fighting. When the North finally conquered the South to unite the country in 1975, some montagnards continued to do battle against the Vietnamese. But they never grew into a major threat. Some members of the devastated montagnard people were forced to flee into Cambodia or seek asylum in the United States in order to avoid punishment.

South Vietnamese soldiers. Some montagnards even organized an open rebellion against the government in Saigon. Hostilities between the montagnards and the South Vietnamese continued to flare up throughout the late 1960s, despite the fact that they both viewed the North as a dangerous threat.

Nixon's decision to intensify American attacks on North Vietnam triggered a new round of demonstrations and protests in the United States. Congressional critics of the war also condemned the president for the escalation. By mid-summer, bills that would dramatically reduce American involvement in Vietnam were circulating in both the Senate and the House of Representatives.

But many Americans did not actively oppose Nixon's choice to retaliate against the North. Relieved that most U.S. troops were no longer in harm's way, they blamed North Vietnam for launching the Easter Offensive in the first place.

In the meantime, America's massive bombing campaign against NVA forces provided invaluable help to the South Vietnamese military. "By the end of June the aerial onslaught had stalled the Communist offensive amid the smoking wreckage of thousands of North Vietnamese tanks, trucks, and self-propelled artillery pieces," Dougan and Weiss reported. These attacks, combined with the surprisingly tough performance of the ARVN, forced North Vietnam to abandon the invasion in September.

A major defeat for the North

The Easter Offensive proved to be a major military setback for North Vietnam. The Communists did manage to gain control of some territory along the Laotian and Cambodian borders, but at a very heavy cost. By some estimates, the North lost 100,000 soldiers and 450 tanks in the assault, which failed to capture any major cities of strategic significance. These losses severely reduced the strength of the NVA for the next two years. North Vietnam's leadership was so upset by the failed offensive that it removed longtime general Vo Nguyen Giap (1911–) from command and replaced him with General Van Tien Dung.

In addition, the performance of the ARVN pleased the Nixon administration. South Vietnam's successful defense of its urban centers and other strategic areas showed that its military was capable of performing well, even under brutal conditions. Still, few observers believed that the South could have prevailed without direction from U.S. military advisors or the awesome power of the U.S. air attacks.

Return to the negotiating table

By the fall of 1972, North Vietnamese negotiator Le Duc Tho signaled a new willingness to resume peace talks with Kissinger, America's chief representative. After all, North Vietnam had suffered heavy losses during the Easter Offensive, and the U.S. bombing campaign was taking a major toll in the North. In addition, the Communists worried that improving relations between the United States and China and Soviet Union—countries that had long supported North Vietnam— might complicate their efforts to take control of the South.

In September 1972, Kissinger and Le Duc Tho resumed their secret negotiations in Paris. A short time later, the United States called a halt to its bombing campaign against the North. As the talks progressed, Le Duc Tho indicated that North Vietnam was now willing to drop its long-time demand for Thieu's removal as part of any peace agreement. Delighted by this change of heart and the rapid progress of negotiations, Kissinger announced on October 26 that "we believe that peace is at hand." But when President Thieu learned of the basic framework for the treaty, he raised objections to the agreement. He did not believe that it provided his government with the level of protection it needed to resist future challenges from North Vietnam. As a result, the negotiators wearily returned to Paris in an effort to address Thieu's concerns.

Meanwhile, Nixon benefited greatly from Kissinger's premature announcement of a peace agreeement. He defeated Democratic presidential nominee George McGovern (1922–)— an outspoken opponent of the war—by a wide margin in the November 1972 presidential election to earn a second term as president of the United States. He won sixty percent of the popular vote and carried every state except Massachusetts and the District of Columbia.

United States launches Christmas Bombing

On December 13, 1972, the Paris peace talks collapsed once again. One day later, Nixon ordered U.S. forces to resume bombing targets in North Vietnam. This campaign was officially known as Operation Linebacker II, but it became better known as the "Christmas Bombing." The Christmas Bombing began on December 18 and continued day and night for two weeks, stopping only for Christmas Day. During that time, American bombers dropped an estimated 36,000 tons of explosives on Hanoi, Haiphong, and other North Vietnamese targets. According to some military experts, U.S. forces dropped more bombs on the North during this two-week period than they had during the entire three-year period from 1969 to 1971.

The timing and intensity of the air strikes drew harsh criticism from antiwar leaders and organizations. After all, Nixon had approved the most intensive bombing of the entire Vietnam War during the holiday season, at a point in time when the American public was extremely tired of the war. Nixon's decision also received heavy criticism from religious organizations, press commentators, members of Congress, and neutral countries around the world. Various voices labeled the bombing campaign as "shameful," "monstrous," and "murderous."

But Nixon and his supporters argued that the Christmas Bombing convinced North Vietnam to resume peace negotiations. "Our bombing achieved its purposes," claimed Nixon in *No More Vietnams*. "Hanoi [the North Vietnam government] quickly accepted our first offer to resume the talks. We had forced Hanoi to come back to the negotiating table." The Christmas Bombing campaign ended on December 29, three days after North Vietnam agreed to resume peace negotiations in Paris.

The Paris Peace Accords

On January 9, 1973, Kissinger and Le Duc Tho reached agreement on a treaty to end the war in Vietnam. The agreement was signed on January 27, almost five years after peace negotiations between the two sides first opened on May 13, 1968. Under the terms of the agreement, North Vietnam agreed to drop its demands for a coalition government (one that included Communist representation) in South Vietnam. In exchange, the United States agreed to allow some North Vietnamese troops to remain in the South as long as they promised not to resume military aggression. This section of the treaty left an estimated 160,000 North Vietnamese troops in various regions of South Vietnam. The treaty also provided for an exchange of prisoners of war (POWs) between the two sides. All U.S. troops were required to leave South Vietnam 60 days after the return of all American POWs.

Finally, the agreement left Thieu in charge of the Saigon government. But it also created a Committee of National Reconciliation that included political representatives from North Vietnam. This organization was charged with supervising elections for a new government in which all parties—including Communists—could take part. Historians agree that this part of the treaty left the political future of South Vietnam very much in doubt.

Thieu forced to go along

President Thieu was outraged by the terms of the peace agreement. He told U.S. officials that he would never agree to its conditions. The Nixon administration reacted to this threat in two ways. First, they tried to reassure South Vietnam's president. Nixon ordered the immediate delivery of $1 billion in military equipment, a gift that left South Vietnam with the fourth largest air force in the world. The administration also promised to provide other military and economic aid to the Thieu government. In addition, the United States promised that it would take "swift and severe retaliatory action" if North Vietnam violated the peace agreement. But second, Nixon administration officials warned Thieu that America was going to go forward with the agreement whether Thieu approved of it or not. Fearful that the United States would simply abandon him, Thieu reluctantly dropped his objections to the treaty.

The Paris Accords did not immediately end U.S. involvement in Indochina. American planes continued to bomb targets in Laos until February 21, when a peace agreement ending that nation's civil war was signed. In Cambodia, meanwhile, the United States continued to bomb Communist opponents of Lon Nol's national government. But to most Americans, the January 1973 Paris Accords marked the end of U.S. military involvement in Indochina. On March 29, the last U.S. troops left Vietnam to return home.

The American public expressed great relief when the 1973 Paris Accords were signed. After all, most people had grown very unhappy with the Vietnam War, which had taken thousands of American lives and plunged the nation into a period of great turmoil. As the last U.S. soldiers returned home, many Americans looked back over the previous decade with deep regret. The country had spent an estimated $200 billion on the war from the early 1960s to 1973. Over that period, more than 58,000 Americans were killed in Vietnam, while another 300,000 were wounded. In addition, about 2,000 U.S. servicemen were still listed as missing in action when the last POWs returned home. Finally, the war triggered bitter divisions in American families and communities that remained deep for years to come.

Nixon's record in Vietnam

When the Paris Peace Accords were signed in January 1973, many Americans—from political leaders and journalists to common citizens—praised Nixon and his administration for their direction of the war effort. The *Denver Post,* for example, praised the Paris treaty as "a tribute to the skill and statesmanship of Henry Kissinger and to the determination, spirit and persistence of President Nixon." The president's supporters argued that his strong leadership—as shown in his defiance of antiwar demonstrators and willingness to use American air power—enabled the United States to negotiate a cease-fire that allowed it to leave South Vietnam "with honor."

Opponents of the war, however, were more critical of Nixon's record in Vietnam. They argued that the war became even more devastating during his first term of office than it had been during the Johnson administration. They charged that Nixon's heavy use of bombing resulted in thousands of civilian deaths and injuries, and that U.S. air strikes virtually destroyed large sections of the country. "The tonnage of bombs dropped on Indochina during the Nixon era exceeded that of the Johnson years, wreaking untold devastation, causing permanent ecological damage to the countryside, and leaving millions of civilians homeless," claims Herring.

Finally, Nixon's critics argued that he spent four years smashing Vietnam and neighboring countries, only to settle for a peace agreement that was similar in most respects to ones that he turned down in the late 1960s. "Four years of the Nixon administration had made only one change from the conditions available to the United States in 1968," comments Robert D. Schulzinger in *A Time for War.* "The United States had not been forced to drop its support for the government of

President Thieu, but that government now had agreed to share power. The final agreement allowed the government of President Thieu a fighting chance to remain in power—no more, no less. U.S. casualties had risen by twenty thousand dead in the four years of the Nixon administration, and an additional three hundred thousand Vietnamese had lost their lives. And still the war went on."

Sources

Aitken, Jonathan. *Nixon: A Life*. Washington, DC: Regnery, 1993.

Ambrose, Stephen E. *Nixon*. 3 vols. New York: Simon and Schuster, 1987–1991.

Andradé, Dale. *Trial by Fire: The 1972 Easter Offensive, America's Last Vietnam Battle*. New York: Hippocrene Books, 1995.

Appy, Christian G. *Working-Class War: American Combat Soldiers and Vietnam*. Chapel Hill: University of North Carolina Press, 1993.

Curry, Cecil B. (as Cincinnatus). *Self-Destruction: The Disintegration and Decay of the U.S. Army in Vietnam*. New York: W. W. Norton, 1981.

Dougan, Clark, and Stephen Weiss. *The American Experience in Vietnam*. Boston: Boston Publishing, 1988.

Eschmann, Karl J. *Linebacker: The Untold Story of the Air Raids over North Vietnam*. New York: Ivy Books, 1989.

Gibson, James. *The Perfect War: The War We Couldn't Lose and How We Did*. New York: Atlantic Monthly Press, 1986.

Herring, George C. *America's Longest War: The United States and Vietnam, 1950-1975*. New York: McGraw-Hill, 1979.

Isaacs, Arnold R. *Without Honor: Defeat in Vietnam and Cambodia*. New York: Vintage Books, 1984.

Isaacson, Walter. *Kissinger*. New York: Simon and Schuster, 1992.

Kimball, Jeffrey. *Nixon's Vietnam War*. Lawrence: University Press of Kansas, 1998.

Schulzinger, Robert D. *A Time for War: The United States and Vietnam, 1941–1975*. New York: Oxford University Press, 1997.

Victory for North Vietnam (1973–75)

14

When the last U.S. troops left Vietnam in 1973, President Nguyen Van Thieu (1923–) and his South Vietnamese government expressed deep unhappiness with the withdrawal. After all, the Communist government of North Vietnam was still trying to take control of the country. Thieu could only hope that continued U.S. economic aid and the threat of American military power would enable South Vietnam to withstand any military aggression by the North.

These hopes rapidly unraveled, however. The U.S. Congress made major cuts in American economic assistance to South Vietnam. Around this same period, the Watergate scandal forced President Richard Nixon (1913–1994; president 1969–1974)—who had vowed to defend the South from northern aggression—to resign from office. Finally, South Vietnam's economy and military suffered a series of setbacks that made the Thieu government even more vulnerable.

In early 1975, North Vietnam launched a major military offensive into the South in hopes of winning the war once and for all. The North Vietnamese Army (NVA) expected the invasion to be a bloody and costly one. But the South Viet-

Words to Know

ARVN The South Vietnamese army, officially known as the Army of the Republic of South Vietnam. The ARVN fought on the same side as U.S. troops during the Vietnam War.

Cambodia A southeast Asian nation located on the western border of South Vietnam. During the Vietnam War, Cambodia experienced its own civil war between its pro-U.S. government and Communist rebels known as the Khmer Rouge.

Communism A political system in which the government controls all resources and means of producing wealth. By eliminating private property, this system is designed to create an equal society with no social classes. However, Communist governments in practice often limit personal freedom and individual rights.

Hanoi The capital city of Communist North Vietnam. Also an unofficial shorthand way of referring to the North Vietnamese government.

Khmer Rouge Communist-led rebel forces that fought for control of Cambodia during the Vietnam War years. The Khmer Rouge overthrew the U.S.-backed government of Lon Nol in 1975.

Laos A Southeast Asian nation located on the western border of North Vietnam. During the Vietnam War, Laos experi-enced its own civil war between U.S.-backed forces and Communist rebels known as the Pathet Lao.

North Vietnam The Geneva Accords of 1954, which ended the First Indochina War (1946–54), divided the nation of Vietnam into two sections. The north-ern section, which was led by a Com-munist government under Ho Chi Minh, was officially known as the Democratic Republic of Vietnam, but was usually called North Vietnam.

NVA The North Vietnamese Army, which assisted the Viet Cong guerilla fighters in trying to conquer South Vietnam. These forces opposed the United States in the Vietnam War.

Offensive A sudden, aggressive attack by one side during a war.

Saigon The capital city of U.S.-supported South Vietnam. Also an unofficial short-hand way of referring to the South Viet-namese government.

South Vietnam Created under the Geneva Accords of 1954, the southern section of Vietnam was known as the Republic of South Vietnam. It was led by a U.S.-supported government.

Watergate A political scandal that forced U.S. President Richard Nixon to resign from office in 1974.

namese Army (ARVN) collapsed, triggering a wave of panic and chaos across much of the country. North Vietnam's forces rolled across the countryside unopposed, capturing city after city. In late April they captured South Vietnam's capital city, Saigon. The fall of Saigon marked the end of the Vietnam War and the beginning of a new era in Vietnam under a single Communist government.

Nixon's final months

In 1973, the United States and North Vietnam signed the Paris Peace Treaty, which provided for the withdrawal of all remaining U.S. forces from Vietnam. In the months following the signing of the treaty, however, both South Vietnam and North Vietnam kept fighting in violation of the cease-fire agreement. These violations concerned U.S. officials. But the continuing hostilities did not prevent American lawmakers from taking a series of steps designed to ensure that the United States would never again become entangled in Vietnam. For example, Congress overwhelmingly passed the Case-Church Amendment, which explicitly prohibited future U.S. military involvement in Indochina. In November 1973, Congress passed the so-called War Powers Act. This legislation put new limits on the president's powers to commit U.S. troops to military operations without congressional approval.

President Nixon opposed congressional efforts to limit his military authority. But by late 1973, he did not have the political power to stop Congress. His administration had become consumed by investigations into the "Watergate" scandal, a June 1972 burglary of the Democratic Party's presidential campaign headquarters at Washington, D.C.'s Watergate Hotel. This illegal break-in had been staged by operatives associated with Nixon's presidential campaign in order to gather secret campaign information. As the investigation into

People to Know

Nguyen Van Thieu (1923–) President of South Vietnam, 1967–1973.

Richard M. Nixon (1913–1994) Elected as the 37th president of the United States in 1969, at the height of the Vietnam War. Resigned from office during the Watergate scandal in 1974.

Pol Pot (1928–1998) Head of the Communist-led Khmer Rouge forces that took control of Cambodia in 1976. As prime minister of Cambodia from 1976 to 1979, he oversaw a violent transformation of society that resulted in the deaths of up to two million citizens.

Richard Nixon, giving resignation speech in 1974 (his oldest daughter, Patricia Cox-Nixon, looks on).
Reproduced by permission of the Library of Congress.

the burglary unfolded, it became clear that members of the Nixon administration—and possibly the president himself—had tried to cover up the burglary. The investigation also showed that Republican agents had engaged in a wide range of illegal activities against Democrats and other political opponents for several years.

By early 1974, Nixon's presidency was in serious trouble. Several of his key aides were indicted (brought up on legal charges) for crimes associated with the Watergate cover-up. In addition, the scandal made him very unpopular with the majority of the American public. Sensing his weakness, members of the Democratic Party kept heavy political pressure on him. Some of Nixon's fellow Republicans, meanwhile, became reluctant to defend him. They worried that supporting the president might hurt them with voters.

In July 1974, the House of Representatives' Judiciary Committee moved to impeach Nixon. The U.S. Constitution says that all federal officials can be impeached (brought up on legal charges) and removed from elected office if they are found guilty of "treason, bribery, or other high crimes and misdemeanors." The House of Representatives brings the charges and acts as prosecutors in an impeachment trial. The Judiciary Committee introduced three articles of impeachment against Nixon, accusing him of obstructing justice, abusing presidential power, and refusing to obey subpoenas (legal directives to appear in court and provide testimony).

On August 5, Nixon released audiotapes showing that he had participated in the Watergate cover-up as early as June 1972. This revelation stunned both the American public and Congress, which moved ahead with its plan to put the president on trial. Convinced that he would be convicted and forcibly removed from office, Nixon decided to resign instead. He made his resignation announcement on August 8, 1974, and left office the next day. Vice President Gerald R. Ford (1913–; president 1974–1977) was promptly sworn in to succeed Nixon. One month later, Ford pardoned (officially forgave) Nixon for all federal crimes he may have committed during his presidency.

Gerald Ford served as president of the United States for two years, after Richard Nixon resigned from office in 1974. *Reproduced by permission of the Library of Congress.*

Growing problems in South Vietnam

President Thieu was disturbed by Nixon's resignation. After all, Nixon had promised South Vietnam continued American protection from North Vietnam. But Thieu believed that the United States would continue to honor its commitments in South Vietnam, no matter who was president.

In the meantime, Thieu ordered a series of major ground and air attacks against areas of South Vietnam controlled by the Communists. The 1973 Peace Accords signed by the United

States and North Vietnam stated that the Communists would be allowed to participate in the formation of a new government in the South. But Thieu believed that he would not have to give the Communists a role in his government if he could regain control of Communist-held areas in South Vietnam.

These offensive operations failed to dislodge captured areas from NVA control. In fact, North Vietnamese forces responded with a series of counterattacks that enabled them to increase the amount of territory under their control. These military clashes disrupted food production and economic activity throughout South Vietnam. At the same time, rising world oil prices and the disappearance of free-spending U.S. military personnel crippled many South Vietnamese businesses. By mid-1974, the South Vietnamese economy was in a shambles, burdened by massive unemployment, terrible inflation (increases in the price of goods and services), and widespread corruption. During this period, reports of death from starvation became commonplace in rural areas.

U.S. financial support drops

South Vietnam was also hurt during this time by a dramatic drop in U.S. economic aid. Congress was sick and tired of pouring money into Vietnam. Many legislators agreed with Senator Edward Kennedy (1932–), who stated that it was time to end America's "endless support for an endless war." In addition, lawmakers knew that the American public wanted to put the war behind them. With these factors in mind, legislators cut financial assistance to South Vietnam from $2.3 billion in 1973 to $1 billion in 1974. In September 1974, Congress voted to cut military aid to South Vietnam for 1975 to $700 million, half of which would be consumed by shipping costs.

Some officials strongly objected to these cutbacks. Defense Secretary James Schlesinger (1929–), for example, called the cuts a "failure of a moral commitment" to the South Vietnamese people. But these arguments were not enough to convince Congress to change its mind.

Combined with South Vietnam's other economic troubles, these cuts took a tremendous toll on the nation's military. Shortages of supplies, nonpayment of soldier salaries, bribery, and corruption became even bigger problems than they had been before. Some South Vietnamese pilots even refused to provide air support for military operations if they were not given bribery payments. In addition, the U.S. aid cutbacks had a negative impact on morale. Many South Vietnamese interpreted the cuts as a sign that their longtime ally was on the verge of abandoning them completely. This feeling became even stronger in January 1975, when President Ford stated that he could not imagine any circumstances under which the United States would reenter the war.

North Vietnam plans a new invasion

By late 1974, most of North Vietnam's leadership believed that the United States would not return to Vietnam. They thought that America's Vietnam War experience had created such deep unhappiness, frustration, and anger that its people would never allow U.S. forces to take part in the war again. With this in mind, the North made plans for another full-scale invasion of the South.

On two previous occasions, the 1968 Tet Offensive and the 1972 Easter Offensive, North Vietnam had launched massive offensives that failed (see Chapter 7, "The Tet Offensive (1968)" and Chapter 13, "America Withdraws from Vietnam (1971–1973)"). But the Communists believed that this invasion would have a different result. First, South Vietnam's military forces were scattered all across the country rather than concentrated in strong defensive areas. This flawed distribution of forces would make it easier for NVA troops to mount

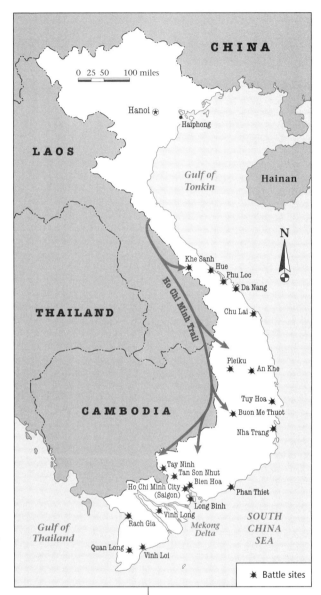

Sites of major battles in the Vietnam War.
Map by XNR Productions, Inc. Reproduced by permission of Gale Group.

effective attacks. Even more importantly, northern leaders felt that South Vietnam would not be able to turn back the invasion without the benefit of U.S. air strikes. In this way, North Vietnam's hopes for a successful offensive rested on its belief that the United States would not respond to the attack with a new bombing campaign.

The capture of Phuoc Long

In December 1974, NVA forces launched an attack on Phuoc Long, a remote city located near the Cambodian border. The Communist forces quickly smashed the city's defenses, killing thousands of South Vietnamese troops in the process. By January 6, the NVA had captured the city and executed a number of provincial and village officials associated with the South Vietnamese government. North Vietnam then settled in to wait for the American response to the attack.

But the United States decided not to punish the attack with air strikes. At this point, North Vietnam's General Secretary Le Duan and other Communist leaders became even more confident that America had no intention of re-entering the war in any capacity. "When Phuoc Long fell in early 1975 it was not important militarily, but it was terribly important as a symbol of America's refusal to carry out this 'massive and brutal retaliation' that Nixon had promised Thieu," said CIA official Thomas Polgar in *Tears Before the Rain*. Vietnam historian Harry G. Summers, Jr. confirmed that the U.S. reaction to the attack on Phuoc Long sent a clear signal to the North. "The United States limited its response to diplomatic notes," Summers writes in *Historical Atlas of the Vietnam War*. "North Vietnam had received the green light for the conquest of South Vietnam."

The attack on Ban Me Thuot

In March 1975, North Vietnam launched its third major invasion of the Vietnam War. The first target of the invading forces, led by General Van Tien Dung, was the central Vietnam city of Ban Me Thuot. Using overwhelming military power, the NVA captured the city on March 11, only one day after they began their assault.

President Thieu responded to the loss of Ban Me Thuot by abandoning South Vietnam's northern provinces and Central Highlands to the invaders. He ordered the withdrawal of all South Vietnamese troops to defensive positions in the Southern provinces. Thieu hoped that by concentrating his forces in the southern provinces, he could keep Saigon and other important cities out of Communist hands. His withdrawal order, however, proved disastrous for South Vietnam and its people.

"In the attack in Ban Me Thuot we surprised the South Vietnamese," recalled NVA Major General Tran Cong Man in *Tears Before the Rain*. "On the other hand, the South Vietnamese troops surprised us, too, because they became so disorganized so quickly . . . . We had expected a very intense and long battle with the South around Ban Me Thuot. But the way Mr. Thieu responded to the attack was not even within our imagination. In fact, his response created a great question in our minds as to whether or not this was a trap, a brilliant tactic to lure us in . . . . But when Thieu withdrew his troops from Pleiku [another city in central South Vietnam], we realized suddenly that there was no trap, and there was no plan, and the South was not up to fighting anymore. That is when we decided to chase them as fast as we could."

The "Convoy of Tears"

Thieu's withdrawal order created chaos. South Vietnamese military units completely fell apart as soldiers scrambled to gather family members—who were permitted to live near where they were stationed—for the flight to the safety of the south. The soldiers and their families were joined by hundreds of thousands of other South Vietnamese who feared the oncoming Communists. As the fleeing soldiers and refugees converged on the roads leading southward, the retreat turned into a miserable experience for everyone involved. Artillery shells roared into the columns of fleeing people, killing dozens of soldiers, women, and children with each blast. Starvation and illness claimed many other lives.

Still, the grim parade of refugees, which came to be known as the "Convoy of Tears," continued southward. "Survivors [of the Convoy of Tears] told of old people and babies crushed and left to die as military vehicles bulldozed through the slowly trudging civilians, who still clutched at cartloads of lifetime possessions," writes Michael Maclear in *The Ten Thousand Day War.* "In the stampede countless lost children died from the shells and from hunger. Only one in four of the vast human convoy reached the coast, with most of the civilians having fallen behind to await capture."

As his nation crumbled around him, Thieu appealed to the United States for help in turning back the invasion. But America refused to take any steps that might suck it back into the conflict. Congress even rejected President Ford's emergency request for $300 million in additional military aid for South Vietnam. "The legislators' vote seems to have reflected the wishes of the American people," writes George C. Herring in *America's Longest War.* "A few diehards [firm supporters of South Vietnam] issued one last appeal to honor the nation's commitments and defend the cause of freedom, and some Americans raised the specter [possibility] of a bloodbath in which hundreds of thousands of South Vietnamese would be slaughtered by the Communist conquerors. For the most part, however, such appeals fell on deaf ears. Weary of the seemingly endless involvement in Vietnam and pinched by an economic recession at home, Americans were not in a generous mood."

Northern forces continue their advance

By the end of March, cities all across the northern and central provinces of South Vietnam had fallen to the advancing Communist forces. On March 19, the North Vietnamese captured Quang Tri City. On March 25, the city of Hue was abandoned, its frightened population adding to the Convoy of Tears. Many of these refugees fled to Da Nang on the South China Sea in hopes of gaining passage on a southbound ship or plane. This flood of refugees swelled the coastal city's population to two million and triggered a complete breakdown in civil order. "People moved about frantically in search of relief and escape," recalls ARVN General Cao Van Vien. "The chaos and disorder were indescribable. Hunger, looting and crime were widespread."

This frightening environment became even worse when the advancing NVA troops began lobbing artillery shells into the

A South Vietnamese Soldier Recalls the Capture of Da Nang

Pham Van Xinh was a security officer with the South Vietnamese military in 1975, when North Vietnam launched its final invasion of the South. In Larry Engelmann's *Tears Before the Rain: An Oral History of the Fall of South Vietnam*, he recalls what it was like when the Communists assumed control of Da Nang:

I was in Danang when it fell to the Communists . . . . We had been stationed at Tam Ky, then we were ordered to go to Danang. But when we got off our ship in Danang, we found that our commanding officers had taken another ship and had gone south. We had been abandoned. We didn't know what we were supposed to do or where we were supposed to go. We were like a snake without a head.

Some of the men got on refugee ships going south. I did not. I was afraid because I knew about the Hue massacre of 1968, when the Communists had killed thousands of Vietnamese. We thought they would do that again, we thought they would kill all of the soldiers first. So we threw away our uniforms and put on civilian clothes.

When the Communists arrived in Danang, at first they did not do anything terrible. Nobody was arrested at first and nobody was sent to a prison camp. But then, after a couple of days, we discovered that the Communists had lists of people who had cooperated with the Americans. Those people were called traitors, and the Communists said they were very dangerous. I don't know how many names were on the lists, but I did see many people arrested. Those who were on a special list were shot right away, right there in the street. The Communists said that those people did not deserve to live. It was not like an execution, really. It was more like a murder in the street. They did not even lead them away as they did in Hue. They just killed them where they found them.

city. These blasts increased the panic of the tens of thousands of refugees who swarmed the city's harbor and airport. An estimated 50,000 refugees and ARVN soldiers eventually managed to escape Da Nang by boat or plane, but most of the city's war-scarred population were not so fortunate. They remained in the city when it fell to the Communists on March 30.

As NVA forces rolled across South Vietnam, U.S. President Ford made another attempt to secure emergency military aid from Congress. He urged American lawmakers to give the South Vietnamese a chance to succeed rather than "doom them to lingering death." But U.S. lawmakers remained opposed to such actions. "Congressmen responded heatedly that the South Vietnamese had abandoned more equipment in the northern provinces than could be purchased with the additional funds, and they argued that no amount of money could save an army that refused to fight," states Herring. Congress eventually approved a modest economic aid package for the South. But those funds were limited to operations for general humanitarian assistance and the evacuation of American reporters, business employees, and diplomatic personnel remaining in Vietnam.

The Battle of Xuan Loc

After capturing Hue and Da Nang, NVA forces continued to move southward. The complete collapse of South Vietnam's military enabled the Communists to capture dozens of towns and villages and huge sections of countryside with each passing day. On April 9, North Vietnam's invasion temporarily stalled at Xuan Loc, a city located about forty miles northeast of Saigon. In this town, a valiant force of South Vietnamese troops mounted a desperate defense. Despite being outnumbered and outgunned, they managed to halt the Communist advance for almost two weeks. On April 22, however, Xuan Loc finally fell to the NVA forces. The Communists then set their sights on Saigon, South Vietnam's capital.

The fall of Saigon

As North Vietnam's military machine continued its steady advance, President Thieu finally realized that the United States was not going to send ground troops or air strikes to rescue his country. Thieu resigned on April 21 after delivering a tearful speech in which he blamed America for South Vietnam's collapse. "The United States has not respected its promises," he said. "It is inhumane. It is not trustworthy. It is irresponsible." Thieu turned the government over to Vice President Tran Van Huong, then fled the country.

By April 27, Saigon was completely surrounded by North Vietnamese forces. A day later, Tran Van Huong resigned the presidency and was succeeded by General Duong Van Minh. "It was commonly—and incorrectly, it turned out—believed that Minh would be acceptable to the North Vietnamese and that he alone of all the political figures in the

South could arrive at a negotiated settlement with the advancing North Vietnamese Army," writes Larry Engelmann in *Tears Before the Rain*. "But that, too, proved to be an illusion. Minh found that there was no one willing to make an agreement with him. He had nothing to offer the advancing divisions of the North but surrender. His most important act in his brief tenure as President was to make an unconditional surrender to the North Vietnamese."

U.S. Navy personnel pushing the *U.S.S. Blue Ridge* helicopter into the sea to make room for more evacuation flights from Saigon.
Reproduced by permission of AP/World Wide Photos.

A North Vietnamese Commander Recalls the Fall of Saigon

Van Tien Dung was commander in chief of North Vietnam's military in 1975, when the North successfully invaded South Vietnam to end the war. In the following excerpt from his book *Our Great Spring Victory: An Account of the Liberation of South Vietnam,* he gives his version of events in the last hours before Saigon fell to his army:

> The American evacuation was carried out from the tops of thirteen tall buildings chosen as landing pads for their helicopters. The number of these landing pads shrank gradually as tongues of fire from our advancing troops came closer. At the American embassy, the boarding point for the evacuation copters was a scene of monumental confusion, with the Americans' flunkies fighting their way in, smashing doors, climbing walls, climbing each other's backs, tussling, brawling, and trampling each other as they sought to flee . . . . [When U.S. Ambassador Graham Martin] left the embassy for the East Sea, it signaled the shameful defeat of U.S. imperialism [the act of extending political

power over another country] after thirty years of intervention and military adventures in Vietnam . . . . They mobilized as many as 6 million American soldiers in rotation, dropped over 10 million tons of bombs, and spent over $300 billion, but in the end the U.S. ambassador had to crawl up to the helicopter pad looking for a way to flee . . . .

> [North Vietnamese forces then captured several important locations in the city, including Saigon's military headquarters and the radio station.] As we looked at the combat operations map, the five wings of our troops seemed like five lotuses blossoming out from our five major objectives . . . . The Second Army Corps seized "Independence Palace," the place where the quisling leaders [traitors under the control of foreigners], those hirelings of the United States, had sold our independence, traded in human blood, and carried on their smuggling. Our soldiers immediately rushed upstairs to the place where the quisling cabinet was meeting, and arrested the whole central leadership of the Saigon administration, including their president, right on the spot. Our soldiers'

On the morning of April 29, the United States belatedly launched a helicopter evacuation of American and Vietnamese civilians and military personnel who remained in Saigon to U.S. Navy ships waiting offshore. In addition, the vessels plucked thousands of desperate Vietnamese refugees out of the waters of the South China Sea, where they had fled on patrol boats, freighters, fishing trawlers, and other boats. Indeed, the evacuation took place in an environment of rising panic and chaos, as tens of thousands of South Vietnamese looked for some way to escape the Communist tanks and

South Vietnamese citizens scaling the wall of the U.S. Embassy in Saigon, April 29, 1975.
Reproduced by permission of Corbis-Bettman.

vigorous actions and firm declarations revealed the spirit of a victorious army. By 11:30 A.M. on April 30 the revolutionary flag flew from "Independence Palace"; this became the meeting point for all the wings of liberating troops.

At the front headquarters, we turned on our radios to listen. The voice of the quisling president called on his troops to put down their weapons and surrender unconditionally to our troops. Saigon was completely liberated! Total victory! We were completely victorious! All of us at headquarters jumped up and shouted, embraced and carried each other around on our shoulders. The sound of applause, laughter, and happy, noisy, chattering speech was as festive as if spring had just burst upon us. It was an indescribably joyous scene. Le Duc Tho and Pham Hung embraced me and all the cadres [core groups of leaders] and fighters present. We were all so happy we were choked with emotion . . . . This historic and sacred, intoxicating and completely satisfying moment was one that comes once in a generation, once in many generations. Our generation had known many victorious mornings, but there had been no morning so fresh and beautiful, so radiant, so clear and cool, so sweet-scented as this morning of total victory, a morning which made babes older than their years and made old men young again.

troops moving just outside the city's outskirts. They feared that North Vietnam's forces would go on a murderous rampage when they entered the city. The operation finally ended in the early morning hours of April 30, a few hours before North Vietnamese tanks rolled through the city streets and the Saigon government formally surrendered.

The evacuation succeeded in rescuing thousands of American citizens and South Vietnamese families. But millions of frightened South Vietnamese were left behind, including approximately 420 men and women who had time and again

Sixteen-year-old Sokly Tum relates his fear of Khmer Rouge and Pol Pot amidst a pile of human bones.
Reproduced by permission of AP/World Wide Photos.

been promised a place on one of the evacuation helicopters. These South Vietnamese ranged from Saigon government officials to secretaries, housekeepers, and administrators who had served U.S. officers and embassy personnel in Saigon. They waited on the embassy roof for hours, scanning the horizon anxiously for the American helicopters that would deliver them to safety. But the helicopters never returned.

North Vietnam's capture of Saigon—which the Communists renamed Ho Chi Minh City—ended the Vietnam War. The North's dream of defeating the South Vietnamese government and its American allies and establishing a single, unified country under Communist rule had finally come true.

Determined to unify the war-torn nation, the Communists did not engage in widespread slaughter of the city's residents, as many South Vietnamese and Americans had feared they would. But they did establish ruthless control over the South Vietnamese people. They imprisoned thousands of

Cambodian Buddhist monks, praying in front of a stall filled with human skulls, observing "Hate Day," at the "Killing Fields." *Reproduced by permission of AP/World Wide Photos.*

people who they viewed as enemies of the new Communist state. The government also sent tens of thousands of former South Vietnamese citizens to "re-education camps," where they endured harsh labor and countless hours of instruction in Communist philosophy. Finally, Vietnam's leadership imposed a strict system of socialism on the newly unified country. Under socialism, the government assumes control over all aspects of a society's economic and political life, and places restrictions on personal freedoms.

Cambodia falls to Khmer Rouge

As North Vietnam's Communist troops seized control of South Vietnam in April, Communist forces also registered decisive victories in neighboring Cambodia and Laos. Cambodia's long civil war ended on April 17, when the government formally surrendered to the Communist Khmer Rouge guerrillas. The Khmer Rouge, led by Pol Pot (1928–1998), immediately instituted an almost unbelievably cruel and ruthless reign of terror that nearly destroyed Cambodia and its people.

Upon taking over, the Khmer Rouge renamed the country Democratic Kampuchea and reset the calendar at "Year Zero" to symbolize the beginning of a new era in the nation's history. They then forced all Cambodians out of cities and towns to labor in rural work camps under terrible conditions. The Khmer Rouge government also launched a policy to execute all educated people within the nation's borders. Soldiers subsequently tortured and murdered tens of thousands of teachers, doctors, engineers, government officials, police officers and anyone else who they viewed as a possible threat. The murderous policies of the Khmer Rouge created a tremendous flood of terrified refugees and resulted in the deaths of an estimated one million Cambodians (one-seventh of the entire country's population) by execution, starvation, or disease by 1978.

Communist triumph in Laos

A new Communist government also came to power in 1975 in Laos. The Pathet Lao Communists gained control of the central government on August 23, 1975. In December, the Lao monarchy that had ruled Laos for 600 years was formally abolished, replaced by the People's Democratic Republic of Laos. During this time, the Pathet Lao launched a ruthless campaign to kill perceived enemies of their Communist rule. As in Cambodia, the main targets of this campaign were teachers, engineers, and other educated people. Fearing for their lives, an estimated 350,000 Laotians (10 percent of the country's population) fled the country. Many settled in refugee camps in Thailand, but an estimated 150,000 eventually resettled in the United States, where they tried to build new lives for themselves.

Sources

Butler, David. *The Fall of Saigon: Scenes from the Sudden End of a Long War.* New York: Simon and Schuster, 1985.

Chandler, David P. *The Tragedy of Cambodian History.* New Haven, CT: Yale University Press, 1992.

Dung, Van Tien. *Our Great Spring Victory: An Account of the Liberation of South Vietnam.* New York: Monthly Review Press, 1977.

Engelmann, Larry. *Tears Before the Rain: An Oral History of the Fall of South Vietnam.* New York: Oxford University Press, 1990.

Ford, Gerald R. *A Time to Heal: The Autobiography of Gerald R. Ford.* New York: Harper and Row, 1979.

Hamilton-Merritt, Jane. *Tragic Mountains: The Hmong, the Americans, and the Secret Wars for Laos, 1942–1992.* Bloomington: Indiana University Press, 1993.

Herring, George C. *America's Longest War: The United States and Vietnam, 1950–1975.* New York: McGraw-Hill, 1979.

Hosmer, Stephen T., et al., eds. *The Fall of South Vietnam: Statements by Vietnamese Military and Civilian Leaders.* Santa Monica, CA: Rand, 1978.

Isaacs, Arnold R. *Without Honor: Defeat in Vietnam and Cambodia.* Baltimore, MD: Johns Hopkins University Press, 1983.

Maclear, Michael. *The Ten Thousand Day War: Vietnam, 1945–1975.* New York: Avon, 1981.

MacPherson, Myra. *Long Time Passing: Vietnam and the Haunted Generation.* New York: Doubleday, 1984.

Snepp, Frank. *Decent Interval: An Insider's Account of Saigon's Indecent End.* New York: Random House, 1977.

Summers, Harry G., Jr. "Final Days of South Vietnam," in *American History* (April 1995).

Summers, Harry G., Jr. *Historical Atlas of the Vietnam War.* Boston: Houghton Mifflin, 1995.

Vickery, Michael. *Cambodia, 1975–1982.* South End Press, 1984.

Wiesner, Louis A. *Victims and Survivors: Displaced Persons and Other War Victims in Vietnam, 1954–1975.* New York: Greenwood Press, 1988.

Vietnam Since the War (1976-Present)

15

The war in Vietnam finally ended in 1975, when North Vietnamese troops captured the South Vietnamese capital of Saigon. The following year, the Communist leaders of North Vietnam reunited the two halves of the country to form the Socialist Republic of Vietnam (SRV). They also introduced a series of changes designed to transform Vietnam into a socialist society. For example, the government took control of all farmland and business activities and placed restrictions on the lives of the Vietnamese people.

These changes created terrible hardships for the Vietnamese. "Rebuilding Vietnam would have been a stupendous task under the best of circumstances. The war shattered its economy, disrupted its social texture, and exhausted its population in both the north and the south," comments Stanley Karnow in *Vietnam: A History.* "The war left Vietnam in shambles, and the Communists aggravated the devastation after their victory." Before long, hundreds of thousands of Vietnamese people decided that they could not live under the new government. Many tried to escape the poverty and repression (denial of their basic rights and freedoms) by fleeing the coun-

Words to Know

Cambodia Southeast Asian nation located on the western border of South Vietnam. During the Vietnam War, Cambodia experienced its own civil war between its pro-U.S. government and Communist rebels known as the Khmer Rouge.

Communism A political system in which the government controls all resources and means of producing wealth. By eliminating private property, this system is designed to create an equal society with no social classes. However, Communist governments in practice often limit personal freedom and individual rights.

Hanoi The capital city of Communist North Vietnam during the Vietnam War, and the capital of the reunified Socialist Republic of Vietnam afterward.

Indochina The name sometimes given to the peninsula between India and China in Southeast Asia. The term narrowly refers to Cambodia, Laos, and Vietnam, which were united under the name French Indochina during the colonial period, 1893–1954.

Khmer Rouge Communist-led rebel forces that fought for control of Cambodia during the Vietnam War years. The Khmer Rouge overthrew the U.S.-backed government of Lon Nol in 1975, but were removed from power by Vietnamese forces in 1979.

North Vietnam The Geneva Accords of 1954, which ended the First Indochina War (1946–54), divided the nation of Vietnam into two sections. The northern section, which was led by a Communist government, was officially known as the Democratic Republic of Vietnam, but was usually called North Vietnam.

Saigon The capital city of U.S.-supported South Vietnam during the Vietnam War. Also an unofficial shorthand way of referring to the South Vietnamese government.

Socialist Republic of Vietnam (SRV) The country created in 1976, when North Vietnam won the Vietnam War and was reunited with South Vietnam.

South Vietnam Created under the Geneva Accords of 1954, the southern section of Vietnam was known as the Republic of South Vietnam. It was led by a U.S.-supported government.

---

try by water in small boats. These Vietnamese refugees became known around the world as the "boat people."

In the meantime, old rivalries and disagreements heated up between Vietnam and its neighbors, Cambodia and China. In 1979, Vietnam successfully invaded Cambodia and overthrew its brutal government. But China and other nations reacted angrily to Vietnam's actions. In fact, Chinese troops invaded the northern part of Vietnam. The United States and other countries established an economic embargo (a legal order preventing trade) to punish Vietnam.

The situation in Cambodia only complicated the problems within Vietnam. By the mid-1980s, the situation had become so desperate that the Communist leaders reversed their earlier policies and introduced a series of economic reforms. Since then, Vietnam's economy has recovered significantly. In addition, the Vietnamese government has improved its relationship with a number of foreign powers, including China and the United States. Although Vietnam continues to struggle with poverty and other problems, many people feel that the country is well on its way to recovering from the devastation of the Vietnam War.

People to Know

Nguyen Van Linh (1915–) Leader of the Communist Party who was the man behind Vietnam's *doi moi* economic reform program.

Pol Pot (1928–1998) Head of the Communist-led Khmer Rouge forces that took control of Cambodia in 1976. As prime minister of Cambodia from 1976 to 1979, he oversaw a violent transformation of society that resulted in the deaths of up to two million citizens.

The Socialist Republic of Vietnam

In April 1975—two years after American troops left Vietnam—North Vietnamese forces captured the South Vietnamese capital of Saigon to win the Vietnam War. North Vietnamese political leaders immediately began making plans to reunite the two halves of the country. In July 1976, they announced the formation of the Socialist Republic of Vietnam. The capital city of the new nation would be Hanoi (pronounced huh-NOY), which had served as the capital of North Vietnam during the war. Many figures in the new government were former officials of the North Vietnamese government and leaders of the Communist Party. But a few politicians from South Vietnam were assigned positions in the government as well.

Although Vietnam was reunified fairly quickly after the war ended, the country still faced a number of serious problems. For example, its land and cities had suffered heavy damage during the war. In the South, 25 million acres of farmland and 9,000 villages had been destroyed. In the North, all six major industrial cities had been severely damaged. In addition, many areas of the country continued to experience negative effects of the war. Each day, farmers were injured by land mines and unexploded bombs that littered the countryside. Many Vietnamese children were born with birth defects because their mothers had been exposed to defoliants and herbicides (poisonous chemicals used to kill trees and other vegetation) during the war.

In addition to the physical damage to the people and the land, Vietnam also faced tough economic problems after the war. In the South, about four million people were unemployed. Many of these people, including former government officials and soldiers in the South Vietnamese Army, had depended on aid from the United States in order to survive. But when the Americans left and North Vietnam took control, there was very little money to support them.

South Vietnamese are "re-educated"

As North Vietnamese leaders took steps to reunite the two halves of their battered country, they expressed a willingness to work with the people of the South. They emphasized that their victory in the Vietnam War was a victory for all Vietnamese people over foreign invaders. Many people in the South were happy to have peace at last. Some had secretly supported the Communists during the war by hiding guerilla fighters (guerrillas are small groups of fighters who launch surprise attacks) or providing them with supplies. As a result, many people in the South seemed hopeful about the reunification of their country under Communist rule. They believed that their lives might get better with a new political system.

Before long, however, North Vietnamese leaders began punishing people who had fought against them during the war. "When the Communists drove into Saigon in 1975, they were prudently [wisely] greeted by a dazed population yearning for peace and prepared to cooperate," Karnow notes. "But instead of proceeding gently, they embarked on a program of wholesale repression."

Amerasians

Many Vietnamese people found living conditions very difficult in their country after the Vietnam War ended. But the situation was even worse for the mixed-race children known as Amerasians. Amerasian children had American soldiers as fathers and Vietnamese women as mothers. The approximately 30,000 children born out of these wartime relationships were treated as outcasts in Vietnamese society.

In Vietnamese culture, a person's identity comes from his or her father. But the fathers of the Amerasian children had either died in the war or returned to the United States in the early 1970s, when American troops were withdrawn from Vietnam. Most of these children had very little information about their fathers. In fact, some of them were abandoned by their mothers after the war ended. As Vietnam struggled to recover from the war, many Vietnamese people resented anything that reminded them of Americans. For this reason, they looked down upon Amerasians as "children of the enemy."

The children of African American fathers received especially poor treatment in Vietnam. "All my life people had been mean to me [in Vietnam] because of my color," an Amerasian named Huong told Steven DeBonis in *Children of the Enemy.* "My skin is black, and my hair is curly, not like the Vietnamese, and they didn't like that."

Because of the poor treatment they received, most Amerasians wanted to leave Vietnam for the United States. U.S. policy toward Amerasians evolved during the 1980s. The Amerasian Immigration Act of 1982 recognized Amerasians as American citizens, but the lack of diplomatic relations between the United States and Vietnam prevented many Amerasians from immigrating. The Amerasian Homecoming Act of 1987 put specific programs in place to help Amerasians and their families leave Vietnam and adjust to life in the United States.

By 1990, about 22,000 Amerasians had settled in the United States. Unfortunately, only about 2 percent were able to locate and establish relationships with their fathers. Without ties in either American society or the community of Vietnamese immigrants in the United States, many Amerasians had trouble adjusting to their new home.

Within a short time, about 400,000 South Vietnamese people who were viewed as threats to Communist rule were sent away to be "re-educated," or forced to go along with the government. These people included not only former South

Modern-day Vietnamese schoolchildren, riding bikes past a poster celebrating Vietnamese independence from French rule.
Reproduced by permission of AP/World Wide Photos.

Vietnamese government officials and army officers, but also doctors, lawyers, teachers, journalists, engineers, and other intellectuals. They were held in prisons that had been used during the war or sent away to work farms. Many were forced to perform hard labor and received very little food.

North Vietnamese leaders initially planned to re-educate people they viewed as political enemies for five years. But many South Vietnamese citizens ended up being held for much longer periods. Communist Party officials worried that these people would try to overthrow the new government if they were released. As it turned out, keeping these skilled and educated people in jail also hurt the government, because their talents could have contributed to the country's recovery.

Socialist reforms of agriculture and industry

After forming the new Socialist Republic of Vietnam, Communist leaders in Hanoi launched a wide-ranging program to transform Vietnamese society. Mainly, they wanted the southern half of the country to operate on the same sort of political system as the northern half. Under this system, known as socialism, the government controls all resources and means of producing wealth. By eliminating private property, it is designed to create an equal society with no social classes.

In 1978, the SRV government nationalized all industry and commerce. This meant that the government would own all factories and businesses. It would also set prices for goods and control other aspects of trade. Vietnam's economy would be centrally planned by a group of Communist Party officials, and individual citizens would be required to go along with their decisions. Many people resented the government controls, particularly in the South. Some people found ways to work around them. Corruption and bribery became common in Vietnamese business.

The Vietnamese government also placed socialist controls over the nation's agriculture. They took land away from individual farmers and combined many small plots into large, collective farms. They believed this would make the land more productive and ensure that farmers grew a variety of crops that would benefit all the people. After all, collective farming had worked well in the North during the Vietnam War to supply food to the North Vietnamese Army.

But farmers in the South resisted joining collective farms because they had always farmed their own land. They did not understand why the government required them to grow crops that were not well suited to their land. They resented having to sell their crops to the government at official prices, because these prices were not high enough to allow them to purchase tools, fertilizer, and seeds. Agricultural production declined very rapidly in Vietnam following the socialist reforms. Hunger became a widespread problem. In fact, food rations in 1978 were twenty-five percent lower than they had been during the hardest years of the war.

The crisis of the "boat people"

The socialist reforms put in place by the new Vietnamese government had disastrous results. People in the South who had once run their own shops or businesses felt that the government regulations made it impossible for them to make a living. Rural farmers and villagers also resented the government controls and increasingly suffered from hunger and disease. Before long, many groups of Vietnamese citizens had become very unhappy with the Communist programs and the hardships they had created.

Shortly after the socialist reforms went into effect, large numbers of Vietnam's citizens decided that they could not live under the new government. The widespread poverty and the repression of basic individual rights and freedoms created what Karnow calls a "massive exodus [departure] from Vietnam—one of the largest migrations of modern times." Over the next few years, more than 1.5 million people risked their lives to escape from the country.

One of the first waves of people to leave Vietnam were ethnic Chinese. Many of these people were successful traders and merchants who operated businesses in southern cities. There was a great deal of political tension between the Socialist Republic of Vietnam and its neighbor to the north, China. The new Vietnamese government placed especially harsh restrictions on ethnic Chinese merchants because they worried that China would use them to influence politics in Vietnam. As a result, hundreds of thousands of ethnic Chinese fled across the northern border into China in 1978. Some of them paid bribes to Communist officials in order to buy their way out of the country. Others tried to reach China by sea in poorly equipped boats.

Huge numbers of ethnic Vietnamese also tried to leave the country. Since Vietnam's closest neighbors—Cambodia and Laos—were also having severe economic and political problems during this time, most of the refugees left Vietnam by water. They usually had to give up all of their personal belongings to afford the trip, and many were forced to leave family members behind. At times, more than 50,000 people per month set sail from the Vietnamese coast on small boats and rafts. As the international media picked up on the story, the refugees became known around the world as "boat people."

Since their vessels were too small to handle storms in the South China Sea, thousands of Vietnamese boat people drowned. Others died of hunger, thirst, or exposure to the elements. But many refugees landed safely on small Southeast Asian islands. Unfortunately, some neighboring countries refused to accept the boat people. For example, Malaysia sometimes turned the Vietnamese boats around and sent them back out to sea. Countries like Malaysia, Indonesia, Brunei, and the

Philippines felt that they should not be forced to take responsibility for unwanted people because they had not contributed to the crisis. In addition, these countries did not have resources to care for the refugees.

When the boat people did reach land, they often had trouble finding a permanent new home. Many of them spent months or years in crowded refugee camps. Wealthy countries like the United States, Canada, France, and Australia increased their immigration quotas in order to accept some Vietnamese refugees. But these countries did not want to appear too generous, because they did not want to encourage more people to attempt the dangerous journey.

Nevertheless, the flow of refugees from Vietnam continued into the early 1980s. The crisis finally ended when conditions within Vietnam began to improve. In addition, the Vietnamese government began allowing people to leave the country legally. About one million refugees from Vietnam and Cambodia eventually resettled in the United States. Some of these people became successful members of American society, but many others continued to struggle with poverty and prejudice in their new country.

War returns to Indochina

As the Socialist Republic of Vietnam struggled with internal problems, it also continued to clash with neighboring countries. Vietnamese leaders felt that Cambodia and Laos—the countries along Vietnam's western border—owed them a debt. After all, the Vietnamese had done most of the fighting against the French and the Americans in Indochina. Now that these foreign powers had left the region, Vietnam expected Cambodia and Laos to support it politically. The Vietnamese government wanted the three countries to form an alliance, with Vietnam recognized as its leader.

Cambodia refused to go along with this plan. Shortly after the North Vietnamese had captured Saigon in 1975, a group of radical Communist rebels known as the Khmer Rouge had taken control of Cambodia's government. The Khmer Rouge, led by a mysterious man named Pol Pot, immediately launched a violent and destructive transformation of Cambodian society. They drove people out of the cities and into labor camps, and they murdered thousands of intellectuals who opposed their rule. Within a short time, more than one million Cambodians had been executed or had died of hunger or disease under the Khmer Rouge.

Cambodia had a long history of disputes with Vietnam. Once the Khmer Rouge claimed power, Pol Pot demanded the return of Cambodian territory that Vietnam had seized generations earlier. In December 1978, the Vietnamese government sent troops into Cambodia to overthrow the Khmer Rouge and protect its borders. By January 1979, Vietnam's invasion forces had captured the Cambodian capital city, Phnom Penh (pronounced puh-NAHM PEN). They immediately put an end to the brutal policies of the Khmer Rouge. They also established a new, pro-Vietnamese government under Prime Minister Hun Sen.

Even though the Vietnamese invasion of Cambodia had removed the violent Khmer Rouge from power, many countries around the world criticized Vietnam's actions. For example, the United States and other countries formed an economic embargo to punish Vietnam. The U.S. government also provided support to Cambodian rebels fighting against the Hun Sen government, including the Khmer Rouge. But the country that was most upset about Vietnam's invasion of Cambodia was China.

China—Vietnam's neighbor to the north—had supported the North Vietnamese Communists during the Vietnam War. In return, the Chinese expected the new Vietnamese government to form an alliance with them against their bitter rivals, the Soviet Union. But Vietnam had a long history of disputes with China. In fact, China had controlled Vietnam by force for hundreds of years. As a result, the new Vietnamese government felt suspicious toward China and was determined to maintain its independence.

When Vietnam invaded Cambodia, China became concerned that it was losing power over Indochina. In February 1979, the Chinese responded by invading northern Vietnam in order to "teach Vietnam a lesson." The Vietnamese army fought off the attack, but both sides suffered tens of thousands of casualties (killed and wounded soldiers). In addition, an area of northern Vietnam that had escaped damage during the Vietnam War was destroyed.

Economic and political problems grow

The fighting with Cambodia and China only made the situation worse within the Socialist Republic of Vietnam. The expense of fighting and maintaining troops in Cambodia reduced the money available to solve problems at home. In addition, the economic embargo made it impossible for Vietnam to trade with or borrow money from many other countries. Before long, the Vietnamese economy was suffering from terrible inflation (a situation where the cost of goods rises more quickly than people's incomes). By 1986, prices were rising by 600 percent per year. At that rate, one chicken would cost an average Vietnamese worker an entire month's salary.

The Vietnamese government also had trouble uniting the economies and cultures of the northern and southern sections of the country. People in the South tended to resist the socialist controls that the northern government tried to place upon them. "Historic differences between north and south were exacerbated [made worse] during three decades of war, and even the most heavy-handed methods could not force the freewheeling and resilient south into a made-in-Hanoi mold," George C. Herring explains in *America's Longest War*.

By the mid-1980s, even people who had supported North Vietnam during the war began to feel that the Communist leaders were doing a poor job of running the country. After all, the government had promised to reunite Vietnam and return it to peace and prosperity. But instead, conditions for many citizens were worse than they had ever been before. "By the time Vietnam's rulers staged huge public ceremonies to celebrate the tenth anniversary of their victory, it was no longer possible to conceal—even from themselves—how poorly their leadership had repaid the enormous sacrifices that had given their revolution its victory," Arnold R. Isaacs comments in *Vietnam Shadows: The War, Its Ghosts, and Its Legacy*.

The *doi moi* economic reforms

In 1986, the Vietnamese Communist Party responded to the growing problems by electing new leaders. Nguyen Van Linh (pronounced en-gie-EN VAHN LIN; 1915–) became the new chief of the ruling party. Within a short time, the government announced a series of major economic reforms known as *doi moi,* or "renovation." "The Communist Party bosses recognized that they had squandered [foolishly wasted] the peace and tarnished the reputation they had gained from winning the war," Karnow notes. "Desperate, they introduced an array of pragmatic [sensible] economic reforms."

Under the *doi moi* program, private citizens regained some control over business. The Vietnamese government also made some moves toward improving relations with the United States, China, and other countries. For example, it expressed an interest in withdrawing its troops from Cambodia. In 1988, SRV leaders took another step toward opening their economy and society. Under an initiative called Directive 10, the Vietnamese government took apart the collective farms and returned the land to individual farmers. They also ended all price controls on farm products.

The reforms quickly created positive effects in the Vietnamese economy. As a result of the changes, agricultural production increased by twenty-two percent and industrial output by fifty percent between 1989 and 1993. In fact, Vietnam became the third-largest rice exporter in the world during this period. "This movement toward a more open society and economy, known as *doi moi* in Vietnam, has made the second decade of Communist rule much more agreeable—though by no means perfect—for a great number of Vietnamese," Murray Hiebert writes in *Chasing the Tigers: A Portrait of the New Vietnam.*

Vietnam resumes diplomatic relations with the United States

As the Vietnamese economy became more free and open under *doi moi,* government leaders recognized that the next step involved improving relations with the rest of the world. For their economic reforms to succeed, they needed money, technology, and management skills to flow into the country from overseas. But their traditional source of such support, the Soviet Union, was having economic and political troubles of its own. This situation forced Vietnamese leaders to look toward capitalist countries like the United States and

Nguyen Van Linh: "Vietnam's Gorbachev"

The man behind Vietnam's *doi moi* economic reform program was Nguyen Van Linh (pronounced en-gie-EN VAHN LIN), who became head of the Communist Party in 1986. Born in Hanoi in 1915, Nguyen Van Linh was active in the Vietnamese resistance to French rule during the colonial period. As a result of his activities, he spent a dozen years in French prisons beginning when he was fifteen. During the Vietnam War, he became a member of the Communist Party in North Vietnam.

After North Vietnam won the war in 1975, hard-line Communists made a number of changes in order to create a socialist society. The government took control of all agriculture, business, and industry in the country. Decisions about prices and other aspects of trade were made by government planners. But over the next ten years, these changes resulted in lower production of food and goods, rapidly increasing prices, and widespread poverty and hunger. By the early 1980s, some of Vietnam's leaders realized that the socialist economic policies they had put in place after the war were not working.

Although he was a longtime Communist, Nguyen Van Linh held more liberal, flexible views than many other party leaders. He began working within the government to loosen some of the restrictions on private farms and businesses. But many of the old-school Communist leaders resisted his efforts. They were afraid that allowing reforms would reduce their power. In fact, they kicked Nguyen Van Linh out of the Vietnamese government in 1982.

Rather than giving up, Nguyen Van Linh quietly encouraged the Vietnamese people to push for change. For example, he wrote an anonymous column

Japan, as well as successful Southeast Asian neighbors like Singapore, Taiwan, and Indonesia.

For Vietnam, the first step in improving relations with the rest of the world was to withdraw its troops from Cambodia. After all, the invasion of Cambodia had angered many other countries and led to an economic embargo against Vietnam. Vietnamese leaders began the process of removing occupation forces from Cambodia in 1987 and completed it by 1989. In 1991, Vietnam signed a formal peace agreement that led to free elections and a new government for Cambodia in for the Communist Party newspaper in which he criticized government leaders and their failed economic policies. When he called for citizens to write letters of complaint to party leaders, the government received thousands of messages describing the people's poverty and suffering.

By 1985, it had become clear that the socialist economic policies were causing all kinds of problems and hardships for Vietnam. Nguyen Van Linh was allowed to return to his position in the government, and the following year he became the new head of the Vietnamese Communist Party. Under his leadership, the government took a number of steps toward opening up Vietnam's economy.

Nguyen Van Linh introduced an economic reform program known as *doi moi*, or "renovation." This program reduced the authority of central government planners, encouraged private businesses, and attracted foreign investment. "I think that we have to push away the darkness in just the way that we have to weed a rice field so that the rice grows strong," Nguyen Van Linh said about the reforms. "The good man and good works need room to grow—we must push away bad people and bad works to make way for them." Vietnam's battered economy began to recover soon after the *doi moi* program was put in place.

Because of his success in opening up the Vietnamese economy, Nguyen Van Linh has been compared to Mikhail Gorbachev (1931–). As president of the Soviet Union from 1988 to 1991, Gorbachev introduced reforms that made Soviet society more democratic. He also improved his country's relations with the United States and other nations, receiving the 1990 Nobel Peace Prize for his work.

1993. Unfortunately, the Cambodian government has changed several times since then and remains unstable. With the death of Pol Pot in 1998, the Khmer Rouge is no longer a factor in Cambodian politics. But Cambodia is still one of the poorest countries in the world.

Making peace with Cambodia had several positive effects for Vietnam, however. For example, Vietnam and China resumed normal diplomatic relations and began trading in 1991. In addition, Vietnam developed a strong trading relationship with other Southeast Asian countries. In 1995, Vietnam formally joined the Association of Southeast Asian Nations (ASEAN), a cooperative organization of countries that includes Indonesia, Malaysia, Singapore, Brunei, the Philippines, and Thailand.

Withdrawing from Cambodia also helped Vietnam to improve its relations with the United States. Due to continuing hard feelings about the war, the U.S. government established several conditions for formally recognizing Vietnam and resuming diplomatic relations. One of these conditions was that Vietnam had to help account for all the U.S. soldiers who were listed as "missing in action" during the Vietnam War.

As Vietnam worked to satisfy American demands, the U.S. government gradually eliminated the political barriers between the two countries. U.S. President Bill Clinton (1946–; president 1993–2000) ended the economic embargo in early 1994, and he resumed normal diplomatic relations on July 11, 1995. Twenty years after the Vietnam War, the Socialist Republic of Vietnam and the United States opened a new chapter in their relationship.

Vietnam today

In some areas, Vietnam shows signs of a strong economic recovery. For example, many of its major cities are booming. The streets of Ho Chi Minh City (formerly known as Saigon) are crowded with people riding motorbikes to work. There are fancy office buildings and hotels, shops selling high-tech electronic equipment, glittering dance clubs and karaoke bars, and huge billboards advertising Coca-Cola and other Western products. The capital city of Hanoi is less busy but still highly developed, with business offices of many large foreign companies.

In the 1990s, the Vietnamese government began trying to attract Western tourists to the country, including former U.S. soldiers and their families. They even offered tours of the extensive systems of tunnels that were used by Viet Cong guerilla fighters. Observers have noted that the Vietnamese do not seem to resent Americans, although many continue to express sorrow about the war's enormous cost to both nations. For the most part, however, the Vietnamese people seem to

New Year 2000 in Ho Chi Minh City (formerly Saigon). *Reproduced by permission of AP/Wide World Photos.*

have moved past the war. Part of the reason may be that more than half of the Vietnamese population of seventy-six million was born after the Vietnam War ended. Many people in this younger generation appear to be more interested in learning English and establishing good careers than in worrying about the past.

One project, launched in April 2000, is an attempt to turn the most well-known landmark of the Vietnam War into an opportunity for economic growth. It involves transforming parts of the Ho Chi Minh Trail—the network of jungle trails that moved troops and supplies between North and South Vietnam—into a 1,000-mile-long national highway. Vietnam officials predict that the highway will open up trade and industry to the untapped mountainous western provinces. The estimated three-year-long project is already off to a bumpy start, however, since land mines and unexploded bombs are peppered throughout the trail. This undertaking is one of many initiatives to convert war "relics." Other examples have included turning military bases into factories.

Although Vietnam shows outward signs of prosperity in the cities, it is clear that the government still has work to do. Vietnam remains one of the world's poorest nations, with an average annual income of about $300 per person. Conditions have not improved in the countryside, where peasants work in rice fields as they have for generations. Medical care is limited for the poorer segments of Vietnamese society, and disease and hunger are common problems. While the population of Vietnam has grown rapidly, the nation's farmland and natural resources have disappeared. This means that Vietnam must move toward an economy based on technology in the future. But severe shortages of trained business managers and skilled labor will make this transition difficult.

The Communist Party no longer controls every detail of people's lives, but the government's economic reforms have not been matched by wide-ranging political reforms. Vietnamese leaders do allow students and other groups to criticize their policies in a limited way. But they actively prevent rival political movements from developing. Some people in Vietnam have access to foreign television stations on satellite dishes. But Communist officials often censor the information published in newspapers and magazines.

In 1996, the Vietnamese government took steps to control the people's access to the Internet. "Hanoi is concerned that the information superhighway will not only link one of the world's poorest nations to the economic data it needs, but also give Internet surfers access to human rights reports, pornography, and the many World Wide Web sites created by overseas Vietnamese groups hostile to the government," Hiebert explains.

Despite such efforts to control opposition to their policies, the Communist Party still appears to be losing power in Vietnam. The collapse of the Soviet Union helped increase people's doubts about the wisdom of the Communist political system. In addition, many Vietnamese blame the government for causing the country's economic problems after the war. The government continues to face problems with corruption, as dishonest officials give the best land and jobs to their friends. The younger generation of Vietnamese has become interested in Western culture rather than traditional Communist ideas. As a result, membership in the Vietnamese Communist Party has decreased steadily over the years.

Some observers predict that the Vietnamese people will soon begin demanding greater freedom and individual rights. "As Vietnam's society modernizes, receives information, and joins the outside world, it seems likely that economic change will beget [produce] greater participation in the Vietnamese political process," Frederick Z. Brown predicts in *Vietnam Joins the World*.

Sources

Chandrasekaran, Rajiv. "Highway to the Future Built on Vietnam's Past." *Washington Post*, [Online] April 6, 2000.

DeBonis, Steven. *Children of the Enemy: Oral Histories of Vietnamese Amerasians and Their Mothers*. Jefferson, NC: McFarland, 1995.

Herring, George C. *America's Longest War: The United States and Vietnam, 1950–1975*. New York: McGraw-Hill, 1979.

Hiebert, Murray. *Chasing the Tigers: A Portrait of the New Vietnam*. New York: Kodansha International, 1996.

Isaacs, Arnold R. *Vietnam Shadows: The War, Its Ghosts, and Its Legacy*. Baltimore, MD: Johns Hopkins University Press, 1997.

Karnow, Stanley. *Vietnam: A History*. New York: Viking Press, 1983.

Morley, James W., and Masashi Nishihara, eds. *Vietnam Joins the World*. Armonk, NY: M. E. Sharpe, 1997.

Young, Marilyn B. *The Vietnam Wars, 1945–1990*. New York: Harper-Collins, 1991.

America Since the War (1976–Present)

16

Even after the Vietnam War ended in 1975, memories of the conflict continued to haunt the United States. Troubled by the U.S. defeat, the war's terrible destruction, and its shattering impact on national unity, the American people entered a period of self-doubt and disillusionment. This attitude made America's Vietnam War veterans feel even more neglected and isolated.

The American people continued to feel uncertain and depressed about both themselves and their political leadership into the 1980s. During that period, however, attitudes about both Vietnam veterans and the U.S. war effort began to change. Americans continued to disagree about U.S. actions and attitudes in Vietnam, but they showed a greater willingness to move on and look to the future together. Veterans, meanwhile, finally began to receive recognition for the sacrifices they made in service to their country.

Nonetheless, historians agree that the wounds the United States received in Vietnam have not completely healed, even a quarter-century after the war's conclusion. U.S. foreign policy decisions continue to be shaped by memories of the

Words to Know

Cambodia Southeast Asian nation located on the western border of South Vietnam. During the Vietnam War, Cambodia experienced its own civil war between its pro-U.S. government and Communist rebels known as the Khmer Rouge.

Khmer Rouge Communist-led rebel forces that fought for control of Cambodia during the Vietnam War years. The Khmer Rouge overthrew the U.S.-backed government of Lon Nol in 1975.

MIAs Soldiers classified as "missing in action," meaning that their status is unknown to military leaders or that their bodies have not been recovered.

Watergate A political scandal that forced U.S. President Richard Nixon to resign from office in 1974. In June 1972, Republican agents associated with Nixon's re-election campaign broke into the Democratic campaign headquarters in the Watergate Hotel in Washington, D.C., to gather secret information. Nixon and several members of his administration attempted to cover up the burglary.

war. In addition, the conflict still evokes emotions of sadness, anger, and regret in many American families and communities.

American self-image and Vietnam

The United States entered the Vietnam War in the mid-1960s as a tremendously self-confident nation. Over the previous two decades, America had become the most economically successful and technologically advanced nation in the world. Moreover, the country was proud of its role in the defeat of Germany and Japan in World War II (1939–45), which was widely viewed as a triumph of good over evil. The memory of this great military triumph—and other American military victories throughout the nation's history—combined with the prosperity of the 1950s to create a feeling of optimism, pride, and self-assurance in most American communities.

In the early 1960s, all of these factors led the United States to see itself as both the most moral and the most powerful nation in the world. Americans believed that they "could not be beaten in war—not by any nation, and not by any combination of nations," notes Loren Baritz in *Backfire*. "We thought that we could fight where, when, and how we wished, without risking failure." The United States thus entered the Vietnam War with the full expectation of rolling to a quick and relatively painless victory.

But the war in Vietnam shredded America's belief in its military invincibility, its moral goodness, and its status as a unique and special country. The nation lost more than 58,000 soldiers and endured great internal divisions and turmoil over the war, only to see North Vietnam roll to victory in 1975. North Vietnam's triumph intensified the feeling that America had wasted thousands of lives and billions of dollars in the conflict. It also marked the first time in history that the United States had been on the losing side in a war.

A disillusioned country

In the years immediately following Vietnam, many Americans felt great disappointment and anger toward their country. They expressed doubts about the trustworthiness of the government, the morality of American institutions and society, and the future of the nation. "The Vietnamese War produced a profound moral crisis, sapping worldwide faith in our own policy and our system of life, a crisis of confidence made even more grave by the covert pessimism [secret gloominess] of some of our leaders," claimed U.S. President Jimmy Carter (1924–; president 1977–1981) in 1977.

The Vietnam War was not the only reason for these feelings of anxiety and self-doubt. The Watergate scandal, changing gender roles, unsettled race relations, economic troubles, fast-changing business trends, and new standards of conduct and taste all transformed American society during the 1960s and 1970s. Some of these developments—such as improved opportunities and rights for women and minorities—greatly improved the nation as a whole. But other events—like the Watergate scandal and gasoline shortages—contributed to the United States' post-Vietnam crisis of self-confidence. Combined with America's nightmarish experience in Vietnam, these changes convinced many people that the stable and patriotic society of the pre-Vietnam era had been lost for good.

People to Know

George Bush (1924–) President of the United States, 1989–1993; also served as vice president under Ronald Reagan, 1981–1989.

Jimmy Carter (1924–) President of the United States, 1977–1981. In 1977, he pardoned people who had resisted the draft during the Vietnam War.

Bill Clinton (1946–) President of the United States, 1993–2000. In 1995, he resumed full diplomatic relations with Vietnam.

Ronald Reagan (1911–) President of the United States, 1981–1989.

It wasn't until 1982 that the Vietnam Veterans Memorial Wall was dedicated. This statue, by Frederick Hart, representing the racial makeup and the service branches of the U.S. forces in Vietnam was unveiled in 1984.

Photograph by Kathleen Marcaccio. Reproduced by permission.

American veterans in the 1970s

The years immediately following the conclusion of the war were especially difficult for American Vietnam veterans. Some veterans suffered from the nagging sense that they had let their country down. As Arnold Isaacs explains in *Vietnam Shadows,* America entered Vietnam at a time when "the towering triumph in World War II was still the dominant image in the imagination of most Americans—and their soldiers, as well. The great majority of men who fought in Vietnam were born between 1945 and 1953, growing up in [a time] of postwar prosperity and national self-confidence. A large number were certainly the sons of World War II veterans. Virtually everything in their culture—novels, movies, family stories, childhood games, schoolbooks, the traditional patriotic rhetoric [message] of Veterans Day speeches and graduations and political campaigns—conditioned young men entering military service in the mid-1960s to think of Vietnam as their generation's turn to be, as one veteran said, 'the

Ronald Reagan helped improve the country's attitude toward Vietnam veterans by publicly commending them for fighting for their country.
Reproduced by permission of the Ronald Reagan Library.

good guys against the bad guys.' . . . And when Vietnam turned out to be such a different and disappointing war, the contrast with their fathers' experience made the disillusionment even sharper."

Many veterans also felt neglected and isolated from their fellow Americans in the years after Vietnam (see Chapter 10, "Coming Home: Vietnam Veterans in American Society"). They often returned home to families and communities that offered little sympathy or understanding of their experiences. "After an unpopular, unsuccessful, and morally confusing war, most Americans . . . just wanted to forget it as quickly as possible," Isaacs explains. "The veterans were an uncomfortable reminder of a subject no one wanted to speak about, or remember. Though the failure of American policy was surely not the fault of the young men who were sent to do the fighting, they were often made to feel as if they alone carried the stigma [mark of disgrace] of failure and the moral burden of violence."

Night Sounds in Postwar Vietnam

In 1999, veteran and author Philip Caputo returned to Vietnam, where he had been a marine platoon leader in 1965 and 1966. Writing in *National Geographic Adventure,* he talks about the vast difference between wartime Vietnam and its postwar atmosphere:

> At two in the morning . . . I pad outside through the courtyard gate and down a pitch-black path. If ever I'm going to suffer a flashback, it would be now, but I don't. Hearing crickets sing and frogs chirrup near the riverbank and in the paddies, I recall listening to those sounds on watch [during the war]; listening for them to fall silent. When the frogs and crickets stopped, it meant that someone—or a whole battalion for all you knew—was moving around out there in the black unknown beyond your foxhole, and you waited with every sense alert, every nerve tensed for a burst of gunfire, a grenade to come arcing out of the underbrush. But now the chorus goes on without interruption, the ceaseless song of ordinary and peaceful night.

This sense of abandonment was made even worse by the way that American films, television shows, and other media portrayed Vietnam veterans throughout the 1970s. Their wartime experiences rarely were given any serious attention. Instead, movies and television shows typically portrayed them as pitiful, drug-addicted losers or homicidal maniacs. To the many veterans who had served their country honorably in Vietnam despite enormous hardships, these sorts of characterizations seemed particularly cruel and unfair.

Changing attitudes toward veterans

The image of America's Vietnam veterans finally began to change in the early 1980s. One important factor in this transformation was the increased public support that veterans received from some of the nation's political leaders. Presidential candidate Ronald Reagan (1911–; president 1981–1989) declared in 1980, for example, that the effort in Vietnam "was a noble cause . . . . We have been shabby in our treatment of those who returned. They fought as well and as bravely as any Americans have ever fought in any war. They deserve our gratitude, our respect, and our continuing concern."

Another event that changed American attitudes toward Vietnam veterans was the Iran hostage crisis. In November 1979, militant Iranians, angered over U.S. support for Iran's previous government, took 66 Americans hostage. Thirteen of the prisoners were soon released, but the remaining hostages were held captive for 444 days. They were finally released in

January 1981, on the same day that Reagan was sworn in to succeed Jimmy Carter as president of the United States.

When the Americans who had been held hostage returned home, they received a tremendous reception. Many U.S. communities celebrated their release, and dozens of former hostages were treated to parades and patriotic ceremonies. But these celebrations reminded many Americans of how Vietnam veterans had been treated when they returned home. "The hero's welcome given the former hostages dramatized by contrast the point expressed by a growing number of veterans," writes Christian G. Appy in *Working-Class War.* "They returned from Vietnam in virtual isolation, received no national homecoming ceremonies, and lacked adequate medical and psychological care, educational benefits, and job training." With this in mind, American communities began taking steps to make up for their previous treatment of the veterans.

The Wall

The single biggest factor in America's changing perception of its Vietnam veterans was the creation of the Vietnam Veterans Memorial. This memorial is commonly known as "The Wall" because its dominant feature is a vast V-shaped wall of reflective black granite on which the names of all Americans killed in Vietnam are listed.

The push to create a Vietnam Veterans Memorial was led by Jan Scruggs, who was himself a veteran of the war. At first, the plan for the wall was controversial. Some veterans and other Americans objected to the design, which they saw as an insulting change from more traditional monuments. But others defended the design, which had been submitted by a young Chinese-American art student named Maya Lin. After months of bitter debate, the memorial was dedicated on November 13 (Veterans Day), 1982.

In the months following the unveiling of the memorial, the American people gave the memorial a ringing endorsement. Family and friends of the dead soldiers and millions of other Americans whose lives had been changed forever by the war agreed that the monument was a powerful and moving

tribute to the men and women who died in Vietnam. "Criticism was quickly overwhelmed by the public's reaction," writes Isaacs. "Rarely in the long history of art, if ever, has an object crafted from stone affected a society's emotions so widely and deeply as the Vietnam memorial. Most intense and dramatic, perhaps, was its impact on the veterans themselves, for whom the wall represented a place for healing and the end of the long silence in which most had shrouded their experiences for many years."

Americans reconsider Vietnam

In the months and years following the unveiling of the Vietnam Veterans Memorial, a wave of new films, television shows, and works of literature about the Vietnam War also appeared. As with earlier movies and books, these works portrayed the Vietnam conflict as a terribly violent, depressing, and morally confusing war. Unlike earlier works, however, many of the books, films, and television shows of the 1980s portrayed veterans in a positive or even heroic way.

By the mid-1980s, it was clear that the American people had adopted a new attitude toward the men and women who had served in Vietnam. They now recognized that most American soldiers had done their best in Vietnam under circumstances that were often terribly frustrating and frightening. As Reagan declared in 1988, " For too long a time, they [the American Vietnam veterans] stood in a chill wind, as if on a winter night's watch. And in that night, their deeds spoke to us, but we knew them not. And their voices called to us, but we heard them not. Yet in this land that God has blessed, the dawn always at last follows the dark, and now morning has come. The night is over. We see these men and know them once again—and know how much we owe them, how much they have given us, and how much we can never fully repay. And not just as individuals but as a nation, we say we love you."

Of course, the American people—and Vietnam veterans themselves—continued to disagree about nearly every other aspect of the war. Friends, family members, and communities remained divided about the morality of U.S. actions in Vietnam. They also disagreed about the motivations and influence of the antiwar movement of the 1960s and early 1970s. In addition, historians, military and political leaders, veterans, and peace activists continued to express great differences of opinion on American military strategy, Vietnamese hopes and desires, American press coverage of the conflict, and a range of other war-related subjects. "On both sides [supporters and opponents of the war], there were some who found moral clarity in the wartime choices they had made, or that circumstances had imposed on them," notes Isaacs. "But for most, . . . the issues of an anguished time continued to defy easy or comfortable judgments, remaining as painful and morally confusing—or more so—as during the war itself."

U.S. foreign policy after Vietnam

In the years following the war's conclusion, memories of Vietnam also had a major impact on U.S. foreign policy decisions. Whenever the United States debated using military force in another country, critics compared the situation to Vietnam. In almost every case, American policymakers decided not to commit its troops. As novelist and journalist Jack Fuller commented, "[America] sees Vietnam everywhere, a ghost in every conflict. Vietnam in Angola. Vietnam in Nicaragua. Vietnam in El Salvador, in Guatemala, in Beirut. The ghost whispers contradictory messages. To some it says, 'Stay out [of the conflict].' To others it says, 'Fight this one to win.' . . . From time to time, politicians have proclaimed that we have finally put the war behind us. But we have always proven them wrong."

As the years passed, each new American president insisted that the United States was prepared to use its military might to protect its interests around the globe. They pointed out that many nations looked to the United States—as the world's leading superpower—to intervene in conflicts that threatened innocent peoples. But each administration reacted very cautiously whenever military solutions were proposed for international problems. After Vietnam, U.S. lawmakers simply did not believe that the American people would tolerate any military operations that endangered American soldiers. "Our ineptness [incompetence] in Vietnam led many Americans to question the wisdom of using our power at all," explains former President Richard Nixon (1913–1994; president 1969–1974) in *No More Vietnams*. "Many of our leaders have shrunk from any use of power because they feared it would bring another disaster like the one in Vietnam."

The Vietnam War also had a lingering effect on the attitudes of America's military leadership. Many members of the nation's armed forces believed that the U.S. military was not to blame for the defeat in Vietnam. They rejected charges that America's failure in Vietnam could be traced to flawed military strategies or clumsy military leadership. Instead, they blamed America's loss in Vietnam on timid civilian leadership and weak public support for the war effort. This opinion was shared by conservative legislators and many ordinary Americans.

This attitude led American military leaders to insist that certain conditions be met before committing U.S. troops to hazardous duty in foreign lands in the future. They told lawmakers that they never again wanted to commit troops without overwhelming public support (although critics pointed out that the American people voiced broad support for the

Vietnam War throughout the first three years of that conflict). They also stated that before any military intervention, they wanted clear military objectives and permission to use overwhelming military power. Finally, they expressed determination to exercise greater control over the news media in future military actions. Many U.S. military leaders believed that media coverage of the Vietnam War had poisoned the American public's attitudes toward the conflict. They wanted to prevent that from ever happening again.

Vietnam and the 1991 Persian Gulf War

In January 1991, the United States launched its largest military operation since the Vietnam War. This operation in the Middle East came in response to Iraq's August 1990 invasion of Kuwait, an American ally that was a major source of oil for the United States. When Iraq seized control of Kuwait, U.S. President George Bush (1924–; president 1989–1993) organized a massive military build-up of forces on the border of Kuwait. American military units accounted for most of this build-up, but they were joined by forces from a number of other nations as well. They warned Iraq's President Saddam Hussein (1937–) to remove his troops from Kuwait, but Hussein refused to do so.

During the final months of 1990, Bush repeatedly assured the American people that if the situation in Kuwait exploded into war, "it is not going to be another Vietnam." A vocal minority of American citizens protested the U.S. military presence in the Middle East. But Bush succeeded in convincing most Americans that important U.S. national interests were at stake in Kuwait.

In January 1991, the United States and its coalition of allies launched a major air bombing campaign against Iraq. A month later, they mounted a ground invasion of Kuwait.

George Bush, who served as president of the United States from 1988–92, launched the military action called *Desert Storm* **in January 1991, resulting in the Iraqi withdrawal from Kuwait.**
Reproduced by permission of AP/World Wide Photos.

These military actions quickly smashed the Iraqi military and forced it to abandon Kuwait. With Kuwait freed from Iraqi control, some observers wanted the United States and its allies to enter Iraq itself and overthrow the government of Iraqi President Saddam Hussein. But this idea did not have broad support. Arab members of the coalition objected to the idea of overthrowing another Arab government, and the United States worried that targeting Hussein might involve it in another long and costly war.

Reaction to the Gulf War

The battle to liberate Kuwait—commonly known as the Persian Gulf War—proved enormously popular with the American public. The war ended quickly, with the U.S.-led forces registering a decisive victory over the enemy. Moreover, the successful attack on Iraq resulted in only light casualties for the United States (148 American soldiers were killed; 458 were wounded). Americans were relieved and delighted by the outcome of the war. As Anna Quindlen noted in the *New York Times,* the Gulf War let Americans see themselves "as the leaders of the world again, assured of their inherent [basic] greatness and the essential evil of the enemy."

Both during and after the Persian Gulf War, American communities flew millions of flags and yellow ribbons to show their patriotic support for the U.S. troops operating in the Middle East. As Isaacs observes, "there was a palpable [detectable] national thirst to make the war a successful and satisfying event—the exact reverse of its experience in Vietnam." This attitude could clearly be seen in American news coverage of the war, which Isaacs termed "more celebratory than skeptical . . . . The vision of the war reaching the home front was pretty clearly just what the public wanted. What it did *not* want, unmistakably, was the kind of painful, morally confusing information it remembered receiving about Vietnam . . . . The war on Iraq was everything Vietnam had not been: a triumphant display of American resolve, skill, and technology, responding to a clear-cut act of aggression and waged against a dictator who could plausibly be pictured as a sinister thug."

After America's big Persian Gulf victory, Bush declared that the United States was no longer haunted by Vietnam. "The specter [ghost] of Vietnam has been buried forever in the

desert sands of the Arabian Peninsula," he told American troops in a radio broadcast. As it turned out, however, the victory over Iraq failed to change basic American doubts about military operations in foreign countries. U.S. economic troubles drained away Bush's post–Gulf War popularity, and he lost the 1992 presidential election to Democrat Bill Clinton (1946–; president 1993–2000).

The American people, meanwhile, remained opposed to any military operations that risked U.S. lives or long-term involvement. This attitude convinced most observers that the victory in the Persian Gulf War had failed to erase America's dark memories of Vietnam. As *Newsweek* columnist Meg Greenfield noted in 1994, "Merely mention the possible use of our military now any place on Earth and you will hear the pessimistic refrain: it will mean 500,000 ground troops, the military will fail, the wily enemy will prevail, the terrain is inhospitable, we will be hated, etc." In fact, most experts agree that these feelings were a major factor in America's decision to

Soldiers wearing chemical masks and protective combat uniforms, Operation Desert Shield, 1990.
Reproduced by permission of AP/World Wide Photos.

American Veterans Return to Vietnam

Since the Vietnam War ended in 1975, some American veterans of the conflict have returned to Vietnam to revisit the jungles, villages, and cities that dominate their wartime memories. In fact, tourism officials estimate that several thousand U.S. veterans returned to Vietnam each year in the late 1990s. There are many different reasons for their decisions to return to Vietnam. Some of the veterans have made the journey to assist in the rebuilding of the nation's war-torn communities. They have helped build medical clinics, schools, and bridges. Others have gone to Vietnam to seek out former allies and enemies in hopes of reaching a greater understanding of the war.

But most veterans have returned to Vietnam to mourn the deaths of comrades and to come to terms with their own grim memories of the war. "Going back to Vietnam helped veterans put the war behind them simply by letting them see that it was over," writes Arnold Isaacs in *Vietnam Shadows*. "The scenery they remembered—charred timbers that had once been farmers' houses, sandbagged bunkers and sprawling coils of concertina wire, little hills of expended shell cases heaped untidily along blackened gunpits— was no longer there. In its place was a landscape of orchards, shimmering fields of ripe rice, peaceful villages, gleaming-eyed children on the swaying backs of water buffaloes." "For most [veterans], it is a journey to see a land at peace that they last saw in turmoil," confirmed an American who organizes tours of the country.

avoid large-scale military intervention in the war-torn nation of Bosnia during the mid-1990s. It also has led the United States to secure broad support from other nations before it considers military intervention in foreign countries.

Reestablishing diplomatic ties with Vietnam

In the mid-1990s—more than twenty years after the last American troops withdrew from Vietnam—the United States finally established normal diplomatic relations with the Vietnamese government. Reaching this agreement took much longer than Vietnam had hoped. In fact, Vietnam repeatedly tried to establish better relations with the United States during the late 1970s and 1980s. Vietnam's leadership recognized that America's diplomatic actions against their nation—including an economic embargo (suspension of trade with a country) that had begun in 1975—were hurting its economy and its ability to interact with other countries.

But many U.S. political and community leaders resisted Vietnam's attempts to reach agreement with America. They claimed that Vietnam was interfering too much in Cambodia's internal affairs, even though Vietnam had removed the brutal Khmer Rouge from power. Other opponents of normalizing relations with Vietnam charged that American soldiers from the Vietnam War are still held in captivity by the Vietnamese government. This controversy over the fate of American soldiers classified as MIAs (Missing in Action) in Indochina became a major barrier to establishing diplomatic ties, even though many experts reject the theory that American soldiers remain imprisoned in Vietnam as a myth. Finally, some Americans resisted normalizing relations with Vietnam because they were still angry about the outcome of the Vietnam War.

As time passed, however, U.S. business leaders and many political and community leaders declared their support for normal relations with Vietnam. These supporters of normalization ranged from people who had been at the forefront of the Vietnam-era antiwar movement to Vietnam veterans who had endured imprisonment and torture during the war.

In the early 1990s, the United States and Vietnam reached agreement on a general plan to improve relations between the two nations. As part of the plan, Vietnam agreed to help investigate the fate of American MIAs in Indochina, as well as to return the remains of U.S. soldiers to American soil. The Vietnamese government also agreed to free all prisoners who had been jailed for wartime activities or affiliations. According to most observers, the Vietnamese government cooperated in all of these areas.

In 1992, the Bush administration approved U.S. dealings with Vietnam for "humanitarian" purposes. It also relaxed restrictions on travel, communications, and relief agency activities in Vietnam. A year later, President Clinton changed U.S. policies so that American firms could participate in development projects in Vietnam. In February 1994, Clinton completely removed the embargo. On July 11, 1995, complete diplomatic relations were established between the two countries. Since then, on July 12, 2000, the United States and Vietnam signed a sweeping trade agreement, granting Vietnam the same trading rights with the United States that most other nations have. Congress is expected to approve the pact.

Some Americans strongly disagreed with Clinton's overtures to Vietnam. These opponents included anti-Communist lawmakers, some Vietnam veterans, and organizations associated with the MIA issue. But the majority of Americans—including large numbers of Vietnam veterans—expressed support for normalizing relations. As one U.S. veteran of the war commented, establishing normal diplomatic and trade relations with Vietnam does not "dishonor the memory of our fallen or missing comrades. It is to recognize the truth. The war is over."

Sources

Appy, Christian G. *Working-Class War: American Combat Soldiers and Vietnam.* Chapel Hill: University of North Carolina Press, 1993.

Baritz, Loren. *Backfire: A History of How American Culture Led Us Into Vietnam and Made Us Fight the Way We Did.* New York: William Morrow, 1985.

Ehrhart, W. D. *Passing Time.* Jefferson, NC: McFarland, 1989.

Franklin, H. Bruce. *M.I.A. or Mythmaking in America.* Brooklyn, NY: Lawrence Hill, 1992.

Hellman, John. *American Myth and the Legacy of Vietnam.* New York: Columbia University Press, 1986.

Isaacs, Arnold R. *Vietnam Shadows: The War, Its Ghosts, and Its Legacy.* Baltimore: Johns Hopkins University Press, 1997.

Kahn, Joseph. "U.S. and Vietnam are Said to Agree on Normal Trade," *New York Times,* 13 July 2000. national edition.

Kovic, Ron. *Born on the Fourth of July.* New York: McGraw-Hill, 1976.

MacPherson, Myra. *Long Time Passing: Vietnam and the Haunted Generation.* Garden City, NY: Doubleday, 1984.

Marshall, John Douglas. *Reconciliation Road.* Syracuse, NY: Syracuse University Press, 1993.

Nixon, Richard. *No More Vietnams.* New York: Arbor House, 1985.

Palmer, Laura. *Shrapnel in the Heart: Letters and Remembrances from the Vietnam Veterans Memorial.* New York: Random House, 1987.

Scruggs, Jan. *To Heal a Nation: The Vietnam Veterans Memorial.* New York: Harper & Row, 1985.

Turner, Fred. *Echoes of Combat: The Vietnam War in American Memory.* New York: Anchor, 1996.

Where to Learn More

The following list of resources focuses on works appropriate for middle school or high school students. These sources offer broad coverage of the Vietnam War. For additional resources on specific topics please see individual chapters.

Aitken, Jonathan. *Nixon: A Life.* Washington, DC: Regnery, 1993.

Ambrose, Stephen E. *Nixon.* 3 vols. New York: Simon and Schuster, 1987–1991.

Anderson, David L. *Trapped by Success: The Eisenhower Administration and Vietnam, 1953–1961.* Lawrence: University Press of Kansas, 1991.

Appy, Christian. *Working-Class War: American Combat Soldiers and Vietnam.* Chapel Hill: University of North Carolina Press, 1993.

Becker, Elizabeth. *America's Vietnam War: A Narrative History.* New York: Clarion, 1992.

Berman, Larry. *Planning a Tragedy: The Americanization of the War in Vietnam.* New York: W. W. Norton, 1982.

Billings-Yun, Melanie. *Decision against War: Eisenhower and Dien Bien Phu, 1954.* New York: Columbia University Press, 1988.

Braestrup, Peter. *Big Story: How the American Press and Television Reported and Interpreted the Crisis of Tet 1968 in Vietnam and Washington.* Boulder, CO: Westview Press, 1977.

Butler, David. *The Fall of Saigon: Scenes from the Sudden End of a Long War.* New York: Simon and Schuster, 1985.

Buttinger, Joseph. *The Smaller Dragon: A Political History of Vietnam.* New York: Praeger, 1958.

Caputo, Philip. *A Rumor of War.* New York: Henry Holt, 1977.

Carroll, James. *An American Requiem: God, My Father, and the War That Came Between Us.* Boston: Houghton-Mifflin, 1996.

Caute, David. *The Year of the Barricades: A Journey Through 1968.* New York: Harper & Row, 1988.

Chandler, David P. *The Tragedy of Cambodian History.* New Haven, CT: Yale University Press, 1992.

Dareff, Hal. *The Story of Vietnam: A Background Book for Young People.* New York: Parents Magazine Press, 1966.

DeBenedetti, Charles, and Charles Chatfield. *An American Ordeal: The Antiwar Movement of the Vietnam Era.* Syracuse, NY: Syracuse University Press, 1990.

Dougan, Clark, and Stephen Weiss. *The American Experience in Vietnam.* New York: W. W. Norton, 1988.

Dougan, Clark, and Stephen Weiss. *The Vietnam Experience: Nineteen Sixty-Eight.* Boston: Boston Publishing, 1985.

Downs, Frederick. *Aftermath: A Soldier's Return from Vietnam.* New York: Norton, 1984.

Doyle, Edward, and Stephen Weiss. *A Collision of Cultures: The Americans in Vietnam, 1954–1973.* Boston: Boston Publishing, 1984.

Duiker, William J. *The Communist Road to Power in Vietnam.* 2nd ed. Boulder, CO: Westview Press, 1996.

Dung, Van Tien. *Our Great Spring Victory.* New York: Monthly Review Press, 1977.

Dunn, Peter M. *The First Vietnam War.* New York: St. Martin's Press, 1985.

Ebert, James R. *A Life in a Year: The American Infantryman in Vietnam, 1965–1972.* Novato, CA: Presidio, 1986.

Ehrhart, W. D. *Passing Time.* Jefferson, NC: McFarland, 1989.

Emerson, Gloria. *Winners and Losers: Battles, Retreats, Gains, Losses and Ruins from a Long War.* New York: Random House, 1976.

Engelmann, Larry. *Tears Before the Rain: An Oral History of the Fall of South Vietnam.* New York: Oxford University Press, 1990.

Eschmann, Karl J. *Linebacker: The Untold Story of the Air Raids over North Vietnam.* New York: Ivy Books, 1989.

Fall, Bernard. *Hell in a Very Small Place: The Siege of Dien Bien Phu*. Philadelphia: J. B. Lippincott, 1966.

Figley, Charles R., and Seymour Leventman, eds. *Strangers at Home: Vietnam Veterans Since the War*. New York: Praeger, 1980.

Fitzgerald, Frances. *Fire in the Lake: The Vietnamese and the Americans in Vietnam*. Boston: Little, Brown, 1972.

Franklin, H. Bruce. *M.I.A. or Mythmaking in America*. Brooklyn, NY: Lawrence Hill, 1992.

Freeman, James A. *Hearts of Sorrow: Vietnamese-American Lives*. Stanford, CA: Stanford University Press, 1989.

Gardner, Lloyd C. *Pay Any Price: Lyndon Johnson and the Wars for Vietnam*. Chicago: Ivan Dee, 1995.

Garfinkle, Adam. *Telltale Hearts: The Origins and Impact of the Vietnam Antiwar Movement*. New York: St. Martin's Press, 1995.

Gibson, James William. *The Perfect War: The War We Couldn't Lose and How We Did*. Boston: Atlantic Monthly Press, 1986.

Gitlin, Todd. *The Sixties: Years of Hope, Days of Rage*. New York: Bantam, 1987.

Goulden, Joseph C. *Truth Is the First Casualty: The Gulf of Tonkin Affair—Illusion and Reality*. Chicago: Rand-McNally, 1969.

Halberstam, David. *The Best and the Brightest*. New York: Random House, 1972.

Halberstam, David. *The Making of a Quagmire: America and Vietnam During the Kennedy Era*. Rev. ed. New York: Knopf, 1988.

Hammer, Ellen J. *A Death in November: America in Vietnam, 1963*. New York: Dutton, 1987.

Hawthorne, Lesleyanne, ed. *Refugee: The Vietnamese Experience*. New York: Oxford University Press, 1982.

Hellman, John. *American Myth and the Legacy of Vietnam*. New York: Columbia University Press, 1986.

Helmer, John. *Bringing the War Home: The American Soldier in Vietnam and After*. New York: Free Press, 1974.

Hendrickson, Paul. *The Living and the Dead: Robert McNamara and Five Lives of a Lost War*. New York: Alfred A. Knopf, 1996.

Herr, Michael. *Dispatches*. New York: Alfred A. Knopf, 1977.

Herring, George C. *America's Longest War: The United States and Vietnam, 1950–1975*. 3rd ed. New York: McGraw-Hill, 1996.

Herring, George C. *LBJ and Vietnam: A Different Kind of War*. Austin: University of Texas Press, 1994.

Herrington, Stuart A. *Silence Was a Weapon: The Vietnam War in the Villages.* Novato, CA: Presidio Press, 1982.

Hiebert, Murray. *Chasing the Tigers: A Portrait of the New Vietnam.* New York: Kodansha International, 1996.

Hubbell, John, with Andrew Jones and Kenneth Y. Tomlinson. *P.O.W.: A Definitive History of the American Prisoner-of-War Experience in Vietnam, 1964–1973.* New York: Reader's Digest Press, 1976.

Isaacs, Arnold R. *Vietnam Shadows: The War, Its Ghosts, and Its Legacy.* Baltimore: Johns Hopkins University Press, 1997.

Isaacs, Arnold R. *Without Honor: Defeat in Vietnam and Cambodia.* New York: Vintage Books, 1984.

Isaacson, Walter. *Kissinger.* New York: Simon and Schuster, 1992.

Johnson, Lyndon B. *The Vantage Point: Perspectives of the Presidency, 1963–1969.* New York: Holt, Rinehart & Winston, 1971.

Kahin, George M. *Intervention: How America Became Involved in Vietnam.* Garden City, NY: Doubleday, 1987.

Karnow, Stanley. *Vietnam: A History.* Rev. ed. New York: Viking, 1991.

Kearns, Doris. *Lyndon Johnson & the American Dream.* New York: Harper & Row, 1976.

Kimball, Jeffrey. *Nixon's Vietnam War.* Lawrence: University Press of Kansas, 1998.

Kolko, Gabriel. *Anatomy of a War: Vietnam, the United States, and the Modern Historical Experience.* New York: Pantheon, 1985.

Kovic, Ron. *Born on the Fourth of July.* New York: McGraw-Hill, 1976.

Kutler, Stanley I., ed. *Encyclopedia of the Vietnam War.* New York: Scribner's, 1996.

Levy, David W. *The Debate over Vietnam.* 2nd ed. Baltimore: Johns Hopkins University Press, 1995.

Lewy, Gunter. *America in Vietnam.* New York: Oxford University Press, 1978.

Maclear, Michael. *The Ten Thousand Day War: Vietnam, 1945–1975.* New York: St. Martin's Press, 1980.

MacPherson, Myra. *Long Time Passing: Vietnam and the Haunted Generation.* Garden City, NY: Doubleday, 1984.

Marshall, John Douglas. *Reconciliation Road.* Syracuse, NY: Syracuse University Press, 1993.

Mason, Robert. *Chickenhawk.* New York: Viking, 1983.

McMahon, Robert J., ed. *Major Problems in the History of the Vietnam War.*

Lexington, MA: D. C. Heath, 1995.

McNamara, Robert S., with Brian VanDeMark. *In Retrospect: The Tragedy and Lessons of Vietnam*. New York: Times Books, 1995.

Moore, Harold G., and Joseph L. Galloway. *We Were Soldiers Once . . . And Young*. New York: Random House, 1992.

Morley, James W., and Masashi Nishihara, eds. *Vietnam Joins the World*. Armonk, NY: M. E. Sharpe, 1997.

Ngo Vinh Long. *Before the Revolution: The Vietnamese Peasants Under the French*. Cambridge, MA: MIT Press, 1973.

Nguyen Qui Duc. *Where the Ashes Are: The Odyssey of a Vietnamese Family*. Reading, MA: Addison-Wesley, 1994.

Nixon, Richard. *No More Vietnams*. New York: Arbor House, 1985.

Oberdorfer, Don. *Tet!* New York: Doubleday, 1971.

Olson, James, and Randy Roberts. *Where the Domino Fell: America and Vietnam, 1945–1990*. New York: St. Martin's Press, 1996.

Palmer, Laura. *Shrapnel in the Heart: Letters and Remembrances from the Vietnam Veterans Memorial*. New York: Random House, 1987.

Prados, John, and Ray Stubbe. *Valley of Decision: The Siege of Khe Sanh*. New York: Houghton Mifflin, 1991.

Prochnau, William. *Once Upon a Distant War*. New York: Times Books, 1995.

Rust, William J. *Kennedy in Vietnam*. New York: Scribner's, 1985.

Schell, Jonathan. *The Real War: The Classic Reporting on the Vietnam War*. New York: Pantheon, 1987.

Scruggs, Jan. *To Heal a Nation: The Vietnam Veterans Memorial*. New York: Harper & Row, 1985.

Shandler, Herbert Y. *The Unmaking of a President: Lyndon Johnson and Vietnam*. Princeton, NJ: Princeton University Press, 1977.

Shawcross, William. *Sideshow: Kissinger, Nixon, and the Destruction of Cambodia*. New York: Simon and Schuster, 1979.

Sheehan, Neil. *A Bright Shining Lie: John Paul Vann and America in Vietnam*. New York: Random House, 1988.

Simpson, Howard R. *Dien Bien Phu: The Epic Battle America Forgot*. Washington, DC: Brassey's, 1994.

Snepp, Frank. *Decent Interval: An Insider's Account of Saigon's Indecent End*. New York: Random House, 1977.

Spector, Ronald H. *After Tet: The Bloodiest Year in Vietnam*. New York: Free Press, 1993.

Starr, Paul. *The Discarded Army.* New York: Charterhouse, 1974.

Terry, Wallace. *Bloods: An Oral History of the Vietnam War by Black Veterans.* New York: Ballantine, 1984.

Thompson, James Clay. *Rolling Thunder.* Chapel Hill: University of North Carolina Press, 1980.

Turner, Fred. *Echoes of Combat: The Vietnam War in American Memory.* New York: Anchor, 1996.

VanDeMark, Brian. *Into the Quagmire: Lyndon Johnson and the Escalation of the Vietnam War.* New York: Oxford University Press, 1991.

Wells, Tom. *The War Within: America's Battle Over Vietnam.* Berkeley: University of California Press, 1994.

Westmoreland, William. *A Soldier Reports.* New York: Doubleday, 1976.

Wicker, Tom. *One of Us: Richard Nixon and the American Dream.* New York: Random House, 1991.

Wiegersma, Nancy. *Vietnam: Peasant Land, Peasant Revolution.* New York: St. Martin's, 1988.

Wiesner, Louis A. *Victims and Survivors: Displaced Persons and Other War Victims in Vietnam, 1954–1975.* Westport, CT: Greenwood,1988.

Wolff, Tobias. *In Pharoah's Army.* New York: Alfred A. Knopf, 1994.

Young, Marilyn B. *The Vietnam Wars, 1945–1990.* New York: HarperCollins, 1991.

Zaroulis, Nancy, and Gerald Sullivan. *Who Spoke Up? American Protest against the War in Vietnam, 1963–1975.* Garden City, NY: Doubleday, 1984.

Index

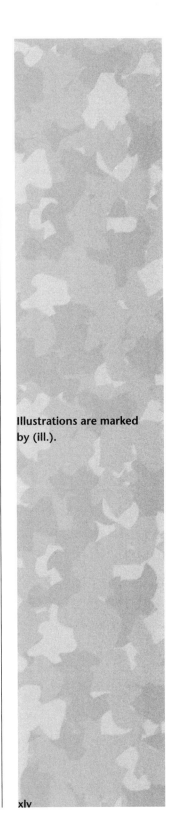

Illustrations are marked by (ill.).